SIN BRAVELY

A MEMOIR OF SPIRITUAL DISOBEDIENCE

MAGGIE ROWE

SOFT SKULL PRESS
AN IMPRINT OF COUNTERPOINT

Library of Congress Cataloging-in-Publication Data

Names: Rowe, Maggie Wallem, author.
Title: Sin bravely : a memoir of spiritual disobedience / Maggie Rowe.
Description: Berkeley : Soft Skull Press, 2017. | Includes bibliographical
   references and index.
Identifiers: LCCN 2016040120 | ISBN 9781593766597 (alk. paper)
Subjects: LCSH: Rowe, Maggie Wallem. | Christian biography. | Mental
   illness--Religious aspects--Christianity. | Psychiatry and religion.
Classification: LCC BR1725.R683 A3 2017 | DDC 270.092 [B] --dc23
LC record available at https://lccn.loc.gov/2016040120

ISBN 978-1-59376-659-7

Cover design by Michael Fusco Straub
Interior design by Tabitha Lahr

SOFT SKULL PRESS
An imprint of Counterpoint
2560 Ninth Street, Suite 318
Berkeley, CA 94710
www.softskull.com

Printed in the United States of America
Distributed by Publishers Group West

10 9 8 7 6 5 4 3 2 1

To my parents, who never departed.

DISCARDED

CONTENTS

PART ONE

CHAPTER ONE: **ONE CONDITION**

JESUS'S EYES SEEM KIND, but I will not let myself be fooled. I will not be taken in by the graceful features, by the healthy conditioned hair spilling over soft shoulders, by the gentle protection He seems to offer His flock of wide-eyed sheep, who bury themselves into the folds of his robe.

I know better.

I know that the Jesus in this painting, just like the real Jesus, could turn on me at any moment; that He is kind until He is not, that He is absolute love until He is absolute vengeance. I know He could effortlessly toss me into hell for all eternity before turning back to nuzzle his beloved sheep—all without messing up His Pantene hair.

I am in jeopardy and I will not let myself forget it.

The waiting room presents itself dimly, in hushed tones, as if being careful not to further disturb its disturbed visitors. I am one of those visitors, sitting on a hard high-backed couch that seems designed to reprimand slouches. My mother sits next to me, her jaw tight, crossing and uncrossing her slender fingers, as if focus on this simple gesture could resolve the complicated mess I've gotten us into. My mother doesn't deserve this. She deserves a daughter she can be proud of. Not the quivering skeletal mess who returned from college after her sophomore year begging for help. My mom and I should be waiting together for me to be admitted to an honor society, not a psychiatric ward. But here we are.

I remind myself that I am lucky my parents found this place. I remind myself that the doctors at any other hospital wouldn't understand my issues. Here, however, at Grace Point, as they proclaim on all of their marketing materials, the Bible comes first. And to prove it, the *t* in *Grace Point* is formed into a cross, and that cross has a teeny-weeny little Jesus hanging from it.

I am here for one reason, which is elegant in its simplicity, or ludicrous: I am scared of going to hell.

It's not that I think I'm definitely going to hell. It's just that I can't prove to myself that I'm *not*—a distinction I will attempt to clarify to therapists many times in the months to come. This elegant ludicrous reason is why I'm terrified and why I'm sitting on this uncomfortable couch, staring at this painting of Jesus.

The first time I heard about hell was when my Sunday school teacher Miss Trimly warned my class *not to be afraid of those who will kill your body, but rather fear God who can kill your soul in hell.* Before that moment, I hadn't been all that worried about people killing my body. But now there was an even-greater danger to comprehend.

Miss Trimly was a pinched, thin-lipped woman whose bun pulled at her face with a force I suspect must have given her a chronic headache. She told our group of squirmy six-year-olds that if we denied Jesus, we would be condemned to an eternity in hell; that God would say to unbelievers on Judgment Day, *Depart from me. I do not know you,* and then toss them into a fiery pit, where there would be weeping and gnashing of teeth forevermore (*gnashing* being a word far too frightening to inquire into its exact meaning).

Miss Trimly, her face ever taut and pained, held out a felt storyboard and began telling us the parable of Lazarus and the Rich Man. She trotted a fuzzy figure of a leper up to a big fat man in a fancy coat and began the tale.

"Lazarus goes every night to the Rich Man's mansion, begging for scraps of food, scraps that even the dogs reject. Time and again, the Rich Man turns Lazarus away. Later, when the two men die, Lazarus is sent to heaven and the Rich Man goes to hell. The Rich Man in his agony cries out to Jesus, 'Have pity on me, and send Lazarus to dip the tip of his finger

in the water and cool my tongue because it is burning and I am agony.'"
Miss Trimly swooped a pearly white figure of Jesus down onto the board
and said, "Jesus looks at the Rich Man and says, 'No, not for you. You have
made your decision and now it is too late.'"

Too late? The words knotted my stomach.

Miss Trimly said we needed to be prepared because Jesus could come
back at any moment to judge the world. No one knew the hour of His
return, only that He would come like a thief in the night, in the twinkling
of an eye, and when He did, if we were one of the unbelievers, no one—not
even our parents—could help us. I imagined my parents being pulled up
into the sky as I was being sucked down below.

Down and down. Like the doomed astronaut from *The Twilight Zone*.

I had recently seen the episode where an astronaut is repairing a hole
on a spacecraft's hull when he accidentally cuts his own tether. He tries
to grab onto the mother ship and pull himself in to safety, but the surface is slick and metallic with nothing to hold, so his grasping only ends
up pushing him further out. The astronaut floats away into never-ending
space, his limbs thrashing in futile protest of his fate. The severed rope, I
remembered, dangles uselessly behind.

Miss Trimly, satisfied that she had sufficiently spooked her charges,
assured our trembling group we didn't need to be afraid because God had
also given us an unconditional gift. A gift called grace. The only string was
we had to accept it by saying the Sinner's Prayer: *Dear Jesus, I believe in
You and accept You into my heart as my personal savior. Please forgive my
sins and cleanse me from all unrighteousness.*

I said the prayer. Of course I did.

But what if I didn't really mean it?

So I concentrated and said it again.

And again.

But my mind wouldn't rest. Maybe I'd gotten it wrong. I'd been wrong
before. Plenty of times. Like in math class, when I was sure that five minus
four was nine so I wrote down nine on the test. But I was wrong. I had
confused subtraction with addition. What if the same type of thing was
happening now?

The following Sunday Miss Trimly elaborated on the "good news," informing us that true repentance meant committing to "sin no more," reciting, *Not everyone who cries to me, 'Lord, Lord,' will enter the kingdom, but only those who do the will of the Father.*

Wait, *what*? I thought the whole idea was that you just had to cry, *Lord, Lord,* and then you were okay. Wasn't that the one condition of unconditional grace? The one string of the no-strings-attached gift? But no, I was wrong again. Five minus four is one. Not nine. And now, apparently, unconditional gifts sometimes require action on the part of the receiver.

The following Sunday I burst into class and panted out the question I'd been desperate to ask all week, the question I was hoping had a swift and easy answer that would let me move on and focus on candy and recess, like a normal first grader. "Miss Trimly, how do we know for sure that we got it right? The prayer, I mean." Miss Trimly's reply sounded sweet but felt like a threat: "Mark says *you will know a Christian by his fruit.* Christians have good fruit, not bad fruit. Christians are drawn to things *good and pure and lovely.*" This was not reassuring. I knew I wasn't always drawn to what I should be, even during the Bible stories Miss Trimly illustrated on the felt storyboard.

Most of the felt figures were prophets or saints or dutiful mothers, clothed in the plainest shades of beige, bowing their heads modestly before the Lord. But then there were the harlots—Mary Magdalene, Delilah, Bathsheba, Jezebel, the sister-prostitute team Oholo and Oholibah; colorful figures decked out in low-cut purple dresses, goddess sandals, painted faces, and fabulous gold bangles. Their bold eyes gazing straight ahead, irreverently, over the mounds of their substantial cleavage. My favorite was Mary Magdalene, the one who poured perfume on Christ's feet and then dried them with her hair, the woman whom Jesus seemed to be constantly protecting from criticism and stoning. Even when Judas seems to have a very reasonable objection to her actions, when he points out, "This woman just poured perfume worth a year's wages onto your feet, money that could have been given to the poor," Jesus simply replies, "Don't talk bad about Mary."

While the felt stories played out, I would imagine myself as one of the harlots, decorated and painted, my own eyes unaverted, my breasts spilling over a plummeting purple neckline. As far as I could make out, this was the opposite of being drawn to what was "pure and lovely." Miss Trimly told us, "A woman's greatest gift is her purity, a gift she will one day bestow on her husband." *Purity* meant not having sex outside of marriage but also, I gathered, not *acting or dressing* like someone who has sex outside of marriage. So no high heels. No heavy makeup. No short skirts. All indicators of premarital sex.

A verse from the call-and-response song we used to sing perhaps said it best:

> *(Solo) Oh you can't get to heaven*
> *(Group) Oh you can't get to heaven*
> *(Solo) In a miniskirt*
> *(Group) In a miniskirt*
> *(Solo) Oh you can't get to heaven in a miniskirt cause God*
> *don't like no silly flirts.*
> *(Solo and Group) All my sins are washed away; I've been*
> *redeemed.*

My interest in the bad women from the Bible stories was evidence of bad fruit and clear proof that the prayer did not take. I knew that having good fruit alone wouldn't save me—that if I had good fruit, it was only an indication that I had already been saved: a tricky and frightening distinction. But I figured maybe I could work from the outside in: maybe good fruit could backwardly produce genuine conversion. I knew reading the Bible every day was an example of good fruit, so when I was eight I begged my parents to take me to the Christian bookstore to buy me my own Bible.

My parents took me that weekend and guided me to an aisle made entirely of Bibles, then let me loose like they did at the indoor playground at Wonderfun. My mission here, however, was more serious than my inconsequential time on swings and superslides. I needed to pick the smartest, most magical Bible I could find.

I walked up and down the aisle, pulling out different Bibles, flipping through the pages, considering, until finally I found it: *The Ryrie Study*

Bible compiled by theologian Charles Ryrie. *The Ryrie Study Bible* had four different translations of the Word printed side by side: King James, New International Version, Living, and Revised Standard. Plus, in addition to the traditional glossary, index, and maps at the back, this whopper of a Bible offered verse-by-verse commentary at the bottom of each page, comparing and contrasting the four different translations and offering more than ten thousand footnotes by the author himself. As I heaved the weight of my new book up into my chest, I felt Jesus looking down upon me proudly. Even He would have to say, "Whoa, that's some Bible!"

There were a lot of words I didn't understand in my *Ryrie Study Bible*, but I had a dictionary and a glossary, so I set to bearing good fruit, making sure I was saved. Some verses I loved for the reassurance they offered, but also for the sound—the King James Version always sounding the loveliest. One of my favorites was Romans 8:38, where it says, *For I am convinced, that neither death, nor life, nor angels, nor principalities, nor powers, nor things present, nor things to come, nor height, nor depth, nor any other creature, shall be able to separate us from the love of God, which is in Christ Jesus our Lord.* The verse just keeps rolling along, emphatic and assuring, even after its point seems to have been made, as if trying to calm a frightened girl.

But then there were other verses. Like Revelations 3:16 where at the Final Judgment Jesus says, *So then because thou art lukewarm, and neither cold nor hot, I will spew thee out of my mouth.* I read the verse commentary at the bottom of the page that said, "Many falsely assume they have received salvation. 'Lukewarm' should be read as not on fire for the Lord, a condition more perilous than that of the unbeliever." What if I was lukewarm? I didn't really think I was on fire for the Lord. I was only studying this Bible to make sure I was not going to hell—when what I really wanted to do was microwave two Hostess Suzy Q's from the basement freezer and then watch *The Brady Bunch.* That didn't sound like a girl "on fire for the Lord."

My scalp began to burn, dampening the roots of my hair. Lugging my monstrosity of a Bible, I lumbered to the kitchen. My mom was cooking fried flounder while trying to keep my two-year-old sister Trisha, who was painting a picture on an easel by the stove, from painting our basset hound Nicholas instead.

I wiped the flop sweat from my face and chest with both hands, fighting the added heat of the kitchen and nausea from the smell of the fish. "I found this verse and it says that if you're neither hot nor cold, Jesus will spew you out of His mouth and you'll go to hell."

"I don't know that verse." Mom splatted a filet into the frying pan, the cold flounder making a sharp sizzle when it hit. My sister kept painting, eyeing my mother for a chance to return her brush to Nicholas, a far more interesting surface to paint than a white piece of paper.

"It's Revelations 3:16. It says, *So then because thou art lukewarm, and neither cold nor hot, I will spew thee out of my mouth.* What if I'm spewed out of Jesus's mouth?"

My mom turned to see Trisha slap a dollop of red paint on the dog's nose. My sister was only two, so disobedience was not yet a sin. She was blameless no matter what and didn't even realize how lucky she was, how free.

My mother turned back to me. "Sweetheart, your dad and I have told you, you don't need to worry about going to hell. You accepted Jesus into your heart, and that means you're going to heaven."

"But what if I'm lukewarm?"

Mom flipped the flounder, creating another angry sizzle, then stepped aside to narrowly avoid a spray of grease. "You're not lukewarm. I'm sure of it."

"But how do you know?"

"I know."

"But what if you're wrong like last night when you said *The Joker's Wild* came on after *Tic-Tac-Dough*. It came on *before*."

"This is different."

"Can you just look at the verse?"

I held up the leviathan Bible to my mom's face, my muscles almost collapsing from the weight. Mom looked past me to see my sister applying red tempera to Nicholas's tawny back. "Trisha, no!" she said and reached over, grabbing the paintbrush from Trisha's clenched fist. My sister fell to the floor, stung by the injustice, screaming in outrage, and in the process knocked over the easel, spilling paint everywhere, paint which Nicholas was thrilled to lap up.

"Maggie, can we talk about this a little later?"

And we did. We talked about it often. My parents patiently listened to all of my worries about my salvation, continually reassuring me I was fine, and urging me to try not to think about it. And I did try not to think about it, chanting my parents' assurances in my mind like sacred mantras: *We're your parents. We know. Trust us. We know.* But then sometimes the thoughts would overwhelm me and their spells would fail.

One night I was sleeping over at my best friend Sophie's house, honey-haired Sophie whose green cat eyes could turn mischievous in a second. We slept over regularly at each other's houses, staying up far past even our parents' bedtimes until the sky turned inky black and witchy—Sophie in her pink My Little Pony sleeping bag and me in my blue one with a hundred little Smurfs in different states of merriment.

I liked Sophie's mother Mrs. Palladino quite a bit, even though I knew she was not what could be called "nice." I liked how she chucked rocks at squirrels that ate her tomato plant and yelled, "Take that, assholes! Now go tell your friends." I liked how she forced the neighbors to "shut their stupid mutt up" by blasting country music over the fence until they relented. When I slept over, Mrs. Palladino would cook Sophie and me her specialty, Kraft Macaroni and Cheese, before pouring herself a vodka and retreating to the TV room.

On this night, after her mom had left us with our bowls of mac 'n cheese, Sophie suggested that instead of eating the macaroni, we should use the noodles to create an art project on the table, her cat eyes turning more feline than normal as she conceived the crime. I knew we shouldn't play with our food, but maybe it would be okay just this once—*since it was a sleepover.* Sleepover rules were different. Bedtimes were extended. Desserts were unlimited. As long as we cleaned the macaroni up afterward, I figured, there would be no harm.

Sophie and I began arranging our gooey orange dinner into a lopsided heart on the table. We had just spooned out the last of it when Mrs. Palladino came in for a refill.

"That's enough," she said in a voice as stiff as her drink. "The macaroni either goes in the bowls or in your mouths. Got it?"

We began dutifully picking up the macaroni and returning it to the bowl and into our mouths as Mrs. Palladino navigated her way back to the television, carefully measuring each step to keep the majority of the drink from spilling out of her glass.

When she was out of earshot, Sophie said, "My mom's poopy. Poopy Pat," sending us into hysterics. We were high on rebellion, giddy over our audacity, and triumphant in the alliterative wit of *poopy* and her mother's first name, *Pat*. "Poopy Pat!!" we shrieked, overcome with laughter and delight. Then Sophie had another idea. Her eyes narrowed again.

"You want to do something?"

"Um, sure." Though I wasn't.

"Let's spell out *P. P.* with the macaroni." Then upping the ante, "Let's spell it out on the floor."

This was exhilarating, the kind of forbidden activity that made sleepovers great. But Mrs. Palladino had just told us the macaroni belonged in our mouths or in our bowls and not on the table—sleepover or no.

But then again, Mrs. Palladino would take a while before she came back to fill up her drink again, so we'd have time to clean up. Therefore, what difference would it make if she would never even see it?

Then before my racing mind could again criticize its already-many-layered rationalization, I cried, "Let's do it," lifting my bowl like an Olympic torch.

We set to work realizing Sophie's vision, not even trying to contain our laughter. But then, just as we were putting the final touches on our *P. P.*, Mrs. Palladino and her drink sloshed in. When Sophie's mom saw us crouched on the floor over the evidence of our guilt, she stopped and looked, swaying back and forth—irregularly, as if in time to her own rhythm-less and equally intoxicated inner drummer—while we waited for the explosion.

But she just tilted her head to one side and asked, "P. P.?"

Sophie and I froze, knowing we couldn't possibly admit to her mother what the letters stood for. I raced through other ideas of what it could be. Parent Pat? Peacock Pat? Pinwheel Pat? Then I had it.

"*Pretty* Pat," I said in a sugary voice I knew adults found pleasing, "because we were thinking about how pretty you are."

Sophie and I watched expressions cycle across her mom's face, as if in slow motion, while my words made their way through her vodka-saturated thoughts, waiting for one reaction to form and hold. Then . . . Mrs. Palladino laughed—laughed hard, hard enough that she had to put down her drink and pour another. Tears streamed down her face as she put her hand on her heart and mushed out the words, "Pretty Pat. That's great. That's so great, girls," delighted, melted at being called *pretty*, if only by her eight-year-old daughter and her eight-year-old daughter's friend—if only in an acronym on the floor, spelled out in a calligraphy of macaroni and cheese.

Sophie and I started laughing too, and the three of us all laughed together, like we were spinning on a carnival ride that had gone off its center, a moment of perfect sleepover-night abandon. We laughed until Mrs. Palladino, almost but not quite falling down, gave us an uneven thumbs-up and added an encouraging, "Keep it up!" before turning to balance her way back into the TV room.

That night in our sleeping bags, after Sophie had fallen asleep, I began thinking about what Sophie and I had done. It had been fun, but had it been right? I started sweating and thinking some more. Mrs. Palladino had clearly said not to put the macaroni anywhere but in our mouths or in our bowls, and we had flagrantly disobeyed her.

Yes, but she wasn't upset, so we didn't hurt anyone, so maybe that was all right.

Yes, but disobedience is still disobedience. And on top of that, I lied about what *P. P.* stood for.

As this litigation raced on, my temples drummed with regret over my sins while my scalp didn't itch, didn't prickle, as some people will say, but felt instead as if innumerable tiny birds of prey had begun with invisible talons to claw at the skin.

I pressed my palms together inside my sleeping bag, unprotected by the army of Smurfs that lay over my hands, and prayed, "Dear Lord, please forgive me for my sins and for disobeying Mrs. Palladino and for lying to her about what *P. P.* meant. Please forgive me for all of that. Amen."

Had it worked? It seemed it may have.

I turned to go back to sleep but almost immediately the talons began digging into my scalp again. Something was very wrong. My head stung. The Smurfs seemed suddenly cold and warlike, angels of the Lord assembled in ranks to descend on me through the fabric. I started thinking about the Rich Man scorched by flames and calling up, "Please send Lazarus to fetch a bit of water to cool my tongue," and I thought about God denying him, "Too late."

Too late. Too late banged about in my head. God saying to me, *Depart from me. I do not know you*, and sending me down to the flames. I again imagined my parents receding, while I plummeted downward through the pitch darkness. There would be nothing to grab on to. I would fall and they would rise and we would be separated forever.

How could my parents allow such a fate? How could they leave me? Because they would have no choice. They would have to go along with God because, well, He was God. I imagined my mom weeping, sympathizing with her child, recalling how much she had once cared for me, how we liked reading the George and Martha books together, how we laughed when George the elephant poured his wife Martha's pea soup into his slippers instead of admitting he'd never liked pea soup. Then I pictured my dad choking back tears as he remembered the nights the two of us had stayed up late watching *Odd Couple* reruns and how we always laughed in the opening credits when Felix stabbed Oscar's discarded cigar, which I believed to be a hot dog, with his cane. I imagined my dad saying, "Sorry, kid," in a regretful but helpless tone, knowing that despite our connection, "this was the only way." I imagined both my parents turning their backs on me, proceeding down the golden streets of their salvation, and joining the chorus of angels that had been waiting to greet them—my sister cartwheeling behind.

I opened my eyes to blink away the vision but only grew more scared by the thought of forgetting. I forced myself to return to the imagined catastrophe. How bad would it be? How long was forever? I was convinced that the only way to protect myself from the peril I was in was to picture the size of my punishment. I tried to measure what *eternal* meant. If I could measure it, I could endure it.

I started small, imagining one day, without my parents, crying, alone, in the middle of a fire. That was horrible, but I could comprehend it. One day has an end.

"But that's not eternal," I reminded myself. "Eternal has no end."

So I tried a week. I didn't like the thought of a week of burning exile, but I could frame it. One week was like summer camp. I had an idea about how long that was.

"But a week of summer camp ends, Maggie."

I built up to a year.

"No."

I put three zeroes after it.

"No."

A million.

"No, you're still adding an end. A cap. A stop. That's not right! Eternal goes on after that. *Eternal* means *without end.*"

I pictured the horror continuing beyond the point where I had inserted the false stop—millions, billions, trillions of years beyond it— and yet each time I expanded the frame, my mind slipped in the prospect of an ending.

Why was I doing this? I needed to understand. *Eternal means without end.*

The burning in my scalp ignited into a blaze, so I unzipped my sleeping bag and threw off the cover. I snuck through the dark to the phone in the kitchen, next to our unwashed mac-'n-cheese bowls congealing in the sink, and called my mom. I told her how I knew I had been bad but also that Jesus would forgive me if I was saved, if I had said the Sinner's Prayer, but that maybe I wasn't actually saved because I hadn't said the prayer right. Maybe I hadn't meant it.

My mom assured me that I couldn't say the prayer wrong, that I was a Christian, and that if I didn't truly believe in the first place, I wouldn't be worried about it. Mom's comfort made some sense. People don't worry about things they don't believe in. So with this little fistful of assurance, I decided I could make it through the night.

I hung up and immediately pictured a time when she would be up in heaven and God wouldn't let her listen. I knew there were some promises even mothers couldn't keep. I looked at the plates in the sink, crusted with leftover macaroni and cheese. Then I made my way through the dark back to my sleeping bag and willed the sun to finally rise.

My hell fears only increased over the next year, and so did my Biblical research. On one windy Chicago evening when I was nine, I flopped opened the *Study Bible* on my desk to Romans 10:14. I'd been waiting all day—while riding to school on the bus, then in Algebra class, and through English and Social Studies and Science and gym, and then again on the bus riding home—to further research this verse I couldn't dislodge from my mind: *How will they be saved if they do not hear? And how will they hear unless they're told?*

"How will they hear unless they are told?" was a great question. What would happen to all of the people who had never heard of Jesus? How could they accept Him into their hearts if they didn't even know He was there? What about all those kids in Africa? Or India? Or the North Pole? What about kids who believed more in Santa Claus than they did Jesus because their parents took them to the mall at Christmas instead of to church on Sunday?

I pored over commentary on the verse and found the scholars had anticipated my question. The children in Africa and India and from the North Pole—and the boys of irreligious families and little girls whose parents never read from the Bible—they will all go to hell. This was more unfair than I could comprehend. But then again, who was I to judge God? I knew I'd better stop these questions or He would start judging *me*.

I heard a knock at my door and slid the purple ribbon down, bookmarking the page before heaving my Bible shut and calling, "Come in." My mom and dad entered ceremonially, sitting down side by side on my bed, a united front. I picked up a highlighter from my desk to clutch while I waited.

Mom said, "We were thinking maybe you might want to get . . . baptized." Her fingers clasped around her knuckles in prayer position.

I didn't understand. My first thought was that this was an honor, an award for my dedication to my faith. But it could be the opposite. Lots of things turned out to be the opposite of what I thought they were.

"But I'm only nine. Most kids don't get baptized until they're twelve."

"We were thinking that since you've been having all these worries, getting baptized might be good for you. It might make you feel better," Dad said.

"It might make you feel closer to God." Mom's eyes rested warmly on me. "And you can start taking communion on Sundays. That might be good for you, too."

Wow, I thought. Declaring before God, my parents, and the entire congregation that I was a Christian. Maybe that would make me feel better. Maybe that could do the trick. I imagined all my worries being washed away as the water flowed over me, emerging a new and worry-free nine-year-old. Yes.

My mother looked at me gently, then patted the space between her and my father, her eyes welling with tears. I went over. My dad put his arm around my shoulders and drew me in. "Pastor Womac counsels everyone who gets baptized." He squeezed me tighter into his chest, crunching my shoulder up to my chin. "We've tried to help you with your worries, kid, but we don't know what to say. Maybe Pastor Womac can help you more."

My mother skimmed her hand over my hair, and I nodded. "Okay."

I prepared for my private counseling session with ferocity, determined to make the best use of my time with the pastor. I lay in bed at night staring up at the dark ceiling, rubbing the bottom of one foot over the top of the other, making an inventory of the questions I wanted to ask. Finally, I narrowed the infinite cascade down to the top three.

Number one, the biggie, addressed my most urgent doubt. How could I know if I was truly a Christian? Was I actually only lukewarm?

Number two considered the beneficence of God. Why would He send anyone, even a sinner, to hell? Why would He make such a place? How could He be so cruel?

Number three, which was related to number two, focused on the question of innocence. What would happen to the people who have never heard about Jesus in the first place? Would God send them to hell? How could something like that make sense?

The following Sunday after church, I went for my private meeting with Pastor Womac. In case I forgot my questions, I took out my pink Hello Kitty sticky notepad and with my matching Hello Kitty pen I wrote down reminders: *1. Lukewarm. 2. Cruel. 3. Kids in Africa or North Pole.* I stuck the pink note with Hello Kitty's face smiling up at me on the corner of my monstrous Bible and walked up the winding stairs to Pastor Womac's office. I squeezed the handrail hard even though I didn't need it for balance.

A genial man with a broad salesman's grin, Pastor Womac welcomed me into his office, offering his hand to shake just like I was a grown-up. "So I hear you've got some pretty big questions." I nodded, my hand wagging up and down in his, hopeful that my pretty big questions would shortly have some pretty big answers. Pastor Womac gestured with a broad sweep to a leather chair and said as if I were a valued customer, "Have a seat, Miss Rowe. Make yourself comfortable." I hoisted myself up onto a chair clearly made for adults, my Bible overwhelming my lap, my feet dangling, straight-backed and resolved to settle accounts.

"So tell me what you've been thinking."

I launched in, pushing myself forward to the edge of the chair but still unable to touch my toes to the floor. "Okay, well, the big thing is I'm worried I might not really be a true Christian. I said the prayer accepting Jesus into my heart probably like a thousand times, and I say all the words perfectly, but I'm not sure I believe enough. I want to believe, but I'm not sure I totally do. What if I'm not really burning for the Lord? What if I'm lukewarm?"

"Lukewarm?"

I heaved open my Bible, using the force of my entire body, to Revelations and read the verse.

"Hmmm." Pastor Womac rubbed his temples, his salesman's grin beginning to falter. "You have to understand that Revelations is a complicated book. It's a difficult book even for adults to decipher."

He nodded, as if putting a period on the comment, and I sensed him hoping I would accept it and be happy, and I wanted to please him, and I certainly knew that I shouldn't be rude, but at the same time I might never get another chance like this again. Like at miniature golf, I thought to myself, you have to hit your ball before the castle gates or the pelican's beak closes. Go now!

"Yes, but that doesn't answer my question. In my Bible, the commentary says those who are not on fire for Christ are lukewarm. It says those people will all go to hell. How do I know if I'm lukewarm?"

"It seems to me you're awfully concerned about your salvation for a girl your age. You don't seem lukewarm to me at all."

The pastor himself just said that I'm not lukewarm.

No, he didn't. He said I didn't *seem* lukewarm. This was nice enough, but I wanted more. I wanted it solved.

"But how can I know *for sure*?"

"Because you believe in Jesus as your savior."

"Yes, that's true. I do believe. But . . . I'm not sure I believe 100 percent. Sometimes it's like I believe more than other times. Sometimes less. Plus *faith without works is dead*, right? And maybe I don't have enough works. I know it's not works that saves me. It's faith. But still if I don't have works, then my faith is dead. What if my faith is dead?"

Pastor Womac withdrew a blue handkerchief from his pocket and dabbed his already-dry forehead and neck. After a moment, he folded up the handkerchief and returned it to his pocket. "I want to tell you the story of Doubting Thomas. Do you know that story, Miss Rowe?"

I didn't.

"Thomas was one of Jesus's disciples, and after Jesus rose again, Thomas saw him in the flesh and said, 'Master, I cannot believe it is really you.'"

And then Pastor Womac stood up and took several steps away from me onto a shag rug, turning it into a sort of pulpit. "And Jesus said to Thomas, 'Touch the holes in my hands where the nails have pierced me, and the rip in my side where the sword has sliced me. Stop doubting and believe.' Thomas felt the wounds and said," —here the Pastor opened his arms for effect— "'I believe. Help now my unbelief.'"

It was like my own private sermon.

Pastor Womac brought his hands together in a resounding clap and said as if touting the virtues of an industry-leading new-car warranty, "Doubts can even make your faith stronger. That's what's great about God!"

His smile was triumphant, as if closing the deal.

But I wanted to look at the contract. Laboriously lifting my Bible, I asked, "Can you show me where that is?"

Pastor Womac crossed back to where I sat, leaned over beside me, turned the pages to Luke chapter 8, and tapped his finger under the verse, *I believe. Help now my unbelief.*

I said the words out loud, rolling them in my mouth like candy.

"Okay, well, that's something for me to think about, but I was also hoping you could explain why God would send anyone to hell. It just seems so awful and cruel, and I know I shouldn't think that, but I can't seem to forget about the Rich Man. I feel sorry for him—the poor Rich Man."

"Who?"

"The Rich Man in hell who begs Jesus to send Lazarus to fetch water to touch his tongue because it's painfully dry and he's burning up and God just says, 'Too late.'"

Pastor Womac sputtered out a laugh. "Well I don't know that He says, 'Too late.'"

"Really? God doesn't? Does that mean it's not too late? So people still have a chance?"

"Well, I'm not so sure, but I don't think God would say, 'Too late.' Just like that. God is not cruel."

The logic here was difficult. Pastor Womac was saying that, yes, God would cut people off eternally no matter how much they regretted their past decisions or if in their faultless ignorance they could not properly be understood to have been making decisions at all—and he would deny such a person even the smallest of comforts no matter if all they wanted was the tiniest touch of water on their tongues to relieve the incredible heat of unending fire, but He would never say so in an inconsiderate way— because that would be cruel.

It was like when my Aunt Emily wanted company to leave at the end of a night, she would always say, "Well, this was just a wonderful, wonderful night, now wasn't it? I bet you all are wanting be on your way right about now." Instead of "I'm sick of you. I never should have invited you in the first place. Go home." Because she was polite and not cruel.

The fact that God or Jesus or some combination of the two would be *polite* about icing people out eternally for one wrong decision they'd made on earth really did not make me feel better, but it was important for me to please Pastor Womac and to keep this meeting going.

I said with excessive verve, "Okay, well I guess that's just part of my unbelief. Good news!"

Pastor Womac frowned, apparently unconvinced by my display, so I continued to gush ridiculously, "Thank you for telling me the Thomas unbelief thing. That helps. I really love that one. That one helps a lot!"

Pastor Womac studied me. "I don't think what I've said has made you feel any better, has it?"

"Well, sort of, maybe. I mean it's hard to tell, I guess. I mean, I'm still worried."

"About what?"

"Well, even if I'm saved, what will happen to my Jewish friends Tamar Rosenberg and Leah Greenblatt?"

Pastor Womac inhaled deeply. "God feels even more sad than you do about sending people to hell, Maggie. He wants everyone to come to Him."

He must have noticed me drifting because he touched my hand before continuing. "God wants more than anything for all people to accept His sacrifice of His son. But He also wants people to have free will. He gave each of us a choice."

"I see." I nodded, wanting to believe that somehow the concept of free will might solve my problem. "I guess it's good that everybody has a choice."

I suddenly became anxious about time. I wondered if Pastor Womac had planned for this to be a very short meeting. I wondered if he just expected me to ask something like what the bread and wine in communion symbolized and he could say, "The body and blood of Christ. See you next Sunday." Or for me to wonder, "What if water runs up my nose and I can't breathe?" And he could say, "Pinch your nose. That way you can breathe." The back of my neck dampened with a sudden arrival of sweat and my scalp started to sting, but I had to keep going.

"That's really great that God gave us a choice." I nodded again, looking down at point number three on my pink Hello Kitty Post-it. "But what about people who've never heard about Jesus? Like kids in Africa or India? Will they go to hell?"

"Let's see about that. Open that Bible of yours to Romans 1:19 and read me what it says."

I knew the order of the books well by now, so I flipped forward confidently, quickly finding the passage to read out loud: "*For what can be known about God is plain to them, because God has shown it to them. Ever since the creation of the world, God's invisible nature has been clearly perceived in the things that have been made. So they are without excuse.*"

"I think that answers your question, doesn't it, Maggie? Everyone in some way has a chance to accept Jesus as their savior by perceiving God's creation, even if they've never heard the story of Jesus."

I thought for a minute. "Like in nature, you mean? They could see a rainbow or a stream or something and accept Him? Even without knowing to call it Jesus?"

"Exactly." Pastor Womac was emphatic, wanting to wind up this conversation, I guessed, but being too nice to say so. "I think you feel better now. I'm glad you came to talk to me."

I didn't feel better. Making it through my list of questions only made me want to ask more.

He smiled, this time softly, with kindness. "I'm glad you're getting baptized, Maggie. I think you're ready. Baptism will confirm what you already know, that you are a child of God." Then he repeated a phrase he'd used earlier, a phrase I found to be a peculiarly terrifying compliment: "Big questions for such a little girl."

I slid down off the adult-sized chair, covering my disappointment with a big grown-up-girl smile. I was determined to show myself worthy of this meeting, of the honor I'd been given, of baptism.

• • •

A week later, I sat in a white gown on the wooden bench outside the baptismal, the arctic temperature of the unheated portion of the building freezing my toes to an odd lavender hue. I was painfully aware that baptism or "immersion" wasn't going to save me, but rather, that the ritual action could only outwardly manifest the fact that I'd already accepted Jesus into my heart and had been saved. Another tricky and frightening distinction. I focused my thoughts to work it through carefully: *It's not that Jesus forgives you just because you've been baptized or doesn't forgive you just because you have not. It's that you know you're saved once you've been baptized because you only ask to be baptized once you've already been saved.*

But still, I was excited. Something magical might happen in those few seconds underwater. It was possible I could go down the grim, serious child I was and emerge anew. I prayed for it. I wiggled my toes to jumpstart my circulation, disturbed by their veiny color, but they had become senseless and stiff. "Please let me believe, amen."

I thought of my parents, sitting on either side of me on the edge of my bed, and remembered the feeling of their arms on my shoulders and their bodies pressed against mine, and I wanted to believe their confidence. The robe was thin and my toes were numb, but I decided I would not be cold.

I looked down at my knees and realized I could see my boney legs through the white fabric, and a panicked thought seized me: *This thin white robe is going to get soaked with water and I'm wearing the purple bikini underwear I bought at Contempo Casuals with my babysitting money, and when I come out of the water, they're totally going to show through. Everybody is going to see them.* Why hadn't I thought about this possibility when I opened my dresser drawer this morning and chose an entirely-inappropriate-for-a-baptism undergarment? *Especially when God sees everything!?*

Through the curtains, I watched Pastor Womac, wearing what looked like ill-fitting kayaking pants, step down into the baptismal waters and address the congregation. "Today we joyously welcome a young soul bearing witness to the miracle in her heart. Maggie," he flung his arm to the side like Bob Barker on *The Price Is Right*, "come on out!" I stood up from the bench and padded along the cold floor to the water, tugging at my flagrantly purple underpants, desperately scrunching them up, trying to make them smaller. Then I worried I was making them skimpier, their transgression more egregious, and so I attempted to spread the fabric out again, yanking the elastic waistband up around my hips and the bottom edges down to the tops of my thighs.

I held my breath and waded out into the water, the white gown suctioning onto my body exactly as I feared it would. When I reached Pastor Womac and his kayaking pants, he put one hand behind my back and the other around my head and then I was under, surprised to feel water running up my nose. I had thought baptismal water should feel different, more spiritual, less likely to flood the nasal cavities. But no, the laws of physics were oddly the same. I coughed and sputtered, confused and disoriented as Pastor Womac lifted me back up. I opened my eyes to see his big sincere grin.

I instantly remembered my purple underwear and looked down in horror to see that, sure enough, the immodest violet color was blazing right through my transparent linen draping. I felt the eyes of the churchgoers search me, condemning, and I couldn't bear to look up. I was convinced of their judgment, so I pushed through the water. When I did eventually arrive at the steps, I clambered up, dripping water, and in a labored motion leapt out of sight of the congregation, my white gown trailing infuriatingly behind.

But I was not transformed. I was not renewed or cleansed. My fears of damnation were not washed away. Instead, they clung to me, with varying degrees of fierceness, for the next twelve years. And now I am here in the waiting room, even more terrified than I was then, anticipating a different kind of baptism, one I'm hoping will actually take.

CHAPTER TWO: **PEAS IN A POD**

THE GRACE POINT EVANGELICAL Psychiatric Institute waiting room door opens, revealing a mother and her preteen son. The boy charges in first and slumps down on the couch in front of me. He immediately pins his eyes to where his T-shirt is pulled taut against his protruding belly and begins bouncing his leg urgently. The boy's mother, a citadel of a woman, hunkers down next to him. She notices her son's leg and immediately shoots out her paw of a hand, clamping it down on his knee, white knuckles revealing the edge of her patience.

I look back to the picture of Jesus on the wall and am trying to pinpoint why this particular Jesus looks so menacing to me when my mom breaks her anxious habit of crossing and re-crossing her fingers by grabbing my hand. She rubs her thumb back and forth over my knuckles, assuring me that everything will be all right, despite, I'm sure, not believing it herself. I squeeze her hand back in gratitude and apology. This isn't right. We should be sitting in a dentist's office or back at the Young Scholars Institute we went to last year; I should be able to emerge with a thumbs-up and a scholarship check, or at least a *No Cavities!* certificate.

But today might be the day that solves it all. Absolves her. Absolves me. Maybe a psychiatrist here will tell me something that will dissolve my whole problem; perhaps a verse I missed, or a wisdom I haven't yet heard, will assure me that I'm saved and that I can begin my life again. I fantasize about meeting a wise old psychiatrist with rivulets of smile lines traveling easily across his cheeks, someone who's seen cases like mine often over the years, cases of young college girls who thought too much and only needed reassurance, cases that could be resolved in the *twinkling of an eye*. I picture my imagined psychological savior uncovering ancient texts in Aramaic or Hebrew or Coptic from some ancient bookshelf and explaining to me the secret meanings of the original Gospel writers, and how I can let all my fears go.

Doubt has been my personal demon, the fear of damnation a vampire of cognition privately sucking all joy from my life and infecting my mind with poisonous dread. This place could be my silver bullet.

I reposition myself on the cushionless couch, a couch that makes me painfully aware of my weight-loss, which began as the single collateral perk of my anxiety but continued until now I simply look ill—not "chic" ill, just ill. I imagine wanting to eat again. What would I eat first? I decide it would be pizza, pizza with sausage and feta cheese from Papapolis's Perpetual Pies that Cooper and I would have delivered to our dorm, not that long ago. I remember how we would eat the entire perpetual pie, and then leave the greased-stained box on the floor as we climbed to the top of his bunk bed and into the red REI sleeping bag. Then we would curl around each other like the single-celled paramecium in the biology filmstrips in an entirely mindless embrace.

But I can't think about Cooper now. I need to focus. I must be vigilant; the stakes are too high for sentiment. I shake my head and rub my hands over my face, as if I can reset my mind—or my life. The receptionist calls my name. I stand up and walk toward the door, a gateway that glows with promise under the brash fluorescent lights.

"*I am a promise. I am a possibility.*" I remember the song we used to sing in Sunday school and turn back and see my mother, her slender fingers strangling each other in a clenched prayer.

"*I am a great big bundle of potentiality.*"

I give her a weak thumbs-up. She pulls her hands apart and gives me a weaker one back.

I proceed down a hallway, unguided, toward the one room with an open door. This must be it. Through this portal, my wise old psychological savior is waiting. My breath quickens with hope. Yes, this is it. This could be it. Yes. Yes. I need to be open, ready to receive. I enter, bloated with hope. But then my stomach hollows with disappointment when I see a woman not much older than me who bears an uncanny resemblance to my old Sunday school teacher Miss Trimly—except this lady's face is pulled tight even without the bun. She wears a floral blouse whose buttons climb up to a find sweet lace collar, a prairie skirt that reaches modestly below her knees, and has a delicacy of features that display a humble femininity before her Lord. She is the type of pretty that passes as kind, the type of woman I dislike immediately, despite my inability to pinpoint any crime.

The young Miss Trimly smiles at me as if I'm a disabled girl she's welcoming to a potluck, proud to be overlooking my disability. "That's right, Maggie. Right this way. Not as hard as you thought, right?" She gestures to a chair with a bright yellow cross needlepointed into the upholstery and smiles with what seems like a menacing look of good will. I remind myself, however, that my perception has become warped; I've backslid so far that I can no longer tell good from bad. For a second I feel uncomfortable plopping down on the needlepointed cross, on the symbol of Christ's innocent sacrifice for my guilty condition. But I steel myself and ease my butt down with delicacy and respect for the holy emblem, an act for which I am immediately congratulated.

"There you go, Maggie. That's right."

I release the arms of the chair and place my hands in my lap.

"My name is Bethanie. With an *ie*. Not a *y*. I can't tell you how many times people misspell it." She looks at me steadily, expectant, as if it's my turn to say something, as if I've missed my cue.

"I'll remember not to misspell it," I jump in.

"Well, I'd appreciate that. Maggie. Is that short for Margaret?"

"Yes, but I've always gone by Maggie."

"I have an aunt named Margaret."

I give what I feel is the traditional nod of recognition for banal comments necessary in any social contact, but Bethanie clearly desires something more. She sits smiling at me in a way I know she thinks is sweet, but it makes me think instead of the Patti Smith line, "Ugly can be beautiful but pretty never." I keep that thought to myself, however, and explain, "Yeah, I've never liked *Margaret*. It seems like a name for a stuffy spinster, some sad lone woman whose cameo brooch pulls her lace collar too tight." I laugh. Bethanie does not, so I quickly add, "Not that your aunt is stuffy, I don't know your aunt, obviously, it's just my association . . ."

A flash of hostility cuts through Bethanie's sweet facade. "So tell me why you're here."

"I'm experiencing extreme anxiety about my eternal destiny," I explain. "I'm scared I've lost my salvation or that maybe I was never saved in the first place." Then I immediately answer the question I'm certain she's about to ask: "I accepted Jesus into my heart when I was six—then probably eighty to ninety thousand times after that. I've just never been sure that I did it right."

Bethanie leans forward. "What do you mean by *doing it right*?"

"Saying the prayer the right way. Believing enough."

"How much belief would be enough?"

"Well, that's the thing I don't know." I let it all come out; it's too fast, too confusing, but it's coming out and there's nothing I can do about it now. I feel like I've been holding my breath, and I'm grateful and embarrassed to release it in strange, satisfying spurts. "My belief that Jesus is the son of God is somewhere between believing that Pluto is the ninth planet from the sun and believing that Elvis is alive."

I do not expect what comes out of Bethanie's mouth next. "Are you sure that Pluto is the ninth planet from the sun?"

"Well, I mean I'm pretty sure."

"I think it's the planet *closest* to the sun—"

"No, that's Mercury. Mercury, Venus, Earth, Mars, Jupiter, Saturn, Uranus, Neptune, and Pluto. My Very Educated Mother Just Served Us Nine Pizzas."

"What?"

"Oh, it's a mnemonic to remember the order of the planets. *M* for Mercury—"

"But I think Pluto is the closest."

"Well, not according to scientists—"

"Are you sure?"

"Well, no, I'm not sure . . . I'm not sure about anything. Neither are the scientists. That's exactly the point I'm trying to make. It seems like belief is on a scale, that everyone believes any proposition to a certain extent and also doubts it to a certain extent."

Bethanie considers this and then shakes her head. "You sure like to make things complicated, don't you?"

I take the only option that seems possible in the moment: I shrug my shoulders and say, "Yeah, I guess I do."

Bethanie smiles to demonstrate sympathy for a problem she has clearly never had and then asks if I've been baptized. I tell her about my baptism at age nine, and how I'd hoped the immersion would cleanse my uncertainty and wash away all my fears. "But it didn't help," I tell her. "After that, things only got worse. Especially since that was the year my grandmother had her break."

My grandmother was a blue-eyed adulteress and I loved her. I didn't find out about the adulteress part until I was teenager, long after her psychological break, but I had always known there was something "bad" about her. For one thing, she wore makeup—not the light pink gloss my mom occasionally wore, which was only a shade brighter than her natural color. But red, real red, like Snow White's lips, like Dorothy's shoes. And her blue eyes! Blue like the hydrangeas in our backyard I wasn't supposed to pick, a startling color made more magnificent by something she lushly pronounced "*maz-gayer-uh*" that extravagantly splayed her long eyelashes aside. Plus she wore scarves, not to fend off the Chicago wind, not because, like my mom told me, you lose 40 percent of your heat from your neck and head . . . but just because she *liked the colors*.

I worried about my colorful grandmother, however, because she had never accepted Jesus into her heart by saying the Sinner's Prayer. When I asked my grandmother about "accepting Jesus into her heart," she said she didn't like putting it in "those terms." One day I would help her understand it wasn't about her terms, it was about God's terms and that there

was a very specific prayer that needed to be said with a very specific attitude and that we both really needed to figure this out.

We shared the same middle name: LaVee. My grandmother's parents allowed their four girls to pick their middle names when they were
seven. My grandmother's sisters picked May, Jean, and Anne, traditional
Christian names they'd heard before, but my grandma picked LaVee, a
name she made up because she thought it sounded "wild and pretty and
possibly French." I called her Grandma LaVee and she called me Maggie LaVee in a privileged society of two. When Grandma LaVee came to
visit my family, she was pleased to see her son, my dad, but I knew I was
why she got on a plane, even though she was terrified of flying. *I* was
why she came to Chicago in the winter, even though she hated the cold.
She told me once I was her "favorite flavor of ice cream. Better than mint
chocolate chip."

I would anticipate her visit for weeks, and when she arrived, I would
jump up and down until I lost my breath and then I'd launch into a performance of the routine I was learning in my Glenview Park dance class.
Huffing and puffing, I would passionately shuffle ball change, pirouette,
and jeté, occasionally into unsuspecting furniture, making a LOT of facial
expressions. A teacher had once told me to "dance with my face," an instruction I really went to town with. Grandma LaVee would watch my clumsy,
muggy performance, entranced, her blue "maz-gayer-uhd" eyes rapt.

Grandma LaVee did lots of things I knew she wasn't supposed to do.
We would go to the drugstore to get a bag of candied orange slices to
share. Instead of meting them out in appropriate portions like my parents
always did, she'd hand the candy over in fistfuls and we'd eat just as fast
as we wanted, consuming the whole bag until we both felt sick. One time
she let me try on her red lipstick in the park. I looked at myself in her
compact mirror, and then the two of us spun around the merry-go-round.
We were like "two peas in a pod," she said. We were red-lipped and free,
high on orange-slice candy, still whirling even after the merry-go-round
had stopped.

I didn't find out about her history with my grandfather until much later.
The story was this: My dad's father had two sons with a woman in Apex,

North Carolina. Then one day, he met Grandma LaVee, with her eyes and lips and her scarves, then soon after he left his wife and kids. I saw a picture once of him and my grandmother seated together on the hood of an old Mustang, my grandma's leg crossed over his, her scarf flying in the wind.

This is still my favorite picture of her. It's how I like to remember her. Before the break. Before the phone call.

A month before Christmas the phone in our kitchen rang sometime after ten P.M., much later than we normally received calls. My dad picked up the receiver, listened, and when he answered, the sound of his voice changed. His tone was flatter. Deeper. Something had happened to my grandmother. My dad's strange new voice said, "I'm getting on a plane. I'll be there as soon as I can."

Dad flew to North Carolina, brought my grandmother back to Chicago, and admitted her into a hospital near us. This is how I pieced together the story from overheard bits of conversation: My grandmother had gotten really sad, so sad that she didn't know what was real and what was not. So sad that she thought the IRS, which was part of the government, was chasing her because she hadn't paid her taxes, so she hid from them behind a tree in the woods behind her sister Poppy's house. The IRS never came because they don't go looking for people in the woods. But the police do. And the police found my grandmother and told my Aunt Poppy that my grandmother was crazy, but my Aunt Poppy said, "No, you're wrong. She's just fine." Then my Aunt Poppy had called up my Dad and told him the story, and my Dad had agreed with the police officers.

Then I knew; I understood why this must have happened.

It was because Grandma LaVee hadn't accepted Jesus. Or if she had, she hadn't meant it 100 percent.

After two weeks and several rounds of electroshock treatments, my grandmother was able to receive visitors at Garden Grove psychiatric facility. I was excited to see her again, excited she was in town, excited to give her the Christmas present I'd bought with my babysitting money, a box of her favorite candy, ZERO Bars, fourteen ZERO Bars in all. But more important than the candy, more important than the delicious combination of white chocolate and nougat, nuts, and caramel, was ensuring my grandmother's eternal destiny. Someone needed to lead her to Jesus, and that was exactly what I planned to do.

My family arrived at Garden Grove, a modest facility with a smattering of flowers that smelled like old perfume and a fountain that emptied into a small pond with artificial lily pads. Next to the fountain were two wheelchairs, containing two men, one young, one old. Their eyes were open, but all four pupils appeared to be submerged in some unreachable yellow sea. I passed the men and then walked down the Garden Grove halls flanked by parents, the box of candy smashed under my armpit, my step keeping time to the piped-in music of "Jingle Bell Rock."

We found my grandmother slumped on a chair in the visitor's lounge. She wore no scarf. She had on no gorgeous lipstick. No extravagant *maz-gayer-uh* set off her hydrangea-blue eyes. Instead, she sat plain-faced with her lips gummed around a cigarette, yanking the smoke into her lungs, gazing at the wall in front of her or maybe at her own naked eyelashes.

"Look, I brought you a present," I piped, pulling the smushed ZERO Bar box from underneath my sweaty armpit and holding it out. In the old days, her bright blue eyes would have lit up as she clapped her hands before pulling me into chest, with an "Ooh, I love it, Maggie LaVee. My favorite! Better than mint chocolate chip!"

But now, with dull, soulless eyes, my grandma grabbed the box and tore into it, ripping off the wrappers, which she dropped on the floor, and shoving the candy into her mouth, gumming the treats like a goat in a petting zoo. To cover the silence, I told her it was great to see her and that I'd be praying she'd come to know Jesus as her personal savior. As if in reply, a string of caramel dangling from her lower lip swayed back and forth like a strand of crazy golden tinsel.

My family would visit my grandmother at Garden Grove after church on Sundays, sitting in the lounge with the other patients. I got used to the regulars. There was the saucer-eyed fellow who bobbed forward from his waist, as if sipping from a birdbath; the spindly woman who mumbled to herself, something about misplacing her spleen; and the jittery kid who rocked back and forth, roughly blinking his eyes, like he couldn't believe what he was seeing—even if it was just the half-eaten roast beef sandwich that lay on his tray.

At first my grandmother didn't speak. Well, she spoke, just not words. But there were sounds. Especially when she smoked. Sounds of pleasure—odd moans punctuated with an occasional high-pitched squeak. Then after several visits she began making sentences. She had three go-to responses to get her back to the silence she preferred, that would return her to her pure solitary nicotine communion: "I reckon it's all right," "I don't rightly know," and "Sure, that's just fine."

She never seemed exactly . . . crazy. She never said anything that didn't make sense. Nothing frightening. She didn't throw herself about the room. She never saw or heard anything that wasn't there. It was just that she herself was never really there.

On one of our visits, Grandma broke her use of prefab responses to fend off conversation and said, "Grant, can you get me a *National Enquirer*?" My father was clearly pleased, his eyes clouding for a moment, his chest rising with tentative hope. "Of course, Mama," he said quickly. "Of course I'll get you a *National Enquirer*. I'll get you a subscription. I can do that, today. Sure I can."

Grandma's expression lifted from where it had drooped for the last several weeks in an unchanging pout, but instead of achieving a smile, her lips merely stayed flat.

"I'd like that," she said.

On the way home, my mom said, "I think she's getting better; don't you, Grant?" But sadly, as it turned out, that brief conversation, that flat smile, that modest request was as better as she was ever going to get.

When she was released from the hospital, my grandmother moved in with my family. She had her own room with a bed, an ottoman, a television, and a rocking chair that she rocked back and forth in all day. My dad put the television on for her to watch, but eventually she said she preferred it to be off. So that's how we left it, and she continued to rock and stare at the television, just like she had before.

Once my dad suggested moving the television out of her room and replacing it with a table, where a bouquet of flowers could be set. Sunflowers,

he suggested, or maybe lilacs. "Like you used to like, Mama." My grandmother responded with more life than she'd shown in weeks, not with enthusiasm over the prospect of flowers, but in angry insistence that she didn't
want them. She demanded the television stay. My dad, heartened by her display of will, suggested he could maybe put on *Tic-Tac-Dough* or *Joker's Wild*.
Grandma picked at the scabs on her face, festering acne late in life that she
had not addressed, and replied, "No, I reckon it's all right as it is. Sure, that's
just fine." Besides the dark, silent television, she liked two things: Beer. And
Whoppers from Burger King—tomato and ketchup only.

I was scared for my grandmother, scared of what would happen to
her when she died. She didn't recognize the mortal jeopardy she was in
and maybe never would, especially since her mental facilities were so
severely compromised. It became more important than ever to get her to
say the prayer.

Finally, I decided I had to take action. I pulled a Budweiser from the
refrigerator, opened the bottle, and brought it into her room. Then I sat on
the ottoman and asked casually, as if it were an idea I had just alighted on,
"Hey, Grandma, I was wondering if you might want to accept Jesus into
your heart today? What do you think?"

Grandma took a thirsty sip. "I reckon it's all right."

"Great! It'll just take a minute. I mean, you know all about Jesus and
how He died for our sins on the cross and came back to life and stuff. Your
dad was a pastor, so I know you know the story. Not a made-up story. It's
a *true* story. So I think you probably believe in Jesus."

"I don't rightly know."

"Do you . . . believe?"

"Well, sure, that sounds just fine."

This was not convincing. I needed more. "But belief isn't enough; you
have to accept Jesus."

"I reckon that's all right."

Okay. Great. "So . . . do you want to accept Him? You can do it right
here. I'll say the words, and you can say them after me. Then you'll go to
heaven. As long as you mean it when you say it."

"I reckon we could do that another day."

"No, let's do it today. I mean . . ." I looked into her eyes. The color that used to seem so startling, like the hydrangeas in our backyard, now looked drab. The dazzling hue I remembered had been replaced by a tired, smoggy-afternoon blue. I wondered if they had always been that color. They must have. The color of your eyes doesn't change just because you have a mental breakdown.

"Do you believe in Jesus?"

"Sure, it don't matter to me one way or the other."

No. No. No. This was lukewarm. She couldn't be lukewarm. God would spit her out of his mouth if she was lukewarm. She wouldn't be able to understand this now. I needed to understand for her.

"But it *has* to matter to you!" I cried. "You *have* to accept Him."

My grandmother began grinding her jaw, like she was chewing something, despite there being nothing in her mouth. "All right, Maggie, I'm gonna rest my eyes for a while." She shut her eyes for a moment, then popped them open to say, "If y'all go to Burger King, maybe you could get me a Whopper. I reckon that would be all right." Then her eyelids fell again. "Tomato and ketchup only, all right?"

I figured if I pushed my grandma into saying the prayer, it wouldn't count. You can't fool God. Accepting Jesus had to be something Grandma wanted to do on her own. But still, I kept offering to say the prayer with her every now and then. She always declined, shutting me down with either "I reckon not now" or "I like it with tomato and ketchup only." Eventually I stopped asking, and my grandmother gave way to the old woman who lived on the rocking chair in my house. My relationship with her was not unlike the one I had with the ottoman—that is, if the ottoman had been a terrifying warning of what might someday happen to me if I didn't stay on the right path.

My parents insisted that my grandmother's psychotic break and frightening electroshock therapy, and her institutionalization and subsequent hollowing into a heap that rocked in a chair, bore no connection to religion or God, yet I knew that the opposite was true. I knew I was in grave danger if I didn't cleave to my savior with true Christian fire in my heart.

And now here I was at Grace Point Psychiatric, following in Grandma LaVee's footsteps, marching down the same dark tunnel. Grandma LaVee and I were, as she had always said, two peas in a pod.

CHAPTER THREE: **BIGGER THAN YOU THINK**

BETHANIE OPENS THE FOLDER on her lap, runs her finger down a list to the item she's looking for, nods, picks up a pen, and makes a tidy check in the "yes" column.

"Okay," she says with a satisfied smile, "Family history of mental illness."

It occurs to me that Bethanie is one of those people with a capacity for certainty, with an ability to see things simply; a being well-suited for a form with columns of "yes" and "no."

"Did your fears increase or decrease after this?"

"Oh, they got much, much worse."

In eighth grade, I decided the only thing to do about my increasing terror was to commit myself further to Christ. So I signed up for the Hope Valley Baptist youth ministry group, AWANA, encouraged by its thick, glossy brochure, saturated with multi-colored hope. AWANA was led by Mr. and Mrs. Pikenide, a childless couple in their midfifties who prided themselves on making the gospel fun for *young people*. God had called them to minister to *young people*. In reality, all this meant was that us *young people* got a snack break while Mr. Pikenide juggled for us using a variety of fruits, vegetables, and beanbags shaped like crosses. (Mrs. Pikenide bragged that Mr. Pikenide had once been one of the country's most famous Christian jugglers! A claim which, given its narrow scope, I suspect might very well have been true.)

Every week the Pikenides would teach us, using lots of shiny airborne objects, how to convert our friends to Christianity. But the problem was, I didn't want to convert anyone. I didn't want to proclaim to all my friends that I thought my God was better than their God or their family's God or even their lack of God. Middle school was hard enough. I already couldn't drink beer or swear or gossip, and when the popular girls asked me to let them cheat off my tests in biology, I had to reply, "Oh, I so wish I could. But I'm a Christian," and endure their icy glares as I miserably shielded the word *mitochondria* with my elbow.

How much more embarrassment did God want me to endure? But if we complained, Mrs. Pikenide would quote Luke 9:26: *He who is ashamed of Christ on earth, Christ will be ashamed of him on Judgment Day.* Week after week, she drummed her lesson into our heads, equating being ashamed with being tortured eternally in hell until Mr. Pikenide burst through the door juggling cucumbers and stuffed crucifixes. I would sit slightly apart, flop-sweating through my roll-on deodorant in horror, knowing that, above all else, I had to prove to Jesus that I wasn't ashamed of Him.

The Pikenides explained that there were two ways to convert our friends. The first and most desirable was the "direct witness," which meant working Bible verses naturally into conversation. The direct witness was what crazy Ho-sook Namgoong did. Every day during lunch period, Ho-sook Namgoong would pull out the red pocket Bible that was never in her pocket but always open in her hands and cry to whoever wanted to listen and especially to those who did not, "Believe in Jesus or you will perish!" This was not for me.

Less desirable but still acceptable was the "silent witness," which entailed wearing something that indicated we were Christians and then behaving so well that people would nod to each other and wonder, "Hey, what is this Christianity thing? I gotta get me some."

I knew I had to witness if I didn't want to go to hell. And since the silent witness seemed like the easier of the two options, I went to the Christian bookstore to get an inconspicuous silver cross. But on my way to the jewelry section, I saw a blue T-shirt with gold lettering that read, *Feel the Force. Jesus.* I looked at the T-shirt and wondered what its slogan could mean. Was it supposed to be "feel the force *of* Jesus" and they dropped the "of" to give it more of a pop? I flushed with embarrassment at the thought of wearing such a thing to school.

Then . . . I panicked. Did Jesus think I was ashamed of Him because I didn't want to wear this T-shirt? Was He going to be ashamed of me on Judgment Day because I was ashamed of this T-shirt and therefore ashamed of Him? I paid for the shirt at the cash register, bracing even then for my impending humiliation. Then I slumped home, holding the shopping bag away from my body as if it were a sack of shit, determined to prove, with this deliberate act of social self-immolation, that I was not ashamed.

The next morning I walked into homeroom wearing the *Feel the Force. Jesus* T-shirt. My classmates were silent at first as they struggled to puzzle out the shirt's elusive message. Then Eric Kirshenbaum stood up on his desk and began leading the class in singing, "Jesus and Maggie sitting in a tree, K-I-S-S-I-N-G." I joined in, hoping I could be in on the joke and not the object of it. "First comes love. Then comes marriage. Then comes baby and the baby carriage." After the fifth round, I dropped out and just stared at the lines in my hands till the bell rang. Every now and then I looked up at my classmates to acknowledge how funny the joke was.

On the walk home, I relived my humiliation, scrupulously reviewing each horrific component: the smirks I had received at the beginning of each class when fresh eyes landed on my flat chest, flattened further by the ill-fitting T-shirt with the very uncool slogan that no one could understand; the giggles and looks exchanged behind my back; and Errol LoPiccolo saying in his most understanding tone, "Hey, I don't care what anyone else thinks. I think your T-shirt is cool," before shouting, "Just kidding!" and laughing so hard he almost fell down.

I recognized that despite my mortification—or indeed, because of it— my project had been a success. From the moment I had put on the shirt in the morning and all through the day, fear of damnation had not appeared in my mind. I had successfully swept the familiar demon away with the more acute and immediate pain of eighth-grade social humiliation.

Yet as I walked on with a lift in my step, in the moment of calmness that followed I began to wonder if I'd done enough to prove to Jesus that I was not ashamed. It seemed that the only way to ensure my eternal state was to wear yet another T-shirt—one so mortifying, with such overwhelming potential for social suicide, that it would surely convince Jesus of my allegiance to Him once and for all. I went back that night and bought two more T-shirts, unable to decide which one was the worst and, consequently, best suited to my cause. The following morning I showed up at school with silk-screened T-shirt #1, which said, *You think Duran Duran rocks? Try Jesus.* On Wednesday I wore a tank top emblazoned with *Madonna is hot—but Jesus is sizzling.*

And despite wanting to vomit or join a witness protection program where I could start life anew, I still wondered, was it enough? Had I done enough to satisfy Jesus? Which led me to think, *I need to do something so deeply humiliating, so permanently scarring, that I will prove to Jesus beyond a shadow of a doubt that I am NOT ashamed.* My next step became clear. It was time to do the direct witness, to speak in Bible verses, to join forces with Ho-sook Namgoong.

So when Vanessa Vandergraff asked me if I had a flashlight for Outdoor Ed, I replied, "No, I don't, but like Psalm 119:105 says, *Christ's Word is a light unto my feet and a lamp unto my path.*" When Sam Seagal confided in me by the vending machines that he was saving up for a roadster mountain bike, I said, "Well, that's cool, but *Why not store up for yourself treasures in heaven, where neither moth nor rust doth destroy, nor thieves break in and steal at night?*" Sam scoffed and actually pointed his finger into my face and said, "Why not stop being a turd?"

This hurt, but this was good. God was smiling down on me like a warm golden sun, a sun I was determined to keep shining. I became increasingly drunk on the humiliation and the hope that it would save me.

The most painful witness I ever made myself do was with James Kane. James Kane had absurdly thick eyelashes and the sharp, intelligent features of a boy who belongs in prep school brochures. He said I was the only girl in school who "got the beat," an odd expression, but one that made me feel like I was the cool girl drummer in our exclusive two-person band. James would bring in *Far Side* cartoons to our geography class, and we'd discuss them. I'd point out details to James like, "Look how the dinosaur's sticking out his tongue." And he'd say, "Yeah, that's what makes the whole thing so sardonic." I had no idea what *sardonic* meant and I doubt he did either, but I would still gaze at James instead of the maps and imagine us married, trading esoteric comments, both "getting it."

One day toward the end of eighth grade, our class took a field trip to explore ecological footprints at Lake Michigan, an activity which quickly degenerated into students running around unsupervised on the beach while our teachers lay under umbrellas reading mystery novels and smoking cigarettes they thought we wouldn't see. I sat by myself on a towel, while other kids threw each other into the water and had chicken fights. I grimly hunched against my anxiety, a spinster aunt watching her nieces and nephews enjoying the vigor of life, content to sit in the background until her own dry existence was over.

But then . . . James Kane came over and sat down next to me and started running his hands through the sand in the little patch in front of us. James's hands were fascinating. The palms were wider than mine, the fingers longer, and the knuckles squarer, popping out like little screws under the skin. I watched the joints extending and flexing like mechanical hinges and drew a full breath—cool, lake air—into my lungs for the first time that day.

I had a boy with fantastic hands who thought I "got it" sitting on my towel with me—a towel that now seemed like a magic carpet of domestic bliss. I imagined that years from now we would be sitting together on a towel much like this, maybe on a different beach, maybe far away, our vigorous children leaping into the waves, their skin, slightly tanner than mine, glittering under the sun. James would be running his hands, older now but still fantastic, through the sand.

I looked up from James's fingers, over the sand, to the other kids horsing around in the lake, and further to the partly overcast sky, grayish-blue, like a well-worn blanket. *The color of James's eyes*, I thought.

In an instant, panic gripped me so tightly I felt prickles all over my body.

Is Jesus going to wonder why I haven't witnessed to James Kane yet? I mean, I like him, don't I? Maybe even love him.

I tried to take a deep breath, but my diaphragm was frozen.

I knew if I witnessed to James, he would probably never speak to me again. But I also knew that if I did this . . . it would have to be enough for Jesus. This was going to hurt, but it would be worth it in the end. Like when I fell out of the backseat of the car when I was seven and my mom put Bactine on my scrapes and I howled in pain. But it wasn't useless pain; it was pain that would prevent infection, prevent my body from becoming riddled with disease. So as James ran his fascinatingly male fingers through the sand, I dug my nails into my palms and mumbled, "Hey, um, Jesus talked about sand. He said *your sins are as numerous as the grains of sand and your iniquities spread as far as east is from west.*"

James's eyes had widened, but I didn't slow down, "*And God gave Solomon wisdom even as the sand that is on the sea shore*, 1 Kings 4:29."

I felt dizzy, my heart was beating through my skull, and my face must have been shining with madness.

James Kane looked at me with a mixture of pity and revulsion. Then he stood up from my magic-carpet beach towel and walked away as if I had just crapped myself and he was gentleman enough to afford me the privacy and dignity to clean myself up.

Heartbroken, I picked up my towel from the sand, the towel James Kane had been sitting on like a boyfriend or a husband only moments before, and smashed it in my bag, assuring myself that even though I was hurting now, it was worth it. It was a matter of temporal versus eternal reward. I had to prioritize, and I'd prioritized well. God now knew I wasn't afraid to spread His Word—even if it cost me James Kane. I'd sacrificed, like others for centuries before me, like shepherds had sacrificed their sheep, goat-herders their goats, like Abraham, even, who had been willing to sacrifice his son Isaac. Like them, I had proven my dedication, sacrificing romance, acceptance, and social standing. This was an important, serious T-shirt. Eternity lay in the balance, and I was glad I was wearing it. *Feel the Force. Jesus.*

Then I froze. Wait a minute . . . if God was omniscient, wouldn't He know that on the inside, I'd been ashamed this whole time? *He who is ashamed of Christ, Christ will be ashamed of him on Judgment Day.* God is all-seeing and all-knowing. The logic was unavoidable.

I chilled to the bone despite the day's heat. How had I missed the horrible, gaping hole in my proof? My planning, my sacrifice, the humiliation I suffered had all been a waste. Worse than a waste—they had highlighted my shame and multiplied my sins.

"But, no, it's not too late," I told myself. "It's not too late until Judgment Day. Until then there is always a chance. The buzzer has not gone off."

I accept you, Jesus, into my heart. Please forgive my sins and cleanse me from all unrighteousness, I prayed over and over, vowing to begin my devotions anew.

I decided that the more I dedicated myself to Jesus and learned what the Bible said, the safer I would be. The more I tilled the soil of God's verses, the more likely it was that genuine faith would blossom inside me. So I started competing in Bible-verse memorization competitions where teams from different churches would battle it out in cutthroat matchups. The leader would announce a chapter and verse, and the first kid to spit back the answer would score a point. So I made it my business to score thousands of points, accumulating a shelf of Bible Memorization awards in short order. I found my awards shelf a great comfort. A hell-bound girl wouldn't have five blue ribbons and three purple ones for Scripture-reciting contests. She wouldn't have a towering gold trophy shaped like a girl with pigtails holding a Bible aloft.

That year I was cast in a play about Noah and the Great Flood called *100 Percent Chance of Rain*. For the opening song, we all wore rain slickers and danced with umbrellas and sang, "Now the Lord was unhappy with the people on earth. They were not what they ought to be and not what they're worth. They were bad and ugly and mean as could be. So the Lord wiped them out, as you will see."

I attempted to puzzle out the possible rationale from what on first blush seemed like cruel behavior but that I knew must not be. God had told the people on earth to do certain things, but people were imperfect, fallible as God created them, willful and stupid and egocentric and needy and vain. Then, when the inevitable outcome came to pass, God decided to teach them a lesson by drowning them—wives, parents, children—with water dropped from the sky that covered their heads and filled up their lungs until they asphyxiated. God slaughtered every single family but one. And for some reason known only to Him, He also decided to include the animals. He drowned the bears and the elephants and some kid's turtle and some neighbor's golden retriever. And like the Irish Rovers used to sing in what may be the happiest lyric about mass killing, *He drowned the green alligators, the long-necked geese, the humpty-back llamas, and the chimpanzees.* Crazy God even tried to drown the fish.

I told the director, Pastor Bill, that in this whole story about the flood, God seemed pretty cruel, and I told him that it scared me to think of this God as my Father, and I said, it especially scared me to think of this God as my Father who was with me all the time, everywhere I went, watching me even in my sleep.

Pastor Bill nodded with understanding before saying, "Maggie, listen. It is very, very important that you *not* feel the way you feel. God wouldn't like it very much if he knew you didn't want him around." And then he went into that whisper voice that every Baptist pastor uses when he wants to indelibly etch some bit of churchly horror within a malleable child's still-growing skull. "And Maggie," he said, "God sees and knows everything that we think."

So God was a big security camera in the sky whose feelings were easily hurt. He was a jealous God, capable of bitter, barbaric revenge. But the Bible also said God was other things. God was a dove. He was a pearl of great price. A spirit. A ghost. A loaf of bread. A ray of light. A grain of wheat. A glass of wine. A fish. A bridegroom. A lamb. *Yeast.*

I said to Pastor Bill, "I'm really . . . really confused. How can all these things be true at the same time?" Pastor Bill said, "Maggie, those are metaphors. Like when Jesus says, 'I am the bread.' He is expressing the idea that His path offers spiritual nourishment, just as bread that you eat offers physical nourishment."

A wave of relief washed over me. I gushed my gratitude to him. "Ohhh, well, that makes so much more sense. So God didn't really kill all those people and animals so vindictively like that. That's just a metaphor. And He's not literally my Father, who is literally watching everything I do, even when I'm in the bathroom. That's just a metaphor too."

"Maggie," Pastor Bill cautioned me sternly, "Don't blaspheme!"

• • •

My fears began to subside when I got to high school, where the God of the Bible was slowly eclipsed by the God of Glenbrook South Theater, so slowly that I didn't realize the great swap was even happening. By the end of my freshman year, instead of repeating Bible verses over and over in my head, I was reciting lines from Laura in *The Glass Menagerie* and Corie in *Barefoot in the Park*. Instead of repeating the Sinner's Prayer on my way home from school, I was adjusting intonations, honing the dialects, finding emotional substitutions, and above all, rehearsing my spontaneity.

I took high school theater as seriously as I took everything else. I read Uta Hagen and did the acting exercises alone in my room, pretending to lose my wallet (trying to forget I'd placed it under the bed) and then going through the process, the "moment-by-moment" journey of looking for it. I'd endow the wallet with "stakes," just like the book said. I needed the money inside for my infant daughter's heart transplant.

"Little Cara will make it, but you have to find the wallet," I'd imagine my dying husband whispering with his last breath.

"Where is it? Where *is* it?"

I was never able to produce the wet sobs of joy I hoped for, but I once did manage to squeeze out something close to a tear, so I knew I was on my way.

I rehearsed different character walks, leading with alternating parts of my body. I practiced empathy, attempting to feel the pain of every homeless person I encountered, in case I was ever called upon to play someone disenfranchised or abandoned. I read about French theorist Antonin Artaud's "theater of cruelty" and tried to apply the principles of "nerve shocking" to my work in Neil Simon's *Brighton Beach Memoirs*. Mine was a very intense imagining of sixteen-year-old Nora Morton.

The other kids were more interested in goofing off in rehearsal until it was time for the applause and subsequent cast party. I enjoyed the cast parties when they involved discussing the most successful aspects of our performance or trading maudlin insights about no longer inhabiting our characters or living in the world of the play. I did not like them when they involved activities like Truth or Dare, a game in which neither option seemed to be in my best interest, both requiring me to take action I'd certainly avoid under normal circumstances.

My theological anxiety had not entirely vanished, but I was usually able to push it aside to focus on more pressing demands, like creating an emotional biography for my character Mrs. Gibbs in *Our Town*, who I decided dreamed of being an opera singer in Paris but had to settle for singing soprano in a choir led by a drunk in Grover's Corners. Most of the time the demands of Glenbrook South Theater did not conflict with God's laws. I could portray Gwendolen, for example, in *The Importance of Being Earnest* without fear of transgression. If Jesus were to sit in the front row opening night, sandwiched between the Holy Ghost and his Father, I would be able to say my lines proudly, thankful to share well-crafted wordplay with such illustrious company.

But occasionally, I would be given a role that I worried wouldn't be edifying to God, like when I got cast as Miss Gregory in *Tell Me That You Love Me, Junie Moon*. In the play, Miss Gregory repeatedly demands that Warren, a lifetime paraplegic, attempt to walk, even after many failed attempts in which Warren tips forward on collapsing legs and whacks his face bloody on the concrete. Each time this happens, the stage directions say that Miss Gregory gleefully grinds the spoke of her heel into the ground as she squeals, "Yes, Warren, yes! Now again! Again!"

It was difficult to figure out how to make the role of Miss Gregory edifying to Jesus (or why we were doing this play at all in high school). But then I figured God must know that all roles in plays can't be saints. He must understand that drama needs bad guys. He's the One who created Aristotle, as we learned about in Intro to Drama, who said that the most important of the six elements of drama is plot, and that plot is built on conflict, and that conflict needs a villain. God had to know I couldn't always play the hero, and what's more I shouldn't want to. That would be selfish. Sometimes I'd be the hero, but sometimes I'd be the villain, or a townsperson with no lines who peeked through windows to direct audience attention and ascribe importance to the main action, or sometimes maybe just a dead villager down stage right. Like Stanislavski (who God also created) said, "There are no small parts, only small actors."

So sometimes the old fear flickered, but I was able to deftly snuff it out, remembering that God was familiar with the mechanics of dramatic conflict and assuring myself that the Bible instructs us to exercise our God-given talents. *Do not neglect the gift you've been given from heaven.*

I still believed in Jesus, still didn't do anything that I knew to be sinful, and still tried desperately not to *want* to do anything I knew to be sinful. I didn't swear. I didn't drink. I didn't lie. Ever. I didn't gossip. I didn't cheat on tests. I didn't have sex. Or engage in "petting," light or heavy, because my youth group leaders cautioned us to "save the petting for your pets."

I tried to fit in, but I always felt one step removed, like I was doing an imitation of a teenager, the way Canadians always seem like they're doing impressions of Americans, or toddlers appear to be mimicking drunks. I felt grim and dour, but I worked hard at seeming lighthearted and fun, the type of girl who thrills at the mention of a "kegger" or a "rager" or whatever else the other kids called the parties I never attended. I practiced giggling, but I could never sustain more than a "heh-heh" without feeling like a ridiculous fraud. It occurred to me that my disposition was well-suited for the Great Depression era, when a serious attitude was needed for survival, when frivolity was a once-a-year kind of thing if you could afford it—a little swinging around a maypole and then back to business.

Before classes began I would sit at my desk, anxious for the teacher to arrive, watching my normal, lighthearted high school classmates as if through a sheet of double-paned glass. Darcy Devonport was the lightest and most natural. Darcy was a delicate five foot two on tiptoes, which she often was, a butterfly everyone wished would flutter his or her way. She would spread her arms, a wingspan full of uncomplicated luster, gracing everyone's lives with her delightful blond whimsy. Darcy had a great move, a move I dearly wished I could pull off. She would coyly pluck a baseball cap off some lucky boy's head and plop it on her own, seemingly at random, but always at the perfect angle to accent her adorable blond curls and strike an image of pure sugar-spun delight.

The boy sans cap, elated at the attention and not-so-secretively charmed, would pretend to be angry and snatch his cap back. "Come on," Darcy would make a show of complaining, "I'm having a bad hair day.

Not fair!" and frown in a way that did the impossible—it made Darcy look even more fun. Then a second boy, unwilling to let the first claim Darcy's limelight all for himself, would take off his hat, come up from behind, and plop it on Darcy's head. She would then angle the hat so irresistibly over her eyelashes that it would make everyone (even me) want to date her. Then she'd smile and coo a thank-you at the second guy, stick out her tongue at the first, and toss back her wave of blond hair, which I'm still convinced was the color of moonlight.

Sometimes I would have a piece of gossip that I could conceivably use to insert myself into the pre-class festivities. Like when I saw Gina Romano kissing Chuck Cheetum in the stairway, when everyone knew that Gina Romano was dating Gabe Hincapie. This little item would have been a great thing to talk about before class began, but I knew gossip was wrong, so I kept my juicy tidbit to myself and pretended to be interested in sharpening and resharpening my pencil while everyone else around me flirted and laughed and teased and joked.

I had never had a boyfriend. Not because I thought it was sinful. Hope Valley Baptist did not consider having a boyfriend to be a sin, as long as there was no fornication. The problem with me was I still loved James Kane though he had hadn't spoken to me since last year's beach incident. Now, when he brought *Far Side* comics into class, he showed them to Christine Merryweather instead. Plus, in one year I had gone from being an inch and half taller than James Kane to a full five inches taller. I was sprouting out of control, my ever-soaring height knocking out scores of potential boyfriends.

But there was one boy, a petite boy named Ben Filmore who was not bothered at all by the tower of limbs I had become, and, in fact, seemed to view it as a challenge. I was not particularly attracted to Ben, who (although witty and fun to hang out with) was as Sophie and I liked to say, "only slightly bigger than my thumb." Ben himself described his stature as pocket-sized, which I found charming, and I liked how he smiled after he said it. So when Ben asked if I wanted to be his girlfriend, I said yes, hoping eventually love would blossom. Plus, since thumb-sized Ben was playing my husband in *Our Town*, I thought developing an outside relationship with him might add a layer of truth to my performance. As Artaud said, "I cannot conceive of any work of art having a separate existence from life itself." And I really wanted to do a great job of playing Mrs. Gibbs.

After *Our Town* rehearsals, Ben and I would make out in the backseat of his car. One night, he became especially bold and began to drag his teeny hand over the top of my Esprit sweater down toward my breast. I pushed his hand back. In between awkward inarticulate high school kisses and shifting of weight, Ben asked, "Why can't I?" I pretended to not know what he was talking about, continued kissing, and ran my hands over the pimply skin on his back to indicate something he might like to try as an alternative to touching my breasts.

"Why can't I touch your boobs?"

"Because I'm Christian," I answered, jutting my tongue into his mouth, hoping to end the discussion.

"So?"

"So it's a sin."

Then Ben tried an altogether-new tactic, one impressive in both its originality and outrageousness.

"I just think," he ventured, sliding his hand under my sweater, up my stomach towards my right breast, "that since we're playing husband and wife, we should be familiar with each other's bodies, just like we're familiar with all the invisible scenery. I'm sure Mr. Gibbs has touched Mrs. Gibbs's boobs." Ben's hand darted toward my left breast. I blocked.

"I said *no*, Ben."

My stomach knotted as I thought, *I have never witnessed to Ben. I should witness to Ben. God is giving me an opportunity in this moment through this boob-touching discussion to witness to Ben.* So right there in the backseat of Ben's Toyota, my face two inches away from his, my cheeks and chin red from the brush of his adolescent stubble, I asked, "Ben, have you ever accepted Jesus Christ into your heart?" Big pause. Ben looked into my eyes, tucked a piece of hair behind my ear like the sensitive, dashing lead in a romantic comedy, and asked, "If I accept Jesus, will you let me touch your boobs?"

This presented a bit of a moral dilemma. If Ben really did accept Jesus into his heart, wouldn't it be worth letting him touch me? Especially if he only touched me on top of my sweater, which sometimes happened accidentally in gym class or theater improv anyway. Light petting in exchange for someone's salvation seemed like it might be justifiable.

"You can't just accept Jesus because you want to touch my boobs; you have to do it because you believe in Him."

Ben's breath got heavier. "I believe in Him. I believe in Him so, so much."

"Do you want to say the prayer?"

His whisper was hot and wet against my ear. "What prayer?"

"Jesus, I accept you as my personal savior. Please forgive my sins."

Ben spit back, "Jesus, I accept you as my personal savior. Please forgive my sins," and before I could stop him, his hands flew out and grabbed my tiny breasts, squeezing them as if they were two little puff pastries. My first thought was, *That's personal*, the same reaction I might have had if someone stuck his finger in my ear or smelled my armpit.

I broke up with Ben the next day after we got notes on the final *Our Town* dress rehearsal. Our director Mrs. Roebuck said Ben and I didn't seem like we were connected as a couple, and I knew she was right. This wasn't working. Onstage. In life. Before Jesus. I told Ben that I just wanted to be friends—that I would miss him, but that most of all I was glad I was able to bring him to Jesus. Ben watched me with an understanding that belied his years and said with remarkable restraint and economy of language, "Okay, Maggie. I hope you reconsider."

The summer after my junior year I went to a high school theater program called Cherubs at Northwestern University, where a bunch of teenagers squashed in dorm rooms on their own for the first time had classes in vocal technique, scene study, Stanislavski's "What If?", sense memory, and animal inhabitation. I wanted to halt time and stay a Cherub for the rest of my life, to devote myself to art in a continuous Chicago summer, mastering a Brooklyn accent, learning to cry while chopping an imaginary onion, discovering what it feels like to be a flamingo.

The final two weeks of the Cherub program were to be spent rehearsing for a play called *The Mysteries*, an update on the medieval mystery cycle where God and Satan battle for the heart of Man. Georgeanne, the director, was brazen and busty with a sailor's mouth, the kind of immodest woman I knew I needed to stop wanting to be. Georgeanne asked me to read for the part of Satan. I gave my all to the audition, trying to dig in and understand the motivation of evil and how Lucifer came to believe the lie that he was equal to God.

That night, however, sitting alone in my dorm room, the old fear started so smolder. I picked up my journal and began a character biography for Satan, but it seemed like my hand had lost the ability to write. I sat upright in a chair with both feet flat on the ground for a sense-memory exercise focused on falling out of Heaven, but I couldn't get my hands to relax on my thighs. My mind had begun to catch fire, and I could not prevent the smolder from flaring into a blaze.

I held myself and rocked back and forth, my blanket wrapped around me like a straitjacket as I reasoned it out: As an actress, my job was to become my character. But God couldn't want me to *become* Satan, I thought. That had to be the opposite of what He wanted.

The next day at breakfast, I saw Georgeanne standing in line at the cafeteria, her tank top revealing Chinese characters penned across her back, her ripped arms flexing a bit as she heaped her tray with a mountain of eggs, a tower of bacon, and three huge cinnamon rolls. I forced myself to go over to her, holding my own tray with a healthy morning meal of fruit and oatmeal, and stammered, "I'm sorry to bother you while you're breakfast. I mean while you're *having* breakfast."

"I can eat and talk." Georgeanne shrugged, biting into a cinnamon roll, not bothering to wipe the generous icing from her lips. Her face melted with pleasure as she moaned and chewed. "I'm fucking addicted to this shit." I knew it was wrong, but I couldn't help thinking it might be fun to talk like this. Like uncinching a belt that's been drawn too tight.

Georgeanne put the cinnamon roll down and focused all of her attention on me. I launched in. "Okay, so thank you so much for letting me read for the part of Satan. That was amazing. It was a really big honor." I stopped myself and amended, "Not that it's an *honor* to be Satan."

Georgeanne let out a huge, "Ha!"

"I mean I really appreciate your giving me the chance, but if you could just cast me as one of the small parts, it might be better for me. Like maybe I could be a shepherd or one of Noah's daughters-in-law, you know, Shem or Ham's wife."

Georgeanne began munching lustily on a piece of bacon. "Why?"

"I know Satan is a juicy part, and I'm lucky to be considered for it."

"So why do you want to play a shepherd?"

Before I could answer, Georgeanne extended a piece of bacon toward me and asked, "Bacon?" Glancing at my tray, she added, "You gotta eat more than that."

"No, no, I'm good," I said, looking down at my tray. "It's just, I really can't play the part because I am a Christian. I've accepted Jesus Christ as my personal savior, and He wouldn't want me playing the part of Satan. I'm sorry!" I rushed before she could interrupt, "I would never not do a role because it's too small. It's not that. I know Stanislavski says there are no small parts, only small actors. Thanks so much for giving me the chance to read. I really am dedicated to my art."

With a kindness that made my eyes sting, Georgeanne dropped a register in her voice and said, "I know you are, Maggie. I noticed. I'm a Christian too, by the way."

This was difficult for me to process. Georgeanne lived in sin with her tattooed boyfriend. She swaggered and let him grab her ass in public. I'd seen her drink out of a flask. I'd heard her say "fuck" when she bit into a hamburger and the relish spurted green onto her revealing purple tank top. It didn't make sense.

I uselessly attempted to pad my tears off my oatmeal as I asked, "*You're a Christian?*" in a way that could easily have been construed as offensive. But Georgeanne's eyes rested on mine, generous and undistracted, as she told me, easy as a wave in a bathtub, "Yes, I am. And I think one day you're going to find out that God is bigger than you think."

CHAPTER FOUR: DON'T THE TREES LOOK LIKE CRUCIFIED THIEVES?

THE LARGENESS OF GOD is a question Bethanie seems to regard with suspicion. "That must have been hard to have an instructor who has herself fallen off the path."

"No, actually, I really liked Georgeanne. I might have given the wrong impression. I mean—"

"You just told me this woman drank to excess, used foul language, and engaged in lewd behavior with her boyfriend. I think I got the correct impression." Bethanie firmly closes the topic and opens her folder. "It says here you were born in 1971, so that would make you . . ." Bethanie concentrates on the problem for what seems like several minutes before reaching a labored conclusion: "Nineteen."

I support Bethanie's triumph over basic arithmetic with a nod.

"And are you currently in school?"

"Yes, I just finished my sophomore year of college at Cornell. In upstate New York."

"Is that a secular school?"

"Yes."

Bethanie looks at me intently with the same mixture of concern and judgment people at my church did when I told them I wasn't going to a

Christian college. It's not that going to a secular college was in and of itself a sin. It's just that going to a secular college put you in situations where you might be tempted to sin, a constant danger because *the spirit is willing but the flesh is weak.*

"You know, I've heard," Bethanie leans forward, confiding, "that people in those places can be *so* open-minded that their brains fall out!" Bethanie laughs, shaking her head and leaning back in her chair, pleased at a cleverness I'm sure she picked up from someone else. "Have you found the secular environment to be a challenge to your faith?"

"I never really thought of it like that. I never stopped believing in Jesus. Nobody challenged me, but I did fall away, I guess. Drifted away."

Bethanie smiles like someone who has just won a bar bet that even God would be proud of.

At Cornell I had drifted—happily, dreamily drifted—away from thoughts of salvation, of bad fruit, and from my role as Nice Christian Girl, a role I felt desperately miscast in. I lived in Risley Hall, an arts dorm where two hundred college-age artists piled on top of each other in a redbrick Tudor-Gothic building shaped like a giant English castle.

In high school, I had worn only the faintest touches of tasteful makeup, but now, inspired by my artsy peers, I bought the thickest, blackest eyeliner pencil I could find. I had been taught in Sunday school that heavy makeup was prohibited in the Bible: Jezebel had painted her face and then was thrown out a window *so high that her blood splattered on the walls and on the horses.* I found out, however, that there was more to the story, that Jezebel had seduced a King of Israel, Ahab, and roped him into honoring the god Ba'al, a felony count of false worship punishable by wars and famine and death. It was certainly bad to be "a jezebel," I decided, but probably not because she wore makeup.

So I created a new look, inexpertly painting solid black lines on my top and bottom eyelids, pulling them out to meet far beyond the corners of my eyes, almost at the temples. Then I clumped on big globs of mascara, which since I never had the patience to let dry, reliably left a smattering of black smudges on my cheekbones where the lashes hit. It was a look that could be described as "drag queen Cleopatra," if the drag queen had been drunk and reckless during the makeup application process.

The second week of school, I started swearing, rationalizing that there is nowhere in the Bible that says swear words are bad. That was just what my church taught; my church was made up of fallible human beings, just like you and me. And so, in cautious increments, I began peppering my speech with profanity. I started with the word *shit*. I said the cafeteria food tasted like "dogshit," then that my comp lit professor was "pettier than squirrel shit." Then I moved on to *fuck*. David Lynch's film *Eraserhead* was a marvelous "mindfuck." Jethro Tull was divine "fuckery."

The third week, I started going with girls from my dorm to frat parties, but at first I didn't drink, honoring the verse, *Do not get drunk with spirits for that leads to debauchery*. Then after several weeks of glumly saying "no, thanks" anytime I was offered a drink and standing around with empty useless hands, I remembered that Isaiah doesn't say, "Don't drink"—he says, "Don't get drunk." I concluded I could drink alcohol as long as I made sure that I didn't get drunk. So I'd drink with the other girls, but when I started to feel woozy, I'd put down my Styrofoam cup of warm beer and go find a bowl of chips. Standing at the snack table, lining my stomach with Doritos or Fritos, I'd watch the bacchanalia unfolding in front of me. Boys told jokes and offered refills; my girlfriends accepted and teetered on their heels, the boys waiting to catch them.

The following week, I thought about how much I wanted to get drunk, how much easier it would be to fit in. Then I pondered Isaiah's verse, and the more I considered it, the more it seemed Isaiah meant there was nothing wrong with getting drunk, so long as it didn't lead to debauchery. Basically I had God's express permission to get drunk on keg beer if I kept it at that. So at the Delta Chi party that weekend, I drank four Styrofoam cups of Michelob Light. Instead of taking my normal role as tall, dour girl stationed by the chip bowl, I was . . . fun! I did fun things. I pretended to square dance while Lucy Gallagher grabbed the band's microphone and made up nonsensical calls; I licked the frosting off of three marshmallow cupcakes; I stood in front of the stage with my arms over the shoulders of several friends and loudly sang "Stayin' Alive" as the band hammered away at an entirely different song.

I made sure my drinking didn't "lead to debauchery." I didn't behave like my girlfriends, who would openly make out with guys on the dance floor and then go upstairs to check out their stereo systems, wait patiently on the bed while the guys asked their roommates for some time alone in the room, then emerge shortly thereafter with tussled hair, the buttons on their shirts off by one. I knew I shouldn't ever go up to a guy's room. That was certainly debauchery. But kissing wasn't a sin. I'd once heard kissing defined as "shaking hands with your mouth." How bad could that be? Plus, I'd already done it. I'd spent hours kissing Ben in the backseat of his car, guarding second base like an MVP. What did it matter that I knew Ben better than the Delta Chi guy with nice eyes? Kissing, even kissing someone whose name I didn't know, wasn't debauchery, at least not according to the view I tried to convince myself I held. So I took the next step. The next weekend, I started making out with guys at the parties, if there was a good enough reason, like if the guy tapped the keg for me and held the bung because I was too drunk.

I went on several awkward dates. I went for a hike in Buttermilk Falls with a chemistry major who surprised me by having a ferret in his pocket and saying, "Look! My little dude's happy to see you." The following week I went to a New Orleans–style restaurant with a lacrosse player who wanted to suck my earlobes, an activity which I found unsettling despite finding no explicit prohibition in my Biblical crib sheet. Sometimes I discussed my various dates with my upstairs neighbor, Cooper Riley. We decided Ferret Guy had purchased the fragrant animal for the sole purpose of making the "happy to see you" joke and that Earlobe Man was ahead of his time, the vanguard of the earlobe erotization movement.

Cooper was a towheaded freshman with smart blue eyes, his oversized jaw the only feature that prevented his fair complexion and Botticelli bone structure from making him look like an angel. The first time I met him, he was doing his favorite party trick of inserting his fist into his mouth. It was a pretty good trick, one which I requested repeatedly from then on. I liked Cooper and his enormous jaw quite a bit.

The first snow came to Ithaca that year in early November on a night when a group of Risleyites, including Cooper and myself, had gone to a Delta Zeta party. I was trying to decide whether the over-amplified garage band was artfully playing out of time with each other or just drunk when a guy sidled up and said something I couldn't understand.

"What?"

"I'm Eric!" he shouted.

"Hi, Eric. I'm Maggie."

Eric was older than me—a graduate student, I guessed. He was large and unsteady, like an overgrown baby, and when I looked down, I noticed that despite the first snow of the year, he was wearing a pair of flip-flops, which displayed his prominent toe hair.

"Do you want to learn the Chinese art of Push Hands?" Eric lifted my hands up before I could say, "Get away from me, weirdo."

"It works against your natural instinct to resist force with force." Holding his palms flat against mine, he said, "Try pushing me over!" I practiced Push Hands with Eric as the garage band slovenly slapped at their instruments. In front of us, a girl in a Kappa Kappa Gamma sweatshirt puked in a trash can while a dude who looked like Dan Quayle held her hair and tenderly asked if she wanted to check out his stereo system.

Eric then turned to our little group and said, "Hey, you guys wanna come over to my place? It's a lot nicer than this dump." Our gang plodded over to Eric's apartment, which was indeed several levels of sophistication above the beer-soaked frat house. There was a wet bar, leather furniture, high-end electronic equipment, and carpeting that seemed to be made of clouds. Eric explained, unnecessarily, that he had a trust fund.

It would have just been a drunken night in a string of drunken nights I was now having. But instead, it was the night I fell in love. A fall that happened in the span of a mere thirty seconds. Eric had given all of us straight vodka in thick glass tumblers, just the way Sophie's mom used to drink it. Cooper and I sat together against the wall on the cloud carpet, sipping our drinks and watching as Eric played Push Hands in the center of the room with Lucy. Eric would push his right hand forward, Lucy would let her left hand relax, and they would both wobble almost to the point of tipping over before managing to wind themselves back.

Eric asked Lucy if she liked Billie Holiday, and Lucy cooed, "Oh my God, yes, I love him."

I listened for the first time to the song "These Foolish Things." As Teddy Wilson's languid piano meandered up and down and around through the melody and as Billie Holiday spun out the words *A cigarette that bears lipstick traces, an airline ticket to romantic places*, I gazed at a poster mounted in an ornate wooden frame. A dark-haired woman held a naked baby in her lap, her head bent toward him and away from me as she kissed his golden forehead. The baby, suffused in an impressionistic glow, reached with his right hand to pull at his right big toe, relaxed his head backward, and accepted her kiss. I didn't have to guess the name of the painting or the name of the painter because they were both announced in a little framed square of art paper mounted next to the painting, like at a museum: "Mary Cassatt," neat calligraphy noted, "*Mother and Child*, 1906, oil on canvas."

It seemed an odd choice of artwork for a twenty-something male of any sort, much less one who wore flip-flops to frat-house parties in early November, but then I looked over toward the kitchen and saw . . . the same painting, what I now knew to be Mary Cassatt's *Mother and Child*, but I didn't need to know because again right next to it was the same framed label, noting the artist and title, year and medium. It was one of those moments where something is so odd that it's pleasurable, a memorable tick of the clock no one will ever know about but you. Smiling to myself, I relaxed my head back against the wall and gazed back over to my right, and there was . . . the *third* Mary Cassatt reproduction, accompanied by a third framed label. I looked from one to the other to the next.

I finished the first glass of hard liquor I'd ever had and touched Cooper on the arm. *Look!* I mouthed silently, pointing one by one to the three identical paintings, stunned, reverent before this inexplicable bit of outrageousness that had lifted this moment right out of time. Cooper's eyes looked blank for a moment, and then a wave of easy joy bloomed across his face and he began sobbing with laughter. My laughter joined his, and we laughed until we couldn't breathe, until tears ran down our faces, until we were clutching each other for relief. We had witnessed this preposterous revelation together. A graduate student named Eric had a trust fund, beautiful carpet, and three framed reproductions of Mary Cassatt's *Mother and Child*. We laughed for probably three minutes straight before we began kissing.

From that point on, we were a couple. I had slipped into a romance, without trying, without even knowing it was happening. Soon Cooper and I were calling each other "pea" or "peanut" or "sweet pea" or "Suisse pea." When we discovered we both liked black jellybeans, we switched to "jellybean" or "bean." But mostly "pea." He was my pea.

Cooper and I were in a Shakespeare class together, where we were assigned to watch BBC recordings of the plays. We'd go to the library viewing room and sit in a little cubicle together, watching the videos on a small screen and listening with headphones. Once we noticed a teensy sign in one of the cubicles that said, *No petty vandalism*, so Cooper took his pen and changed it to *No pretty vandalism*. I thought this was brilliant. What could be a pettier form of vandalism?

Sometimes as we watched the recordings, we would pass notes back and forth on scrunched-up scraps of paper that said things like, *Do you like me? Yes, no, or I don't understand the question.* And answer with things like, *Yes. Do you like me? Yes, no, or don't be ridiculous.* One time Cooper threw me a note that said, *Will you marry me?* I knew it was a joke, but still, my face flushed with pleasure.

We came up with our own language, which included calling our mothers our "milkhome" and our fathers "Big Taco." We shared a set of social pet peeves and made up our own remedies. We thought it was annoying when people said they liked, for example, all kinds of music and would conspire to one day ask them at parties, "Really? What about amateur polka? Counting songs? How about inappropriate dirges?" Since the school cafeteria allowed students to take a piece of fruit at every meal, we started an exchange in Cooper's dorm room: "Have a fruit, give a fruit. Need a fruit, take a fruit." It was our socialist experiment. We did it together. Like we did everything.

Our only disagreement was over religion. It was true that I hadn't spent much time stewing about Jesus over the previous few years, but I never stopped believing He was real, and was my savior. Cooper thought my continuing faith was childish, like believing in Santa Claus into your teenage years despite having caught your parents placing gifts under the tree. I didn't want my sweet pea to burn in eternal fire, even if that was only a metaphor for endless spiritual suffering, so I relentlessly pressured him to say the prayer. "Why not just say it? What have you got to lose? Please just try to believe it for a moment and say the prayer." I reminded him of Pascal's wager that we learned about in Philosophy 101. "Belief is a wise wager. What harm will come to you if you gamble on its truth and it proves false? If you gain, you gain all; if you lose, you lose nothing. Wager, then, without hesitation, that He exists."

Cooper's response was, "Yeah, but if God doesn't exist, then you've thrown away your one and only life, giving away all your money and praying to a giant load of bullshit." He told me Pascal was a pussy with brain damage: "It's true. They found it in his autopsy. It's why he had chronic headaches and said stupid things." I quickly short-circuited these conversations, not wanting anything to compromise our connection. "Fine," I would say. "Pascal is a pussy with brain damage. Let's talk about something else. Remember how you said animal lovers neglect people and humanitarians hate pets? I think you're right."

At first I would only go so far as kissing with Cooper, heeding the Pikenides' advice to "save petting for the pets." We would roll around kissing on his dorm room bed, inside the giant red sleeping bag he used instead of the traditional sheets and blankets. The sleeping bag was not the thin cotton drivel that Sophie and I used to have at our sleepovers. This was an industrial sleeping bag Cooper had used in Eagle Scouts, designed to maintain one's body temperature even when the temperature dropped to 50 degrees below zero. A bag so heavy it felt like the lead blankets used during X-rays. Squeezing into it was like squeezing into an underground world, where all signs of the outside were shut out.

Then I started to realize that the Bible doesn't actually say anything explicitly about petting. There's no verse referencing either of the two petting categories, light or heavy. Maybe petting was okay. I looked up the word *pet* in the dictionary and found *to pet* meant "to touch gently with affection." That couldn't be bad. Why would that be bad? So one night when Cooper and I were kissing, instead of blocking his hand like I normally did, I left my breasts undefended.

Cooper's hand wandered over my shirt, but this time it didn't feel invasive and weird, like someone was sticking a finger in my ear. I continued my internal debate, now justifying what I wanted to continue happening: petting *is* in the Bible. Solomon in the Song of Solomon talks about his girlfriend the Shulamite's breasts being like two mountains. And then like clusters of fruit. And then like two fawns, twins of a gazelle, that graze among the lilies. And Solomon and the Shulamite weren't even married yet. They weren't even engaged. And Solomon clearly knew a lot about her breasts, and her lips—they *drip of the honeycomb*, he says—and her neck, which is *like the tower of David*, and even the little place under her tongue, where he finds the scents of *milk and honey*. And God was fine with the Shulamite. More than fine. He put her and her breasts in the Bible, and Solomon lying between them all night like a bundle of myrrh. Who were the Pikenides to say anything about petting? That was man's judgment, not God's.

Then I thought, okay, what's the difference between breasts and genitals, when you think about it? So the next night I stopped playing goalie with my pants and it was, like, the Best Sleepover Ever!

But I knew we couldn't have sex. I mean, when the Shulamite tells Solomon all night to *be like a gazelle or a young stag upon the mountains of Bether*, I didn't know exactly what she was talking about, but it couldn't have been more than heavy petting because the laws about fornication were fierce, and I knew the Bible wouldn't give contradicting instructions about one thing. That was a line I would not cross.

Until Cooper gave me a locket for Christmas our sophomore year. Scrunched up inside the locket was the note he had thrown me across the tiny video screening booth that said *Will you marry me?* I stared at the crumpled piece of paper like it was a winning lottery ticket and felt like carbonated soda had filled up my chest.

"I'm not proposing or anything." Cooper brought me down just a little. "But you know, maybe someday."

I went home for Christmas break that year happier than I'd ever been. I wrote things in my journal like, *Being in love is like the first moment of opening your Easter basket over and over*, and *Oooh, now I get why people do this whole "life" thing*, and sometimes, simply, *Wheeeeeeee!*

I took out my big old Leviathan Bible and found that nowhere does it explicitly say you can't have sex before marriage. The text simply states you must only have sex with one person until that person dies or until you die. There's nothing about a government sanction being required. I was committed to being with Cooper forever. God didn't need some paperwork to go through New York State to learn about our commitment. He was bigger than that. He was God.

So by the time I came back from Christmas break, I had made up my mind that if one time when Cooper and I were rolling naked on top of each other in the top bunk under his red sleeping bag, and we ended up having sex, it would be all right. That will just mean we're married in God's eyes, I figured. And that's fine. Cooper and I *want* to get married. Like Solomon and the Shulamite. I'm sure Solomon wasn't just fiddling with the Shulamite's fawn- and fruit-cluster-like breasts. Clearly they were doing it. One night after a particularly lustful roll-around, I wriggled my fingers through Cooper's slightly damp hair and said, "Wow . . . we came pretty close that time."

A bead of sweat from his forehead dropped into my eye. I didn't blink.

"Actually, that was it, Maggie," Cooper finally said blankly, his nose inches above mine.

"Oooh, ooh," I immediately gushed. "Well that was great, then. Soooo great. I loved it." Then for some reason, I decided to add, "Thanks!"

It wasn't that I was disappointed. I just always thought that the thrusting in and out you see in the movies was all just preparation for the actual thing. Like those rev-up Hot Wheels cars that you drag along the ground a couple of times before letting them go and watching them fly into a wall with a big ol' bang. Turned out, that's not how sex worked. But that was fine with me. I'd always hated Hot Wheels anyway.

Later that week, Cooper showed me a play he was reading called *Cowboy Mouth*, written by Sam Shepard and Patti Smith. Patti Smith's character Cavale is a "raggedy street angel," a partly crippled former mental patient, who has kidnapped Slim, "a cat who looks like a coyote," from his wife and child. To Cavale, rock and roll is religion. Her one dream is to find a man who can turn into a rock 'n' roll savior—a Jesus with a cowboy mouth. She thinks Slim is that man.

I tore through the text, high on art and romance, and immediately proclaimed it to be my favorite play ever. When we found out playwright Patti Smith had been a '70s rocker/poetess, we got her first album *Horses*, put the tape in the deck, and sat on Cooper's bed on top of the red sleeping bag. The first several seconds were just the hissing tape player, then a solemn three-chord vamp, then Patti Smith's ragged vocals: *Jesus died for somebody's sins but not mine.* My heart started banging like I was riding the Tidal Wave at Great America, careening upside down. Patti Smith's unfigured voice was a crowbar in the center of my head, a visitation, my own private Revelation.

Melting in a pot of thieves / Wild card up my sleeve. Thick heart of stone. My sins . . . my sins only belong to me.

Cooper grabbed my arm. "I think we should do it."

I was confused, guilty, and light-headed. "I thought we already 'did it.'"

"Not *that kind* of doing it. I think we should do *Cowboy Mouth*."

"What do you mean?"

"You and me. You be Cavale. I'll play Slim. We can do it at Risley Theater."

There had been a lecture at Risley the week before on Oscar Wilde and a reading series of *Star Trek* episodes where the readers were all naked . . . and sitting in a kiddie pool full of water. Clearly the theater administrator was up for anything.

"Let's do *Cowboy Mouth*. Come on, I'll be your rock 'n' roll savior."

I didn't think the play was the sort of material Jesus would be proud of, but I wanted to do it so fiercely. And I didn't want to disappoint Cooper. Christianity was about loving people and not disappointing them, I reasoned, so really, it wouldn't have been very Christian to disappoint somebody I cared about.

I hesitated for a second before dismissing my confused conscience, throwing my arms around Cooper's neck, and squealing "Yes, let's do it! Let's do *Cowboy Mouth*!"

We asked our acting teacher Paloma, an appealing whirl of talent, scarves, and ethnic jewelry, to be our director. Paloma's message to us was that we must set fires of truth on the stage, fires of truth that will blaze throughout the world. I was determined to set such world-blazing fires during the two-night run of *Cowboy Mouth* in Risley's thirty-five-seat black box theater.

According to Paloma, as artists we must "immerse ourselves in our characters," an instruction I took extremely seriously. Because Cavale is described in the stage directions as a chain smoker, I went to the Rite Aid for a pack of Camels and practiced smoking until I could hold the cigarette in my mouth (no hands!) without hacking or tearing up too much. Cavale carries a dead crow with her everywhere, her beloved deceased pet, Raymond. So in the spirit of immersion I went to the school's ornithology department with a note from Paloma and a glint of madness in my eyes and returned with a dead crow in a box. The crow became my constant companion; I perched it in my lap while I studied and tucked it under my arm while I slept. I was buoyed when I overcame my initial repulsion to the carcass, and I was proud when I was able to pinpoint what I felt was a genuine bit of affection for it. The Bible says a mustard seed of faith is all God needs, and I figured the same must be true for acting. I was on my way.

I practiced inhabiting Cavale in front of my dorm room mirror, barefoot in a black tattered slip from wardrobe, smoking inexpertly, coughing and clutching Raymond. In my favorite monologue, Cavale inspires Slim to become the savior the world needs, pleading, "The old God is just too far away. His words don't shake through us anymore. Any great rock 'n' roll song can raise me higher than all of the Revelations." I worked up my passion, reaching for tears, jumping up and down, exhorting my image in the mirror like a revival preacher, before dropping to my knees and flinging my hands above my head. "The old God was selfish. He kept himself hid. You're a performer, Slim. You gotta be like a rock 'n' roll Jesus with a cowboy mouth."

This was my favorite monologue but also the one that scared me most. I worried I was sinning by speaking blasphemous words, words that could lead an audience member away from Christ. I imagined a lonely spinster with a strong Christian faith coming to see our Risley Theater production and becoming so illuminated by the fires Cooper and I set in our limited-seating black box work that she renounces Jesus, loses her spiritual comfort, and spends the rest of her life lonely and bereft. Sometimes after rehearsal, I felt the cold tingling of terror on my scalp—the terror I always felt when I thought of hell.

But now, here in my dorm room, I remembered Georgeanne's prediction: "One day you're going to find out that God is bigger than you think." *Yes*, I thought, *As big as a rock 'n' roll savior with a cowboy mouth.* I said my lines over and over in my head. *A rock 'n' roll savior rocking to Bethlehem to be born.* I loved these words but knew I shouldn't, just like I shouldn't have loved the bangled harlots on the felt boards. The real savior had already been born in Bethlehem—His name was Jesus, and He didn't need updating.

I relapsed into the questions and fear.

"Is it a sin for me to play this part?"

"Is it blasphemy to say these words?" The old fear shot up my spine, and I felt for a moment like I was falling in the dark, falling from the awful height I had tried to clear from my mind and had halfway believed I had forgotten. I looked down and noticed I had dropped my lit cigarette onto the pink velour blanket on my bed, the blanket my grandmother had given me before her breakdown. Not thinking, I stamped the blazing bud of my cigarette out with my hand, but not before it burned a hole in the blanket and singed my fingers.

I reminded myself that it wasn't me saying the words; it was Cavale. Maybe Jesus would work through my performance to show that He is enough of a rock 'n' roll savior for anybody. Was I just rationalizing? I thought back to Miss Trimly telling us that *to rationalize* meant to use good words to support bad actions. *Woe to them that call evil good, and good evil.* But no, this was different, I insisted. This was a justification, not a rationalization. The idea it supported was valid. But then I wondered if thinking a justification was different from a rationalization was just a rationalization.

I tried to shake the unsettling and familiar grip of guilt as I walked across campus to meet Cooper at the Student Cinema, where we had a date and tickets to see Akira Kurosawa's *Dreams*. The sun set as I made my way through the quad, sharpening the cold of the Ithaca wind. I braced myself against the assaulting gusts, wrapping my scarf around my face so only the slits of my eyes showed, peeking up at the looming trees above. The bloody hues of the falling sun distorted the knobs on the tree trunks into what looked like human faces and twisted the turns and lengths of their branches into facsimiles of outstretched arms.

I thought of a lyric from a Warren Zevon song: "Don't the sun look angry through the leaves? Don't the trees look like crucified thieves?" I shuddered as I remembered the two thieves crucified alongside Jesus—the one who believed in Jesus, who Jesus told he would see in Paradise, and the other thief who did not believe, and to whom Jesus said nothing. Was the second promptly cast into the fiery pit, only to begin an eternal torment once his earthly suffering had ended? I didn't want to think about how Mr. and Mrs. Pikenide or Miss Trimly or Pastor Bill would answer that question, so I quickly shifted my thoughts back to Cavale, running through the lines in my head: *The old God was selfish. He kept himself hid. We need a performer, Slim. A savior rocking to Bethlehem to be born.*

I met Cooper at the Student Cinema. We sat in the theater, holding hands freely and easily, thumbs brushing over each other's knuckles. I thought we were inseparable, like my grandmother would have once said, "two peas in a pod." I thought *Dreams* would be just a regular movie, that we'd watch it like we had dozens before. I was certain that afterward we'd walk back together through the cold air, linking arms, our hands in each other's pockets. And that, at the end of the night, we'd wind up hugging, warm and cozy, under the red expedition-grade sleeping bag.

I was wrong, though.

Just like when I thought five minus four was nine.

CHAPTER FIVE: *DREAMS*

"MAGGIE?"

Bethanie is wearing tiny pendant earrings that sway when she speaks, and I've been watching the way they catch the sunlight from the window behind her desk.

"Maggie?"

I return my focus to her face.

As the title suggests, Kurosawa's movie presents a series of vignettes drawn from the filmmaker's dreams.

"I love you, Pea," I whispered as the first title played on the screen, two Japanese characters with a subtitle, *Sunshine Through Rain*.

As the vignette opens, a young boy looks out from the front gate of his home through sheets of rain illuminated by bright sunlight. His busy mother stops with her laundry basket to instruct him.

> *You're staying home.*
> *The foxes hold their wedding processions in this weather.*
> *And they don't like anyone to see them.*
> *If you do, they'll be very angry.*

I was wearing the locket Cooper had given me, and as I read the subtitles, I rolled it between my fingers.

Despite his mother's instruction, the boy sneaks off into a deep forest, where huge trees tower over his small body. At first the boy sees only mist billowing between the trunks, and sun showers and more towering trees. But then they emerge: a procession of men and women dressed in formal wedding garments and wearing fox masks over their faces. As the procession advances to a strangely funereal-like wedding march, the boy peeks from behind a wide tree. His white-and-black patterned kimono stands out against the dark trunk. It was a pastoral scene, lovely and sedate, but I began to feel uncomfortably anxious. I became frightened for the boy. The foxes were going to see him any minute.

And then they do. They whip their heads around and stare right where the boy is standing, pinning him in place with their eyes. A flute shrieks, and as the boy turns to run, I noticed a bloody metallic taste in my mouth, like in gym class when we ran the half mile, which my gym teacher told me came from traces of iron released in my saliva from exertion. But why would I have the taste of blood in my mouth? I hadn't run anywhere. As Kurosawa's disobedient boy races home, my heart accelerated as if I were racing with him. The blood or iron taste in my mouth intensified, and then I started to smell something bitter, like rancid oil. Butter? Could the butter on everyone's popcorn have gone bad?

An angry fox came looking for you, the mother tells the boy. *He left you this.* She hands an object that looks like a baton to the boy. He pulls off one end of the object to reveal a shimmering samurai dagger. *You are supposed to kill yourself.*

My heart rate increased. I could feel the pulse in my temples, as if it were banging out a warning. *Something is wrong, Maggie*, it seemed to be drumming. *Pay attention. Something is terribly, terribly wrong.*

The woman explains that unless the foxes can forgive him, she cannot let the boy back into their home. Then, she slips into the house and pulls the large wooden door shut behind her with a heavy clang. The boy stands helpless as his mother's footsteps recede into the depths of the building.

I remembered Miss Trimly's lesson: "Then God said to the unbelievers, *Depart from me. I do not know you.*"

I remembered how I used to imagine my parents turning their backs on me as I spiraled down into the pit.

I remembered how I had known I could never be angry with them because it would have been out of their hands. God would have cut me off from above. It would have been too late.

After his mother's footsteps have completely faded, the boy pushes against the closed door, which rises above him like an impenetrable fortress wall, but it will not yield. He tries a smaller entrance, off to the side. Nothing.

I thought of the time I was watching *Poltergeist* in the theater and a little boy started screaming out a warning: "Attention, everybody! This is a *very scary* movie! We need to leave this theater . . . IMMEDIATELY!" I'd laughed then, but I heard the genuine terror in his voice through the memory, and now I had the impulse to shout the very same thing. As I looked up and down our row of seats, however, I could see that none of the other students appeared to share my concern, so instead of shouting, I reached over and clasped Cooper's hand. When I gave it a squeeze, though, I only felt the bones.

I looked at Cooper, squeezing tighter, and when he turned toward me, his skin looked pale. His face was blue, and his eyes seemed to peer out from a pair of long black tunnels. He gave me a grin, and I saw his bare teeth glowing and suddenly serrated like a shark's. Spooked, I pulled my hand back. *It must be the lighting in here*, I thought, *the reflection from the screen on Cooper's face.* I stared straight ahead.

In the next vignette, the boy encounters a peach orchard that has been destroyed. Above the fallen trees, frightening doll faces appear. *Hey there, little boy!* they shout. *We have something to tell you. We'll never go to your house again. Why not?* the boy asks.

> *Your family cut down all the peach trees in this orchard.*
> *We are the spirits of the trees, the life of the blossoms.*
> *Those vanished trees are weeping in their sorrow.*

I thought of the Noah's arc story, how God told Noah that the wickedness on the earth was great and then slaughtered all but Noah's family and those few animals he could save. I thought about *100 Percent Chance of Rain*, of death by drowning, and a God who was always watching. Kurosawa's boy cries with remorse, but an unmoved doll says, *It's too late. Your tears won't help.*

The flute music shrieks.

I tried to swallow, but my throat caught. I heard a buzzing sound. I saw the audience as rows of corpses: corpses staring straight ahead, their eye sockets black and bottomless, their discolored skin peeling off their faces in strips.

The third section of *Dreams*, titled "The Blizzard," begins in a wash of gray. The only sound is of wind and labored, panicked breathing. The gray thins enough to see a group of mountaineers hiking through a blizzard, with nothing in front of them but endless drifts of dirty white. They are barely moving and barely alive.

As I watched, I remembered visiting my grandmother at Garden Grove psychiatric facility. I remembered trudging through the snow up to the gray building in my pink rubber boots, the box of ZERO Bars under my armpit. I remembered arguing with my parents about what had happened. I had known that Grandma's lack of faith and refusal to pray with me were directly related to her subsequent shock therapy. I knew they were linked. I hadn't forgotten.

The men on-screen continue their bitter march, their eyes filmed-over and bloodshot, their lips blue, their movement slowly freezing to a standstill. One of the group succumbs to his fate. He falls to his knees, and then onto his face, his nose planting in the snow. The leader of the group shakes him and says, *You'll die. You'll die if you stop!* But it's too late. The man slowly freezes into a motionless, disfigured sculpture of ice.

Had these men accepted Jesus as their personal savior? Where would they go when they died? Outside of small, quickly stifled spurts of contemplation, I hadn't thought much about the afterlife for years. But now the long-buried fears surfaced violently in my consciousness, like the ocean throwing up rot from a scary born-again sea. My mind instantly leapt from *Are these men saved?* to *Am* I *saved?* and I focused all my attention on the only defense I knew.

Dear Lord I believe in You and accept You as my personal savior. I willed the thoughts through my mind. *Please forgive me for my sins and cleanse me from all unrighteousness.*

A wave of hot flashes passed over my body, descending on weird patches of skin—behind my right ear, my left armpit, under my knees.

I grabbed at the armrests to steady myself, but my hands felt like paper. My limbs seemed to belong to someone else.

I needed more air but could manage only a small sip each time I pulled at a breath. I tried to decide whether I needed to breathe in or out, and I became increasingly frantic as I realized I was unable to do either.

The smell of rancid butter intensified as the taste in my mouth became bloodier. The audience of corpses sitting around me seemed to drift further and further away, and in the terrible snowscape on-screen, a second mountaineer succumbs to exhaustion and freezes to death, his last, struggling cloud of breath lingering in the air just longer than his will to live.

The temperature in the theater, however, seemed to soar. I felt the weight of a powerful hand pressing down on my sternum as a third hiker dies, leaving one mountaineer to struggle on, his equipment rattling and clanging, frozen metal against frozen metal, until he too crumples into a heap while ice passes through his body and freezes his blood.

The buzzing in my head became louder and more adamant until it felt like an alarm rattling through me. I didn't understand what was happening. I just knew there was something wrong and I needed to steady myself somehow, but nothing seemed solid enough. I was sweating in the heat like I'd overdressed for the cold and shivering at the same time as if with the chills.

It's a fever, I suddenly thought. Then, a terrified yelp came from my own mouth, and I bolted like a terrified animal.

Frantically, I crawled over the people in my row, stepping on toes and banging against knees, panting, apologizing, thinking all the while about the sins that would surely land me in the lake of everlasting fire—the drinking, the cursing, the sex, the rationalizations . . . what had I done?!

All I could hear was the weeping and the gnashing of teeth, and all I could see was a boy driving a dagger into his stomach because his mother says it's too late, doll-faced peach-tree spirits saying they will never forget, and exhausted men, frozen and preserved forever as corpses, for whom it will be always too late.

I flung myself under the green exit sign, stumbled across the carpeted lobby, and toppled out of the double doorway into the January wind. The cold shocked my body into breathing again, and I greedily sucked in the frigid air. Seconds later Cooper followed, holding my jacket. "What's going on, you crazy weirdo? It's arctic out here. Put on your coat."

I heard his voice as if over an old-fashioned overseas phone line, and then I heard my own, distant and frightened. "I've messed up, Cooper. I've messed up so badly."

The bare, knotted trees, like crucified thieves reaching out through the night, loomed above me, haunting and closing in, until I could see nothing else. All I remember is how cold it was as Cooper carried me back to our dorm and how sorry I was, for everything.

CHAPTER SIX: **UNEQUAL YOKE**

BETHANIE PERFORMS SYMPATHY with a therapeutic nod and fingers the cross around her neck, as if to flaunt her own uncomplicated faith. "It sounds like a terrible movie."

For some reason I feel the need to defend the film that exploded my life. "Well, actually, I think *Dreams* is pretty amazing. It turns out Kurosawa intended the film's imagery to evoke fears of the afterlife." I point at myself and smile goofily, "So . . . mission accomplished with this gal!" I'm hoping to make Bethanie laugh, hoping for some sort of connection, some acknowledgment of the absurdity of my plight. I mean, I'm here because I watched a Japanese art film with unsettling flute music and frozen mountaineers dying in front of cinematic skies. It's crazy. This isn't something that happens to people. If someone would just acknowledge how crazy this is, I'm certain I'd feel significantly more sane.

But Bethanie's mask of forced pleasantry remains uncracked, much as I imagine it would if she actually saw *Dreams*. She'd probably see nothing but the sunshine and the misty rainbows, rainbows that would remind her of God's great promise to Noah to never again drop water from the sky. Just like Bethanie would see only the good in the picture of Jesus in the lobby, the Jesus with the Pantene hair and the flock of sheep—the sheep who had clearly said the prayer, or didn't need to say the prayer because they were sheep who hadn't been granted the tricky gift of free will. Lucky sheep.

Scrunching up her nose like my sister facing a portion of lima beans, Bethanie asks, "So what happened after this inappropriate movie?"

After the *Dreams* debacle, I gave up every behavior I thought could possibly be sinful. I stopped swearing right away, terminating my use of *shit*, *fuck*, and *cockmeister*, which had once felt so glorious to say. I stopped dancing at frat parties. I stopped drinking beer at frat parties. I stopped going to frat parties altogether—opting instead to stay in on weekends and focus my thoughts on guilty feelings and the sensation of shame. Though I did complete the two-night run of *Cowboy Mouth* on the grounds that backing out of a commitment would be a worse sin than repeating unholy words onstage before a maximum of seventy people, I vowed to stop acting in plays that didn't accord with the teachings of Christ. I even stopped listening to Patti Smith.

All this helped, but one night as I hovered on the edge of sleep, feeling my body sink into the bed and my mind release its daylong battle with fear, a stray thought jerked me awake.

What was that?

I blinked at my darkened dorm room. The sensation that I had forgotten something important drove a sharp dose of adrenaline through my body. I sat up in bed and turned on a reading light. There it was: my Marianne Faithfull poster. The haunting beauty who had kept me company since the first week of freshman year stared back at me from under a floppy sun hat, straddling her motorcycle, black eyeliner splashed under her wide, dark eyes.

Scrawled underneath the picture, in her handwriting, was a quote I loved: *I was born in Hampstead. My mother wasn't screaming so they didn't believe she was in labor. Later I went to convent school. Later I rode in leather. Later I took some sleeping pills. I needed to lose . . . M.F.* I loved these sentences in a way I was never able to articulate, even to myself. There was something about the odd tie between the silent labor in which her existence was denied, her need to rebel extravagantly, and then the simplicity of the phrase *I needed to lose.* But even when I'd put the poster up, I suspected it was not the kind of image or quote a young Christian woman should have up on her wall, certainly not one who held the AWANA Midwest Bible Verse Memorization title, one who possessed a gilded trophy of a pigtailed girl, a Bible extended from her arm, leaping in the air.

I looked at the brazen image of Marianne Faithfull astride her motorcycle, the heedless scrawl of the phrase *I needed to lose* written as if no one were watching, and suddenly it seemed terrifyingly reckless—not just of her, but of *me*. I should have put a Christian poster up on my wall—something with footprints on the beach or a sun peeking out from parting clouds, something with an inspiring Bible verse penned in delicate brushstrokes, a verse I had memorized and could share with my peers. Not this wickedness. So I ripped the transgressive poster off the wall, slicing Marianne's face in half and splitting the word *lose* right down the middle.

I also pulled down my poster of Gustav Klimt's *The Kiss*, which I'd bought at the campus store my first week on campus, thinking I'd made a choice in poster art that would set me apart, just like 85 percent of my female classmates. Peeling the Klimt that had once seemed so special off the wall, I thought of Cooper and me cocooned in his red sleeping bag intertwined like the kissing couple in the painting and felt waves of guilt. I ripped the poster in half and then into strips and then into smaller and smaller pieces until nothing remained but a small mound of red and yellow confetti in my lap. I knew what had to be done next. It was unavoidable.

I had told myself it was okay for Cooper and me to have sex because we were married in God's eyes, but *how did I know that?* It may be true, it may not, but now I saw with nauseating clarity that it wasn't worth the gamble. *It's like Pascal said*, I reminded myself as I brushed the confetti off my lap, scattering it onto the floor, *no finite pleasure is worth risking infinite pain.*

So the following morning at the coffee shop, armed with a useless mug of ginger-lemon tea, I reached across the table, grabbed Cooper's hand, and braced myself. What was the right way to tell a college sophomore that he can no longer have sex with his girlfriend? I waited for Cyndi Lauper to finish explaining what girls want to do when the working day is done on the coffeehouse mixtape, and then I spurted out, "I'm so sorry but I can't be intimate with you anymore." *Intimate?* Why did I use that word? Where did that horrible word even come from? *What was happening to me?*

"What?" Cooper asked.

I seemed to be instantly sobbing. "Sex. I can't have sex," I garbled out through a mess of tears. "You can hate me. I don't blame you. *I* hate me. I'm just so scared. It's Pascal's wager . . . finite loss for infinite gain . . . I just can't take the risk . . ."

To my astonishment, Cooper didn't immediately break up with me. "The thing is," he said instead, "I love you, Maggie." Then he added with a valiant smile, "Just don't use the word *intimate* again. It sounds like we're on *The Newlywed Game.*"

I came around the table and hugged him and kissed his mouth and made little wet marks on his neck with as much passion as I thought I could without being inappropriate in the eyes of God—or the boys working the espresso machine and the pre-med looking up from her chemistry textbook.

But was it enough? Had I lost my salvation? Had I backslid so far into a slippery mess of rationalization that I would never be able to slide back into place? Was I calling *evil good and good evil?* "Dear Lord," I prayed, "please forgive me for going astray. I am willing to give up all for You. I'm not lukewarm. And if I am, I will try not to be. Please just take me back." But it wasn't enough. Or maybe it was. Who knew? All I knew was that Jesus would return to earth like a *thief in the night*, as *labor pains on a pregnant woman*, and that I had better figure it out by this unpredictable instant or I would fall—my parents and all I loved would ascend and I would be lost forever.

I fought back with the only tools I knew. *If we confess our sins, He is faithful and just to forgive us and our sins and to cleanse us from all unrighteousness.* Furiously, I confessed everything I could think of. I made confession lists and checked those lists. I repented over and over again and vowed to never consciously do anything sinful ever again. I found some comfort in the feeling of terror itself. You don't worry about God's wrath because you *don't* believe in God—just like you don't scream when you see a rat because you think rats are friendly and clean.

I decided to join the Evangelical youth group Campus Crusade to prove the extent of my renewed dedication, even though being a part of something with the name *Crusade* mortified me. I hated to think what my friends around the dining hall table might say behind my back if they knew I was willing to associate with a group that named itself for four hundred years of invasion and murder and religious subjugation, but what could I do? I had to save myself, so I slipped away from the dining hall one evening and walked the short distance to Chesterson Hall for a newcomers meeting. I found a circle of chairs in the first-floor library and, after trying for several moments to decide where in a circle one might find a seat close to the back, I chose one at random, sat down, smiled at my neighbors without introducing myself, and waited for the meeting to start.

"Whoop! Whoop!" the group leaders, Kyle and Karlee, shouted, each swirling a fist in the air as if they were about to lasso a make-believe pony with an invisible rope. Kyle and Karlee, a fresh-faced brother-and-sister team, had grown up with a Baptist preacher for a father. They excelled at that special kind of manufactured glee only a preacher's kids can summon, and it was their never-ending mission to prove "Christians can have fun, too!" The group chanted back, "Whoop! Whoop!"—like a fun, hip, collegiate version of a hallelujah call-and-response. I did my best to muster enthusiasm but was only able to manage a weak, slightly embarrassed, "Whoop," before returning my hand to my pocket.

Kyle and Karlee announced that the meeting would be about planning for Slope Day, a university-sponsored bacchanalian event held on the first day of spring, in which several hundred students gathered on the slope of Cayuga Hill. For this one day only, alcohol was permitted out in the open, so kegs and coolers full of cheap tequila and wine spritzers were splashed all over the lawn. Cafeteria workers put the trays from the dining hall outside, and the students proceeded to slick the trays with Vaseline, sit on them, and sail down the hill. It was a fantastic day of chaperoned decadence, and several ambulances were always parked nearby so students could pursue the Slope Day Creed, "It's not a party till someone goes to the hospital" with both abandon and relative safety.

For the previous year's Slope Day, Cooper and I had filled up two thermoses, one with Long Island Iced Teas and one with Fuzzy Navels, and we each hung a pair of binoculars around our necks to get a more intense view of the festivities. On our way to the hill we'd grabbed two lawn chairs that were sitting in front of our dorm and hoisted them on our backs, a couple of happy Sherpas. When we got to the top of the hill, we'd deposited our stolen lawn chairs in a spot perfectly situated to see the intoxicated sledders careening down the slope. We'd opened our thermoses and settled into our chairs, and we began betting on which sledders would vomit before reaching the bottom of the hill.

We had stayed on the hill until sunset and then staggered back to the dorm holding onto each other and taking turns with the lawn chairs. Coming back seemed a much longer journey than going out had, and we traded theories about how a lawn chair could double in weight over the course of a day. When we finally reached our dorm, the thought of climbing the stairs to our rooms was so daunting that we plopped the two chairs down on the grass, side by side, and fell asleep under the stars, lulled by the drunken crooning—and hiccupping and burping—of our alma mater: *Far above Cayuga's waters, With its waves of blue, Stands our noble Alma Mater, Glorious to view.*

But this was a new year. This was the year that Kyle and Karlee were determined to prove that Slope Day could be just as wild and crazy and fun without the alcohol—and I was determined to believe them.

"Campus Crusade is gonna rock the Slope," Kyle shouted while he and Karlee readied their invisible lassos. "Can we have a 'Whoop! Whoop!'?" The group responded with collective forced merriment. This was my life now, and I had to get used to it. Eventually, I hoped, I could embrace it without reservation. *Whoop! Whoop!*

Karlee handed Kyle a flag, which he lifted above his head and waved back and forth. *Campus Crusade!* the flag proclaimed in big black letters. *Win the campus today, win the world tomorrow!*

On the big day, as I started up the hill, I passed two hippie girls spinning in a circle, braided hair and beads flying, a two-person salute to Stevie Nicks. I wished I could join them but reluctantly reminded myself that I was on the right path. The righteous path. The path for those concerned about the future, those who weren't frivolously twirling away their window of opportunity. I passed by a lone engineering student wearing a pith helmet and juggling three textbooks with remarkable agility. The textbooks flew in the air, covers flapping, all three aloft simultaneously while his busy hands whirled beneath them.

I believe, Lord. I shot up my old well-worn prayer: *Help now my unbelief.* I stood watching the boy and his flying books with a blank appreciation until the needling thought that I might have never been saved in the first place pricked me back into motion.

I reminded myself of Mathew 17:20—all I needed to be saved was a *mustard seed of faith.*

I passed by a group of sorority girls sitting in a circle, passing a joint around. Every few seconds, one of the sisters would shout, "Wake and bake!" and the others would follow with peals of laughter. I passed a short fat girl lying on top of a tall skinny boy, her lips to his, kissing him hungrily. Then a group of frat boys urging a scrawny freshman, his mouth wrapped around a beer bong emblazed with Greek letters, to "Suck Hard! Life is short!" I wished life really *were* short, but I knew it wasn't; it was horrifyingly limitless.

I finally spotted the bold Campus Crusade flag at the top of the hill, catching the sunlight, and made out Kyle and Karlee beneath it, supervising a stack of lunch trays and a vat of Vaseline. Kyle was dancing around the stash, caught up in the tidal wave of fun he wished he were having. When he saw me climbing toward him, he hooted, "All right, we got Rowe here. Let the party begin!" Appreciating the inclusion in a group I didn't want to belong to but needed nonetheless, I replied, "Thanks, Kyle. Hey, you got an extra tray for me?"

"Do we got an extra tray for Rowe?"

Karlee handed Kyle a tray that he then lifted above his head and waved with as much fanfare as he had the flag. "Uh, yeah, I think we do!" I took the tray and walked over to the top of the hill, determined to participate and desperately trying to knock the nostalgia for last year's preferable festivities out my head.

I got on my tray and sailed down the hill at a surprising velocity, shooting past everyone I'd seen on my way up, my thoughts momentarily suspended. I passed the diminutive beer-guzzling freshman, now lying in a heap, and his ring of boosters, congratulating each other with slaps on the back. I passed the mismatched couple, who had flipped their positions so that his long legs now dangled past her feet. I passed the upper-class girls laughing at nothing, flew by the pith-helmet juggler, and nearly crashed into the twirling hippie girls.

Everything was a blur; whizzing snapshots of typical college life, a parade of kids who were granted the luxury of focusing only on the finite, as free and as happy as dogs on a beach, for whom eternity was as irrelevant as last semester's syllabus. And for a good thirty seconds, I was one of them, my mind wiped clean of worries about my salvation.

My tray slowed down, however, skidding onto level ground, and the fears flooded back, twofold, reasserting control of my thoughts with a punishing grip. I heard Kyle cheering for me at the top of the hill and looked up to see the flag clapping the back of his blond hair, his body contorted with grotesque enthusiasm. "All right, Rowe! Oh yeah! That's what I'm talking about! Whoop! Whoop!" My butt hurt. I was cold. And I didn't want to go back up to the top where Kyle and Karlee would force me to celebrate. Would God understand? Did the "Whoop! Whoop!" sound forced and desperate to His ears, too? Or was this a kind of updated anthem to His greatness, the unreserved kind of hallelujah He had always liked, and which I'd been refusing to sing?

I put the slick, icy tray under my arm and walked back up the hill to rejoin the merry band of crusaders.

I had a new plan. I decided to attack my theological demons with theological learning. I drew my trench-line in a remote corner of the Cornell library, between Dewey decimals 220 and 230, reading what theologians and the early church fathers had written about salvation and hell. I learned that the word *hell* came from the Hebrew word *Gehenna*, and that *Gehenna* was the city dump, where trash was constantly being burned and wild animals would fight over the scraps, producing a genuine gnashing of teeth.

Some theologians, such as John Calvin, wrote that no one can lose their salvation, that the elect are children of God, and nothing can alter their eternal destiny. Once saved always saved, he believed, because God "pre-ordained part of the human race, without any merit of their own, to salvation." But then others disagreed, like St. Augustine, who wrote that you *can* lose your salvation, citing John 15:6 as evidence: *If anyone does not abide in me he is thrown away like a branch and withers; and the branches are gathered, thrown into the fire, and burned.* I loathed St. Augustine.

St. Paul stopped me with a verse I had memorized but never understood: *Be ye not unequally yoked together with unbelievers: for light will be pulled into dark. Yoke* referred to marriage, the commentary explained. Paul was arguing that an unbelieving spouse would inevitably pull the believer down to hell. I pictured myself reaching down from a high scaffold or construction crane or helicopter, like in some action movie, trying to lift Cooper to safety with one arm. Instead of me lifting him up, though, and saving the day, I saw his weight pulling us both inexorably down, our two bodies spiraling into a black pit while the world of goodness and light flashed out of sight.

I dug through the stacks, excavating every bit of commentary I could find on the doctrine of the unequal yoke. Some acknowledged the burdens of interfaith marriage but argued that God approves of all committed relationships. Others maintained that any believer who knowingly marries an unbeliever unequivocally forfeits his salvation, citing 1 Corinthians: *How do you know, wife, whether you will save your husband? Or how do you know, husband, whether you will save your wife?* I thought, *How do you know you can't?* Wasn't saving Cooper a worthy, loving goal? Wasn't *love* supposed to be the lynchpin of the whole dang thing?

But then I remembered: *The road to hell is paved with good intentions,* which wasn't from the Bible, but that did not mean it was not true. My stomach turned and I ran to the bathroom to vomit. With each heave I thought of how much I loved Cooper, but how nothing could be worth the sacrifice of my eternal destiny. As I leaned over the toilet, I tucked my hair back away from my face, the way Cooper used to do after I drank too much, a gesture that had seemed more romantic in its way than any stroll on any moonlit night. I thought about Pascal, his wager, and the damage they found in his brain.

And what about Cooper's soul? What would happen to my Pea, my Peanut, my Bean, spinning away for all eternity? And what about the millions of other people in the world? What about the Asian librarian with the Buddhist yin-yang symbol around her neck who didn't charge me a late fee for my overdue books even when I deserved it, even when I was three weeks late? That was grace on her part; that was undeserved kindness, no caveat, no prayer to say over and over and over again. But . . . unless the Asian librarian repented of her Buddhism and switched out the little yin-yang symbol for a little cross, God was going to cut her off on Judgment Day.

I wasn't going to make the same mistake. I knew that no matter how much I loved Cooper, it wasn't worth jeopardizing my soul. And I knew I shouldn't wait to act on this knowledge.

But instead of lifting my burden as I'd hoped, breaking up with Cooper just made things worse. I couldn't eat. I could hardly sleep, and when I did, I woke up feeling like somebody was sitting on my chest. The only thing that made me feel better was throwing up, perhaps because it's hard to think about anything while you're throwing up, like when you're falling, or sneezing, or going down a slide, or when the doctor keeps jabbing the needle into your arm because he can't find the vein. Out of desperation, I called up Hope Valley Baptist and, knowing that Pastor Womac had long since left, asked for Pastor Bill, the literal-minded director of *100 Percent Chance of Rain*, the one who had warned me God wouldn't be pleased to find I didn't "want Him around" and advised me to avoid having that instinctual reaction.

"I feel like I'm going crazy," I told him. "I'm scared that I'm not really a Christian anymore. Maybe I never was. I don't know, Pastor Bill. I don't know what to do."

Pastor Bill told me that God sends us the Holy Spirit to assure us of our salvation and that if I was worrying about being saved maybe I wasn't really saved.

I hung up the phone, stung to the center of my already-compromised core.

This was the exact opposite of my parents' comforting perspective: that worrying was an indication of my faith, not my lack of it. Now because of Pastor Bill, each worry I had seemed to confirm my damnation. And round and round it went, multiplying my worries until they were, as Isaiah would say, *as numerous as grains of sand in the desert.*

I called my parents for help, and they tried again and again to assure me of my salvation. But how could I trust them? Parents always believe their kids are awesome. Like my dad used to think I was a good softball player even though I would strike out most of the time, sometimes even splatting facedown on home plate after swinging so wildly I fell down. And my mom had thought I was pretty even during the year I had full wraparound braces, a pageboy hair cut with a spiral perm, and budding boobs that sprouted into weird, sad little puckers. I told them I couldn't believe them. Their vision was cloudy. They loved me too much. I needed objective, serious help, and they found it for me: a one-of-kind facility two hours from our home, a facility dedicated to BOTH mental health and Christ.

"Well then," Bethanie clicks her pen closed and attaches it to her folder, "now you're here."

"Now I'm here."

Bethanie composes her thoughts for a moment. "Your situation is quite a challenge, but . . ." she lets me in on a secret, "but I know someone who's going to be a big help." I expect Bethanie to mention a respected staff psychiatrist with experience in religious mania maybe, but instead she blinks both her eyes in a gesture I think she means as a wink and points to the ceiling. "God," she says in tone of exaggerated wisdom, "has a little more experience with this type of thing than I do."

I start having trouble breathing, and so I do my trick of lifting my torso up, popping out my chest to get a rapid shot of oxygen, and holding it to keep from fainting. It's a good trick, and one that reliably prevents me from passing out. As I struggle to maintain consciousness, Bethanie, unaware that I've ceased respiration, tells me that here at Grace Point they focus on God's love, and not on His wrath. Her system strikes me as flawed; if you believe in His wrath, it seems to me you *should* be focusing on it—with diligence. But of course I don't say this out loud. Instead, I smile at Bethanie and attempt to screw my face into an endearing expression of, *Well, Grace Point is the perfect place for me, then!*

Bethanie asks if I have any additional physical symptoms, and I tell her that I feel nauseous pretty much all the time and don't want to eat anything, ever. However, I rush to assure her, I do make myself eat because I must in order to live.

"I drink Ensure," I say, "because it's packed with calories and I can get it down pretty quick. But I can't always keep it down, and—"

Bethanie stops me, interest piqued. She's a detective with a juicy clue, thrilling on the trail of discovery. "What do you mean you can't always keep it down?"

"I vomit."

Bethanie glows with the satisfaction of having penetrated and expertly solved a case (and far faster than her imagined competitors). She nods, almost delirious with a diagnosis that presents itself so easily. "Ah, you look in the mirror and see someone fat."

I protest, "No, I . . . I don't think I'm fat."

Bethanie smiles, warmed with satisfaction. She's been down this road and knows the signposts; she loves them. She is a creature who is certain, for whom all is as clear as a glass of water, a creature I will never be. "You don't think you're fat. You *know* it, right, Maggie? Isn't that what you mean?"

I object weakly, "No, I'm really not that concerned about my weight."

Bethanie smiles, sailing on the high of it all. "Denial is the most common characteristic of bulimia. You are a beautiful young woman, and Jesus loves you just the way you are. We're not all made to be a size six." Bethanie purses her lips and taps them with her finger. "Plus, Maggie, vomiting strips the enamel from your teeth. I suggest you save those pearly whites for the pearly gates."

In an instant, I feel I can see Bethanie's whole easy, non-conflicted life, a life in which the world is never horrifyingly inexplicable, a life composed of lucid patterns where A consistently leads to B, and if you want to prevent B, you just stop doing A. I can see the psychology textbook Bethanie studied in her Christian college dorm room that she shared with her equally faith-focused roommate, a space that both girls agreed to decorate with the theme "The Bible: We Love It." I can see her highlighting a bullet point in the chapter on eating disorders: *Bulimia's common characteristic: Denial. Many bulimics deny their condition.*

I attempt to keep my tone of voice even and without antagonism as I tell Bethanie I'm far more concerned with my eternal salvation than my weight. She nonetheless exclaims, "Ah, so you *are* concerned about your weight!"

Determined not to mess up the chance I wish I didn't have to take, I say simply, "I need to be admitted as soon as possible. Please."

PART TWO

CHAPTER SEVEN: **FIRST DAY**

THE FOLLOWING MORNING, my parents bring me back to Grace Point for the big drop-off.

"You can let me out here," I say at the driveway turnaround. Mom cries. Dad bites his lip until it bleeds and then pretends it's a cold sore, even keeping up the pretense by applying Carmex to it. They both watch until the door of the facility closes behind me with a bang that startles me with its volume and finality.

A boy in his late teens suddenly appears wearing an odd ensemble of brown corduroy pants, high-top gym shoes, and a Green Lantern T-shirt. His face is speckled with acne, and sparse whiskers sprout from his chin. The boy speaks quickly, making eye contact with only one of my eyes. "My name is Bernie. My job is to show you around. Welcome to Grace Point. This is the front lobby, obviously, I guess, and if you come with me this way, we'll go to your—" Bernie stops suddenly and looks back at me, startled. "Are you Maggie?"

"Yes, that's me."

Bernie looks relieved then abruptly heads down the hallway. He takes several steps before turning around to make sure I'm following. "We'll go to your room first, Maggie."

My room is small and clean and appears to have been decorated by a lonely aunt obsessed with daisies and all things Christ. Directly across

from a twin mattress with a daisy-quilted bed cover is a watercolor painting of a small boy on a beach gazing up at the sky. Beneath the image it
says, *Where can I go from Your Spirit? Or where can I flee from Your pres-*
ence? If I ascend to heaven You are there. If I make my bed in Sheol, there
You are. Psalm 139:4. The boy in the painting hugs his chest and looks up
at the heavens. I'm sure the artist intended for the boy to look comforted
by the seascape. I'm sure the image was meant to express the beauty of
God's omnipresence—God in the sky, God in the ocean, God in the waves,
God in each grain of sand. But that's not what I see. All I see is an abandoned boy standing with no adults in sight, looking as terrified as I feel.

"All right," Bernie says. "I'll bring you back here at the end." And then
he's out the door and down the hallway before I can set down my bag.

I hustle to catch up, and I find out that Grace Point looks nothing
like the hospital I imagined. Nothing like the institution my grandmother
stayed in. Certainly nothing like a scene from *Frances.* There are no ice
baths. No lobotomy equipment. No pale women in shackles rocking
imaginary babies while some weird dude masturbates in the corner. Just a
series of tastefully decorated rooms, each with a smattering of chairs and
couches, dimly lit by bulbs under tasseled shades, smelling of too much
potpourri. A perfect place for a tasteful funeral reception, or a murder
mystery, or, I'm hoping, a speedy recovery.

Bernie tells me I have no restrictions other than that from eight A.M.
to eight P.M. Monday through Saturday, I need to participate in the daily
schedule, which includes group therapy, activity therapy, exercise hour,
Bible study, "God, Help Me Stop" group, individual therapy, and psycho-
pharmaceutical consultation. Other than that, I can leave whenever I
want. I can drive the two hours and stay at my parents' or my best friend
Sophie's house overnight if I choose.

"Next door there's a convenience store and a hair salon." Bernie slips me a
coupon that reads *Sunny and Shears: The "I Got You Babe" Special—50 percent*
off a combination cut, blow-dry, styling. Then he leans in and lets me in on a
secret: "My mom says it's the best deal in town. She goes once a month."

I respond with more pep than necessary, "Oh, great. I'll check it out!"

"Would you like to see the cafeteria?" Bernie offers, and he leads me

out of the hushed hallways of Grace Point into a multiple-business building complex the facility shares with dentistry offices, accountants, law
firms, insurance agencies, money-management firms, a graphic design
business, and several corporations of the "someone, someone, and someone else" variety.

I immediately feel out of place in the busy cafeteria where men hurry
to their tables in gleaming loafers and expertly fitted suits and women
with blown-out hair confidently click their pristine pumps on the linoleum floor as they select items from the salad bar. My reflection in the
door of the drink refrigerator, in contrast, shows a tall frazzled-looking
girl in baggy elastic-waist muumuu pants and a *Flashdance* sweatshirt.
Her hair is in a clipped mess of a bun on the top of her head, stray strands
shooting out like sprouts of an untended potato. Nothing about her is
sleek or contained or appropriate for this cafeteria. She looks every inch
the mental patient that I now know myself to be.

"Morning check-in is beginning now," Bernie says with urgency, and
I'm grateful to follow him out of the public glare of the business center
and back to the freak wing of Grace Point, where I appear to belong. He
escorts me into one of the rooms, where I find Bethanie sitting in a circle
with an assortment of seven people you'd only expect to see together on
an airplane or at the DMV. Or in a murder mystery. Bethanie introduces
me to my fellow patients, whom she calls "the gang," and smiles proudly,
evidently pleased with her lack of formality.

Dwayne is an unsettlingly still man who appears to be one of those
wooden Indians come to life . . . barely.

Next, there's Ron and Jon, a pair of freckled red-haired twins, probably in their late teens, who both look as if someone has just beeped a horn
at them and they're in the process of recovering from the fright. Bethanie
points to the two boys and, like an upbeat hostess providing conversation
fodder, says, "Ron and Jon also suffer from obsessive thoughts," in the
same way one might say, "Ron and Jon also enjoy trying new foods and
dipping candles."

Petra is a hairdresser with tanning-bed rust-colored skin and talon-
like nails—put-together, but clearly falling apart.

Mickey is a sixty-ish petite Captain Kangaroo look-alike. "It's nice to meet you, Maggie," he says, offering a broad smile that reveals a bright slab of teeth far too large for an ordinary human mouth. *The joy of the Lord is my strength*, his T-shirt reads, and I wonder how, if that's true, he has found himself here.

Then there's Timbo, a biker-type dude with a red beard, who I can easily picture cheering with vigor at an illegal dogfight.

And completing the circle is Quinn, a warm, doughy woman in her midthirties with perfect Cupid's bow lips and deep blue eyes. Her smile is relaxed, I notice, as if she's just saying hello instead of trying to make an impression. I like Quinn immediately.

Bethanie explains that every morning "the gang" checks in and tells everyone how they're feeling. "If you have trouble, you can always look up here," she says, indicating a poster on the wall listing about a hundred feelings. "Timbo, will you start us off? How are you feeling today?"

Timbo, who is alternating between cracking his knuckles and tugging on his ears in an obvious state of agitation, mutters, "Fine. I'm fine."

Bethanie smiles. "*Fine* is not an emotion."

Timbo blows air through his nostrils like a bull, his face flushing. "Well, what is it then?"

"I don't know what the right feeling word might be for you this morning, Timbo, but *fine* is not on the list."

"Well, who made up the list?" Timbo fumes. "You? What are YOU? The expert on the world?" If this were a cartoon, I think, this is where steam would start pouring out of his ears.

"I'm not any kind of expert on the world, Timbo. I think you know that," Bethanie says affably. "Only God can claim that title. I don't know what you're feeling, but would a word like this help?"

Bethanie points to the word *anger* on the board, and Timbo explodes.

"Well, okay, now I am angry because you're telling me it's not okay for me to be *fine*. Like I have to be on some rollercoaster all the time. Like I'm some *woman*. Fine, you win. I'm *angry*. I'm really *angry!*"

"Okay, Timbo's feeling angry," Bethanie summarizes in a studied calm, which I'm guessing proves to herself that she's a true professional.

Next she turns to Dwayne, the lifelike wooden Indian. "Dwayne, how are you feeling today?"

Dwayne takes a pause long enough for me to wonder if he's still breathing before sighing and attempting an answer. "Um, I guess . . . bored."

Bethanie replies, "*Bored* is also not an emotion."

Timbo, from across the circle, barks, "Oh my God! It's on the board!" He points "*Bored* is on the board. It's after *bitter* and before *brave*. It's right there!"

Bethanie turns and sees that *bored* is indeed on the list and must reluctantly concede, "Well, okay then. Dwayne is feeling bored. And Timbo, I'd like you to think some more about the word *angry*."

Next she addresses the twins, who both wear rubber bands on their left wrists, which for some reason they are snapping repeatedly. "Hey, guys, looks like you've got some stuff happening." She speaks to the twin closest to her, "Ron? How are you feeling?"

Ron wheezes out, "Scared."

Bethanie repeats, "Scared. Ron is feeling scared." Then she turns to Ron's even-less-bold twin, and asks, "And you, Jon?"

Jon manages to sputter, "Same."

Bethanie responds, "Same as . . . ?"

Jon's face turns red. "Same as my brother. *Scared*."

"Wow. You two have a lot in common." Bethanie appears to be attempting a joke. "Has anyone ever told you that you look alike?"

Ron and Jon don't know what to make of this. They look at each other for help before Ron replies lamely, "Yes, we're twins."

Bethanie at least knows to move on when a joke has fallen flat. So she turns to Petra. Petra's troubled eyes turn into two puddles and she chokes out one word, "Lonely."

Bethanie, oddly upbeat, coos, "Ooh, that's a good one. *Lonely*," then winks with both eyes. "I've got to add that one to the list."

Bethanie shifts her focus to Mickey, our resident Captain Kangaroo. "Mickey, how are you feeling this morning?"

"This is the day that the Lord has made," he says, showing his great wall of teeth. "Let us rejoice and be glad in it."

"Yes, let's! But, Mickey, can you tell us, how do you feel *right now*?"

Mickey looks around the room as if in wonder at this thing called life. "Amazed. Humbled. Gobsmacked." Then, looking up toward the ceiling, he continues, "Lord, your wonders truly are unceasing. Your mercies astounding. 'My cup runneth over. Surely goodness and mercy shall follow me all the days of my life and I will dwell in the house of the Lord forever.' That's Psalms 23." Mickey shakes his head in theatrical astonishment at his good fortune and slaps his knee as if to say, *Hot damn!*

"Yes, Mickey," Bethanie persists, "but right this moment, what does it feel like to be Mickey?"

"It feels like being a child of God."

"And what does being a child of God feel like?"

"It feels terrific."

"So right now you feel *terrific*?"

"You betcha!"

"All right. Mickey feels *terrific*."

Mickey clasps his hands above his head and shakes like a boxer who has just won the heavyweight championship of happiness.

Bethanie turns to Quinn. "Quinn?"

"I guess I feel like I'm . . . well, like I'm missing out."

"Missing out?"

"You know that feeling when you look in a picture window and you see kids playing, maybe a little girl trying out her tap shoes or playing the piano, and, I don't know, brothers tackling each other, and it just seems like that's where life is? Inside that window? And you're on the outside?"

"Is that feeling called *envy*, do you think? Are you feeling *envious*?"

"No, more like I'm *missing out*. Not that I specifically want what someone else has, but that there are joys in life that I don't have access to."

"*Jealous*?"

"Well, no, I think jealousy is like being protective over something you already have, and I more have this feeling of *missing out*—"

I'm impressed with Quinn's ability to hold her ground. I would have caved much earlier.

"*Deprived*?" Bethanie asks, with heightened diction as if to impress an unseen supervisor.

"Well, no, *deprived* implies that someone has wronged me in some way."

"Well, what word would you like to go with?"

"Can I just go with *missing out*? Can that be my word?"

Bethanie screws her face up and asks quizzically, as if to point out what she clearly feels is the absurdity of Quinn's response, "You feel *missing out*?"

"Well . . . I feel *like* I'm missing out."

"Okay, Quinn, what we're trying to do in morning check-in is to clue in to what we are feeling in the moment. Right now. *Right now*, how are you feeling?"

"I was trying to explain how I feel—"

"*Jealous*?" Bethanie completes her sentence as if the suggestion hadn't just been rejected.

Quinn starts to throw her hands up in frustration, but then her right hand bats her left back down into her lap, in a very literal show of self-restraint, and she replies evenly, "Okay. Sure. *Jealous*."

"Excellent. Quinn is feeling *jealous*."

Bethanie, pleased with the deftness of her psychological probing, now turns to me. "And Maggie, how are you feeling? If you need help, you can look at the board."

I feel that how I identify myself in this initial meeting is important, first impressions and all that, so I've been thinking it over while everyone's been talking, and I'm ready with my answer. "I'll go with *anxious*. I'm anxious about being here, but also, I mean, overall . . . well, my big problem is I'm anxious about . . . I'm worried, well, *terrified* about going to hell and—"

Before I can complete my sentence, Mickey bleats out, rapid-fire, "Jesus says all you have to do is accept him into your heart and then you're SAVED! That's it! Let's do it right now! You won't go to hell. Do it NOW!"

I clearly disappoint Mickey with my reply. "Oh, I've accepted Jesus into my heart already. Probably like ten thousand times. It's just I feel like I can never be 100 percent sure I got it right—"

Mickey clutches his fingers around the seat of his chair, apparently to restrain himself from pouncing on me and getting some sort of commission on my salvation. "Just say *Jesus, I believe you died on the cross for my sins*," he implores me. "Just say it! Say it now! I'll do it with you!"

I bristle. It's not like I don't know the drill. *I've probably converted more people than he has*, I think with a surprising burst of righteous indignation, remembering my success with creepy single men and oxygen-assisted elderly ladies at shopping malls.

"Mickey," Bethanie interrupts, "there's no cross-talking in morning check-in. Maggie said her feeling. She is feeling *anxious*. Maggie is *anxious*." Hearing my name repeated along with the word *anxious* has the unfortunate effect of making me even more anxious.

In group therapy later on in the day, I learn that Ron and Jon are both troubled by intrusive, obsessive thoughts about having sex with their mother and that, no matter how hard they try, neither can stop fantasizing about screwing dear old Mom. Apparently, it all started when their mother wore a tight Christmas sweater one holiday season that must have really been something, since neither boy can seem to pry the image from his head. I picture a headless cable-knit pullover with two bulging Christmas bells, one on each breast, ringing in an odd sort of family cheer.

The rubber bands Ron and Jon both wear around their wrists, it turns out, are for snapping any time one of these troubling thoughts pops up. This information clears up my question, but now, any time I see either Jon or Ron snap their rubber band, *I* can't help imagining them imagining having sex with their mother.

Timbo tells us he had been a Hells Angel until the day he found Jesus, said the prayer, and accepted Christ into his heart. When I learn that he did this *while he was on methamphetamines*, I can't help but to think that Timbo has a lot more to worry about than I do. But Timbo is not anxious like me. He says he could literally feel Jesus enter his heart at the moment of conversion, and that it was the greatest high of his life. But then, afterward, the weight of his sin hit him hard. That very day he quit drugs, riding, women, and "pounding," a term Bethanie seems pleased he does not expound upon.

Timbo shares that he came to Grace Point to deal with his tendency to fly into maniacal rages over perceived social slights, something that does not go over well in his new Christian social group. He relates the tale of the time his tailor suggested letting out the waist of a pair of his pants. Timbo heard an implication that he was getting fat and so he slapped the tailor . . . with the pants. Timbo shared this experience with his men's group at church, who could *not* relate *at all*, and who contacted their pastor, who, in turn, immediately contacted Grace Point.

Petra shares that she has been married for twelve years and that she recently had an affair with a waiter she met at Bob's Big Boy, but she broke the affair off after six months, breaking her own heart in the process.

Bethanie nods with understanding. "Yes, it's easy to confuse lust with love. The angels are rejoicing in heaven over your repentance, Petra. Of that you can be sure."

Petra shakes her head. "I didn't just lust over Anthony. I loved him."

Bethanie tilts her head and raises an eyebrow, silently and not so subtly communicating, *Come on. We both know you're lying.*

Petra stands her ground. "It was love. It really was. I really loved him, and now anytime I drive past Bob's Big Boy, I can't stop crying, which is hard to explain to my husband when he's with me in the car."

"What do you say to your husband in these circumstances?"

"I tell him I had a bad experience there once. Rotten coleslaw. I say it was brown and that I was sick the next day."

"What is your husband's response to this coleslaw deceit?"

I notice Quinn suppressing a smile at Bethanie's usage of the term "coleslaw deceit."

"He just tells me I should never order coleslaw at diners, that he's told me before that mayonnaise-based foods are always risky at low-end establishments."

Mickey chirps happily, "Your husband makes an excellent point. Also you should never order fish on Mondays."

Bethanie ignores Mickey and turns to her next customer. "Why don't you tell the group what you've been working on with your individual therapist, Quinn?"

"We've been talking a lot about, well, as usual, sadness. Dr. Lakhani gave me an image I really liked. She said the amount of sadness or loss you experience in your life carves out a space, a space that the equivalent amount of joy is given room to flow in. I've suffered a lot, and I like to think that might be worth something."

Bethanie nods as if she's listening, but I can tell she's forming her next insight. Her eyes lose focus, drifting toward the water spot in the ceiling.

"That image gives me hope that perhaps I'm due for a similar degree of joy someday. Maybe soon, I hope."

Bethanie's eyes return and lock back into place. "Can I tell you how I like to spell *joy*?"

"Sure."

Bethanie takes a big ol' pregnant pause, until she's confident she has secured the gang's attention. "I like to spell *joy* J-O-Y—Jesus and Others and You." Bethanie looks each member of the gang in the eye before continuing, "If we can align our priorities with God's, God promises us in His Word that we will experience 'joy that surpasses all understanding.' What do you think of that, Quinn?"

Quinn replies, "Well, that would sure be nice."

"It's more than nice. It's true. Just remember: Jesus and Others and You."

At the end of the day, I stand next to Quinn in the women's bathroom, brushing my teeth, feeling hopeful that maybe this place can save me. Bethanie may not be that bright but, well, who's the one in the nuthouse? I take a moment to thank God for Grace Point, knowing that one doesn't find a born-again psychiatric facility on every corner. If I went to a regular hospital, they would try to convince me that hell doesn't exist, that it's a tool used to control the masses with fear, that the Bible is just a bunch of fairy tales . . . and maybe I'd actually start to believe them, putting my soul in even greater jeopardy. At any other hospital, they wouldn't understand Pascal's wager, that faith is definitely worth the gamble, and that doubt is so, so, *so* not worth the risk. They wouldn't see that this one little life is nothing in comparison to a sprawling, merciless eternity. No, I am lucky to be here. I spit the toothpaste and my distaste for everything that is happening to me into the sink, and as I inhale, I try to breathe in a sense of hope and gratitude.

Quinn begins packing up her toiletries and looks over at me and says, "I don't floss. Don't judge me. I'm on my own case already."

I smile. "No judgment here."

I am pleased when Quinn continues, "I just hate flossing. I always end up using too much force and thwacking my gums and then they bleed. And my gums don't deserve that. It's not their fault that I can't master a basic personal-hygiene technique. Why should they suffer?"

Quinn and I walk together down the hallway back to our rooms, and on our way we see that Mickey has put a chin-up bar in his doorway and he's hanging from it, his arms slack, his face red, his knees brushing the floor.

"Glad you're hanging in there," Quinn quips, and she waits for Mickey to explain what he is doing. Mickey just looks at us and grins, his giant teeth shining. We stand watching him hang like that until Quinn finally gives in to curiosity. "Whatcha doing there?"

"Stretching myself," Mickey answers matter-of-factly.

"Doing what?" Quinn's not sure she understood him right.

"I've always wanted to be tall," Mickey explains, "and now I'm going to be. The spine is the most flexible part of the human body. It can be stretched up to three inches."

"Wow, I've certainly never heard that before. Huh. Well, I guess . . . carry on," Quinn says with a remarkably straight face. When Quinn and I get out of view, she bursts out laughing. "Stretching himself!"

I stifle a giggle. "Oh, the poor man."

"I bet he got the idea from *The Brady Bunch*. There's an episode where Peter hangs from a bar like that because he wants to be as tall as Greg."

"I've seen that one. But I think it's Bobby who wants to be as tall as Greg."

"That's right. Bobby's upset because he's a peewee. He keeps saying, 'I'm a shrimpo . . .'"

We say the line together, laughing: "I'm a peewee! And I always will be!"

"Jinx," she says as fast as a flash, and then she releases me in the next breath: "Maggie Rowe."

• • •

The next day I find out that everybody in the gang gets individual therapy four times a week. I fantasize about who my individual therapist might be, hoping for a witchy woman from Harvard Divinity School whose eyes are shot from years of reading ponderous religious texts so she's forced to wear glasses that bug out her eyes and make her look like a freak—a freak who's going to save my life.

At the end of morning check-in, Bethanie says to the group, "Okay, time to head out to your individual therapists."

As the "gang" members get up and start to move off, I look up at Bethanie. "What about me?" I ask.

"Yes, Maggie, lucky for you, you get . . ." Bethanie places her hand on her heart, tilts her head, and does a stupid little curtsy. "*Moi.*" Even though I fully comprehend Bethanie's meaning and unnecessary use of French, I still say, "Wait, what?" in the foolish hope that this three-second delay will give Bethanie the opportunity to change her mind about my fate. Bethanie interprets my stunned response to mean I'm overcome by my good fortune.

Later that day, I go into Bethanie's office for my one-on-one. She is sitting behind a desk with a full-length mirror propped up against it. I look in the mirror and am taken aback. I appear weak and skittish, like an upright, very tall stray cat, poorly fed.

"Do mirrors frighten you?" Bethanie asks.

"Oh, no, I was just startled. It's always weird to run into yourself." I wait for Bethanie to give a little attempt at a laugh. Not that what I've said is especially funny. It just seems to me that the normative response to a halfhearted joke is usually a halfhearted laugh. But Bethanie just . . . listens. Until I feel compelled to spurt, "I was just surprised to see a mirror in a therapist's office."

"Us therapists have a few tricks up our sleeves." Bethanie shakes the arm of her floral blouse, indicating her sleeve, and winks with both eyes. "Now, look in the mirror and tell me what you see." I instantly realize she's pushing the bulimia insight, and I try to lead back. "I see myself. I really think I look fine. Seriously, my appearance is the least of my—"

"Mmhmm. Okay. Well, we all have things we don't like about ourselves, right?"

I wheeze a deflated sigh before replying, "Yes, definitely. But my main problem—"

"So tell me what you see in the mirror that you don't like."

I figure I'll never get to the issues I care about if I don't go along with my therapist, so I humor her. "Okay, well, I don't like that my eyes are asymmetrical; my right eye is higher and larger than my left. I've tried to make them look less wonky by tipping my head and squinting my right eye a little, but that always makes me look even more wonky."

"Mmhmm, what else?"

"Okay, uh, I wish my upper lip were thicker. When I smile, it rolls up like a window shade, displaying my gums, like I'm doing some stupid commercial for my orthodontist. I've tried to work on that too, by purposely trying to keep my lip down when I smile, but that always ends up making me look, well . . . simple."

"Simple?"

"Simple. You know . . . like mentally deficient."

"You feel mentally deficient?"

"No, no, I just mean I look that way when I try to control my upper lip." Bethanie looks at me blankly. "Never mind. I shouldn't have said anything."

"Maggie, listen to me. You can tell me anything," Bethanie says, placing her hand on her breast and bowing her head, as if humbled by the generosity of her own offer.

"Okay, well, all right, Bethanie. Thanks."

"You bet. Now let's get down to the nitty-gritty. I want you to look in the mirror and tell me how you feel about your *weight*."

Without looking in the mirror I reply, "Seriously, I don't think I'm fat."

"Why don't you look in the mirror and tell me what you see?"

I give my reflection a glance and say, "I see a girl who is skinny. Actually, very skinny. Very tall. A very tall, skinny girl who looks really freaked out." Then, trying to add some levity, I pat the sides of my thighs and say, "I mean, of course, there are *these*. Can't escape the curse of the Southern-lady saddlebags."

Bethanie exults. "Tell me more about this curse."

"Oh, it's not really a curse. That's just what my mom and her sisters call it."

"Maggie, therapy is about going to the difficult places, not running away from them. Now, tell me, what are saddlebags?"

"*Saddlebags* just refers to upper thighs that stick out to the side. I assume like baggage you sling over a horse's saddle."

"How do your saddlebags make you feel?"

"Oh, I really wish I hadn't said anything. On a scale of 1 to 10, my displeasure about my saddlebags is like a .03, whereas my displeasure and anxiety over what will happen when I die is absolutely a 10. If I could have assurance about my eternal destiny, I'd happily weigh four hundred pounds. I'd sign a contract to be the fat lady at the circus." Even as the words come out of my mouth, I am able to predict Bethanie's response, which comes right on cue: "You feel like the fat lady at the circus?"

"No, no, I'm just saying if I had a choice. I mean, I'm five foot ten and 120 pounds. If I were the fat lady at the circus, I'm sure people would want their money back. They could justifiably claim false advertising." I'm hoping Bethanie will laugh, but my perception that humor is not one of her special skills is reinforced when she replies earnestly, "Well, I'll tell you one thing: the mirror is going to be your friend one day. Not your enemy."

After individual therapy, I see Quinn going to the outside courtyard, a small pocket located between our freak wing and the rest of the complex, a haven of open air centered around a single birch tree and spotted with gardenias. I follow her into the courtyard and watch as she takes a pack of cigarettes from her purse and pulls out what is, because I haven't smoked in three days, the most appealing cigarette I've ever seen. Quinn turns, sees my hungry look, and asks, "Do you smoke?"

It feels like she's throwing a ball to me on the playground, and I happily toss it back.

"Yeah, I do. I didn't know if we could smoke here."

"Sure; even felons get to light up. You and me, we're free to be you and me."

"I just didn't know if, you know . . . if smoking was considered sinful."

"It's the only thing keeping me sane, is all I'll say. I thank God for nicotine every day. For sunshine, my husband, and nicotine. The trinity." Bethanie extends a cigarette. I light it and drag greedily.

"I have a pack in my room. I'll totally pay you back."

Quinn waves off my offer, then asks conspiratorially, "Sooo, how was going *one-on-one* with Bethanie?"

I sigh. "She kept trying to convince me I'm bulimic. I'm really not. I just throw up sometimes because my anxiety makes me sick to my stomach."

"Did you tell her that?"

"Yeah. She thinks I'm in denial."

Quinn rolls her eyes. "Bethanie plays the denial card a lot, but what can you say, right? Denying that you're in denial is just proof of the denial."

"Did Bethanie ever do that to you?"

"Oh, sure. During one of the group sessions she told me my depression sprang from difficulty in my marriage that I wasn't acknowledging. I kept telling her my marriage was the one solid thing in my life. And that's true. Jack's been great, completely supportive of my coming here. Amazing. I mean, when people at church ask where I am when everyone's chatting after service with their leaky Styrofoam cups of coffee and their donuts balanced on napkins, he's got to say his wife is in a nuthouse. But he doesn't care. He's really an exceptional man. He's put up with far more than he bargained for. But Bethanie wasn't buying that. So . . . yeah, denial."

I watch the smoke from our cigarettes waft up, escaping into the small patch of sky above the birch tree. "Did you know prisons in the Middle Ages used to have holes in the ceilings of the cells called *God's eyes*?" I ask. Quinn shakes her head.

"The church wardens," I explain, "would starve and torture the inmates, but it was considered cruel to not give them a little hole in the ceiling."

"Small mercies."

Quinn flicks an ash into the patch of dirt around the tree. "Hey, did Bethanie tell you right away that her name was spelled with an *ie* and not a *y*?

"Yes! That's the first thing she said. That was the information she felt she had to get out on the table *right away*!"

"Yeah, it's a bummer that you got Bethanie for individual. But you'll get to see some other people, Dr. Elkins and Dr. Lakhani. It won't be all Bethanie all the time."

Quinn and I say in unison, "Small mercies," then enjoy the last precious drags of our cigarettes under the small square of the God's-eye sky.

CHAPTER EIGHT: **BAD THOUGHTS AND RUBBER BANDS**

ALL DAY LONG, I LOOK FORWARD to eight P.M., when the day's forced march is done and I can have a cigarette with Quinn beside the solitary birch and watch my slender stream of smoke waft up into the uncomplicated patch of sky. Then I can go back to my little room and sleep, each breath lapping me reliably away from the rocky "I" of myself—until my alarm clock rings at seven A.M., slamming me once again against the hard shore of consciousness. Then I yank my body out of bed for morning check-in and begin the new day's march with "I feel *anxious*," or "I feel *fearful*," or I feel *terrified* today."

After morning check-in comes Bible study group, led by Sed, a likeable-enough fellow sporting a bulbous nose and a jet-black mane with tufts of gray over his ears that look like they've been aged for a high school play. At my first Bible study group (called "BS group," a name which only Quinn and I find amusing), Sed begins by leading us in a prayer: "Father, thank You for giving us Your Word so that we may know You. Guide us in our studies today. In Christ's name we pray, amen." I forget to close my eyes because I'm staring at Sed's nose, marveling at its clown-like roundness and copious peppering of blackheads. I find myself spellbound for over twenty seconds as I wonder how much material would come out if

I squeezed the engorged appendage. Until Sed pops open his eyes, which next to his nose seem tiny, like small olive green capers.

"Sometimes I feel so lucky," he says, apropos of nothing, and he throws his arms up in the air.

"It is a good thing to give thanks unto the Lord," Mickey immediately seconds, "and to sing praises unto Thy name, O Most High." Sed takes this in stride, clearly used to Mickey's choral participation, and asks, "Do you know why I feel lucky?" Mickey chimes in, "Because our Lord is great and mighty in His power."

"Yes," Sed continues, unbothered, "and because we have a God who talks to us directly. He doesn't make us guess who He is and what He wants." Sed holds his Bible aloft with one hand and pats it with the other. "And it's all right here. He put the truth in a book. Isn't that amazing? Just one book. And we are lucky enough to *have* that book." Mickey's grin sprawls across his face and he nods in furious support as Sed continues, "He doesn't leave us to wander like sheep." Sed looks around the group again, querying each of us with his small, olive green eyes, "What do we know about sheep?"

Timbo seethes, suddenly angry at the hypothetical sheep for a reason unbeknownst to all. "They're stupid. They wander off. They run into things. They're fu—" Sed, who has been completely impassive in the face of Mickey's introjections, raises a bushy eyebrow, and Timbo's face freezes. "Fu-*ools*!" he revises mid-word. "They don't know anything about anything. They are total fools." Sed laughs good-naturedly as he folds his hairless arms.

"That's the perfect word, Timbo. *Fools*. Sheep are fools. Just like *we're* fools. We wander off without God's Word to guide us."

Timbo's on a roll, high on outrage against the entire sheep population. "They're dumb, stupid creatures. Morons. When it rains, they look up at the sky with their mouths all open, and the rain falls in, and it fills up their throats and then they drown to death."

I'm wondering if Timbo might be confusing sheep with turkeys when Petra chattily asks, "Do you mean turkeys?"

Timbo turns on her, instantly transferring his rage. "What did you say?"

Petra, oddly unaware of the fuse she has clearly lit, twirls a lock of frosted hair around a meticulously manicured finger before answering, "It's turkeys that drown themselves to death in the rain." Timbo's fists clench.

"Who said anything about turkeys?" he shouts, his hands twitching. Petra pulls her perfectly frosted tips into a delightful bunch before replying in her own good time, "Nobody. I'm just saying it's turkeys that do the crazy rain thing. Not sheep."

Timbo explodes, "Turkeys are the only ones allowed to drown in the rain? Who says sheep don't drown themselves, too? Let's get one in here and we can settle this." Timbo stands up and gestures extravagantly toward the door, as if beckoning a sheep who's been waiting outside to settle the argument.

"Gee-uz Loui-uz," Petra unhurriedly replies and then deploys a well-practiced line I immediately admire. "No need to make a thing when there's not a thing."

Timbo looks like a bull whacked from an unexpected side. "*Louise*? Who are you calling *Louise*?"

"Calm down, baby, it's just an expression."

"Baby? Now you're calling me baby?"

"Whoa, cowboy."

"Cowboy? You can't just call me insults because you're some hot piece of—"

"Whoa, whoa," Sed leaps to his feet. "Okay. All right. I think we're getting a little off track. Yeah? I think Timbo's just saying that we are like sheep, right, Timbo?"

Timbo's eyes remain pinned on Petra as Sed continues, "We're lost without a shepherd, but we don't have to stay lost because God gave us a guidebook, and we know it's literally true. Every letter of it. Because He tells us. 2 Timothy 3:16 says, 'All scripture is directly inspired by God.'"

I've always hated this Bible study chestnut. It seems like an obvious logic error to believe a document must be true because the document itself says so. Like believing the homeless dude talking to himself must be Napoleon because he says he just won the battle of Austerlitz.

Sed turns over the dry-erase board. "Our verse for today is Luke 14:8," he says, pointing to the board. "*For this reason I say to you, do not be worried about your life. Look at the birds of the air. The sparrows do not sow, nor reap nor gather into barns, and yet your Heavenly Father feeds them. Are you not worth much more than they?"*

This is another familiar verse that's always driven me crazy. *Yeah,* I want to say, *but awful things happen to the birds of the air* all the time. *People shoot them. Stuff them. Eat them. There's famine and avian flu. And bigger birds, like hawks, that grab them in their claws and tear them apart. And raccoons that suck their little gestating chicklets right out of their eggs. My neighbor, Mr. Marzoni, ran over one once with his lawn mower and only discovered it when he cleaned the mower blades and found an impaled little bird skull.*

"I love this verse," Sed tells us, tapping the board with his pen. "Every time I start to worry about my life, I just think of the sparrows and remind myself that I'm in God's hands and that He's going to take care of me—just like the birds of the air."

Mickey spurts, "Oh, Lord, praise Your Holy Name!" I think of Mr. Marzoni's decapitated sparrow, a small bloody hulk on a suburban lawn.

I meet Quinn in the courtyard for a cigarette. We take a couple of needy drags before Quinn asks, "So did you want to squeeze Sed's nose?"

"How did you know?" I laugh.

"Those poor blackheads. It's like they're bursting, desperate to surrender their pus."

"I couldn't stop staring."

"Me neither."

"We should get him a gift certificate for a facial."

"No, I want to do it myself." Quinn giggles as she takes a drag. "Squeezing blackheads has such a clear reward. It's so *unambiguous.*"

"Right. No second-guessing. It's an activity without competing perspectives."

"Exactly." Quinn puts out her cigarette. "We can get more tomorrow during break. There's a convenience store next building over." Cigarettes: A promise of a clear, unambiguous reward.

• • •

The next day in group, Dwayne tells us he's been working with his individual therapist on getting in touch with his feelings. He says his wife Cricket always complains about his lack of emotional expression and that Cricket goes to the other extreme. The "other extreme" turns out to mean that over the last decade she's been serially treated for multiple personality disorder.

"Your wife has multiple personality disorder?" Bethanie asks.

Dwayne seems puzzled by Bethanie's surprise. "Yeah," he says matter-of-factly, "and during one of our fights she blamed me for it. She said if I could just get one decent personality, she wouldn't have to make up so many."

It *is* a pretty good line. I wonder if Cricket came up with it on the spot, or if she had been holding onto it, like a winning card, just waiting for the right moment to slap it down.

Bethanie folds her hands and leans forward, playing for a close-up no one is taking. "Has your wife actually been diagnosed with multiple personality disorder?"

"Sure. She's been on medication for years. Sometimes it helps, sometimes no."

"Were you aware of her condition before she was diagnosed?"

"Nah, you know. I just thought she was moody."

"Can you tell us about your wife's personalities?"

"Bitches."

"I'm sorry?"

"Mostly they're all bitches."

Quinn and I catch each other's eye and suppress a laugh.

"Dwayne," Bethanie scolds, "that is not the kind of language we use in this group. We've discussed this. If Jesus were sitting next to you, do you think you might make a different word choice?"

Dwayne looks at the empty chair next to him for a long moment, as if genuinely summoning an image of Jesus.

"Do you want to rephrase?"

"Okay, well, most of my wife's personalities I find . . . repugnant." Bethanie scrunches her nose like a ferret, indicating she is unfamiliar with the word *repugnant*.

Dwayne becomes surprisingly animated, "*Repugnant*. You know, like sewage, or what's the slop the Brits use on toast? Marmite. All of her personalities were like that. Sewage. Or Marmite."

Bethanie decides to abruptly cut the conversation off here, a decision that I believe springs from her lack of familiarity with either the word *repugnant* or the British toast condiment Marmite. "Well, this is certainly a lot for us to explore."

The twins are on the hot seat next. I know they're both in the throes of erotic mother fantasies because each is furiously snapping his rubber band, as if determined to commit the world's slowest form of suicide. "Ron, let's start with you. I see you're utilizing your rubber band. Tell me what's going on." Ron wraps one knee into his chest and then an elbow over his mouth, as if trying not to throw up, and shakes his head.

"It's okay, Ron. The gang's all here for you."

"I just . . . I just—" Ron mumbles into his sleeve. "I just can't stop it."

"Do you think you could speak to us, Ron? We can't understand very well when you talk into your elbow."

Ron's eyes glint with anger, but he lifts his head and confesses nonetheless, "I hate it. I hate it so much. I know it's wrong. I know it's sinful, but I can't help it."

"We all have unwelcome thoughts pop into our minds. The only thing that's wrong is continuing the thought, entertaining the sin, inviting it in, instead of sending it away. That's what the rubber band is for. You're saying, 'the show is over.'"

"I know, but the thought-popping, if that's what you want to call it, is pretty constant, so I think I must be entertaining the sin. And I can't figure out how to stop entertaining. I want the show to be over."

Jon nods in agreement.

"You feel the same way, Jon?" Bethanie asks.

Jon looks up, plaintive and confused, like an injured dog that can't understand his pain and why licking the sore spot just makes it worse. "Yeah, same."

Bethanie's takes on her familiar look of unjustifiable certainty and says like a confident salesman, "I want to tell you something I think you're both going to like." The boys lift their eyes, red and watery with hope.

"Philippians 4 says, 'I can do all things through Him that strengthens me.'" The twins continue to look at Bethanie expectantly, waiting for the part she was sure they would like.

But that's all she's got.

"Jon, do you believe the Bible is true?"

Jon stammers, "Y- y- yes."

"Do you believe that God is a liar?"

"No!" Jon blurts out, giving his brother a frightened look. Ron, who looks equally scared, however, can offer no comfort.

"How 'bout you, Ron?"

"No! I know God doesn't lie."

"I've got another verse for you. 'God is truth and in Him is no falsehood.' How does that make you feel?"

Mickey jumps in. "It makes me feel like I want to shout for joy to the Lord, and worship Him with gladness!"

"Thank you, Mickey, but I'm working with Ron right now. Ron, how does it make you feel that God won't lie to you?" Ron, clearly wanting to be out of the spotlight, quickly answers, "Makes me feel good," and before he can finish, Jon sputters, "Same."

Bethanie gives the boys a long, satisfied look and then swivels around to me. "Maggie, I think you might be able to relate to having unwanted thoughts."

I take in the twins' beleaguered wrists and their fatigued faces and answer as empathetically as I can, "Yes, I totally do. Ron, Jon, I totally relate to what it's like."

The twins look skeptical.

"I have the same thing—I mean it sounds like the same thing—where I don't want to think the thoughts, but they keep coming up no matter what I do. And I don't know why it's happening. Am I inviting them? Or allowing, maybe? And how do I send them away?

"And who is it really that's doing all of this? Is it me? I mean, if I don't want the thoughts, but I keep thinking them anyway, who is the *I* in all of that? You know, if you say, '*I* don't like the things *I* think,' what does that even mean?"

Ron and Jon are nodding. They get it. And it's nice for me to let the words flow. But of course, Bethanie wants to help.

"Would you like to tell the group about your saddlebags?"

I feel my face turn red from a combination of embarrassment and outrage. It seems to me therapists shouldn't volunteer information you've revealed in private sessions, especially if the information you've revealed has nothing to do with your psychological issue.

Bethanie prompts me, "Saddlebags are . . ."

"Seriously, I'm not concerned about my weight." I hear my voice rising. "My weight is fine. I mean, I'm skinny. I need to eat. But my body—I think my body is fine."

Bethanie archly raises an eyebrow, an affection I'm sure she's practiced many times in the mirror. But it works, and I feel compelled to turn to the group. "*Saddlebags*," I explain with as little inflection as possible, "is a term that refers to extra weight on your upper thighs. You probably know that. Maybe not. I think it comes from gear you'd carry on a horse. The only reason I brought it up was Bethanie had me look at myself in a mirror and tell her what I didn't like about my appearance, and I couldn't really think of anything, so I said, 'Southern-lady saddlebags.'" I turn back to Bethanie and say as firmly as I am politely able. "I know you're trying to help, but I'm here because I'm not doing very well. I'm in bad shape, actually. Really bad shape, not because I'm worried about my weight, but . . . because I can't stop thinking about going to hell."

Mickey, of course, has an easy solution. "Just say the prayer!"

I smile at him and nod to indicate that this is a well-trod, fully explored road, but Mickey's gunning for his end-of-the-month salvation-sales target bonus. "Say the prayer! I'll say it with you."

I remain calm, despite a ridiculous impulse to jump up onto my chair and say, *It's not that simple! It's not that simple! Why does everyone think everything is so simple?* Instead, I reply with a restraint I'm personally impressed with. "Mickey, I've said the prayer. I've said it a lot. It's just that it doesn't help because how do I know if the prayer took? How do I know if I did it right? And then what will happen? Will I go to hell? Will God spew me out of his mouth? What can I do? And how can I stop thinking these thoughts?! *Saying the prayer for the ten-thousandth time will resolve nothing, okay?* Thank you, but it's complicated."

The group is quiet, and I realize I have exposed a nerve. Bethanie fails to notice, however, because her plan is already in motion. With an annoying twinkle in her eye, she reaches in her purse and pulls out a rubber band, like my grandmother would once have pulled out a bag of candied orange slices. But instead of breaking open the cellophane and bestowing me with a treat, Bethanie walks over, hands me a dirty rubber band, and says, "Here. For anytime you have a bad thought."

Later, alone in my room, I put the rubber band around my wrist, and I have to admit, somewhat resentfully, that I'm happy to have it. Like a new toy, it comes with the possibility of *changing everything*. Plus, I think, it's also a tool. And tools do things. They get results. Cavemen used them, and look where we are now. Tools are about action. They are about hope.

But then again, Ron and Jon have been actively using their tools for months, and their overzealous desire for maternal affection remains the same while their wrists now look like the insides of strawberry pop tarts. I decide this is a "bad thought" worthy of a snap, so I pull the band what feels like a reasonable distance away from my wrist and let it go. The sting is reassuring, concrete. Like eating hot sauce, when the burn erases everything else for a moment, and you can't talk or think for a split second, and you just uselessly wave your hand over your mouth, your mind mercifully numb. I shoot up another prayer. "Thank you, Lord, for the gift of this tool. Please help me use it in service of You."

At my next individual session with Bethanie, I am ready to share my appreciation of my new tool, but before I can get there, Bethanie jumps in with, "So I noticed in group yesterday that you were resistant when Mickey suggested saying the prayer. It made me curious. You told me you accepted Jesus when you were five, is that right?"

"Well, yeah, for the first time. I mean, I've said it literally thousands, maybe like ten thousand times since then."

"Do you not believe God will keep His promise?"

"No, I believe He'll keep His promise."

"Then I guess you don't have anything to worry about, right? You believe God will keep His promise, and you've accepted Jesus into your heart, maybe tens of thousands of times."

"Well, no."

"No?"

"I'm just not sure I've done it right. The Bible says grace is a free gift—*if* I accept it, but what does that mean exactly? My pastor used to say it means you have to 'reach out for it,' so I'd say the prayer, but did I 'reach out' when I said it? There's no way to know—until it's too late. That's what I'm scared of." My shoulders slacken with gratitude for this opportunity to share my experience with someone who is paid to listen to me, who knows the Bible—when Bethanie slides off her seat. For a moment, I don't realize what's happening. At first I think she's passing out, and I lurch to support her weight, but nope, she waves me away. She's not passing out; she's going down on her knees.

"Maggie, let's say the prayer together." Then I realize, ah, we're doing this old-school. I know this move. I've made this move many a time. I join Bethanie on the floor, and both of us kneel together on the itchy Lysol-smelling carpet. Together we fold our hands, and I prepare to say once more the words I've said thousands and thousands of times.

"Repeat after me," she says with reverence. "Dear Lord, I believe You sent Your son to die on the cross for my sins."

"Dear Lord," I fall into step, "I believe You sent Your son to die on the cross for my sins."

Saying the prayer is like riding a bike. But I'm better at this, having had much more practice, motivated by a much deeper fear.

"I accept you, Jesus, into my heart."

"I accept you, Jesus, into my heart."

"Please forgive my sins and cleanse me from all unrighteousness."

"Please forgive my sins and cleanse me from all unrighteousness."

"In Christ's name I pray, amen."

"In Christ's name I pray, amen."

We open our eyes and look at each other. Bethanie smiles. "There. How do you feel now?"

I look to Bethanie to see if we should continue our conversation down here on the increasingly unpleasant carpet or move back up to our seats. Bethanie tucks her petite heels beneath her and pops back up into her chair. Good. I follow.

"Well, I feel appreciative," I say. "I appreciate your taking the time to help me with my issue. Thank you for saying the prayer with me."

"You're welcome."

"Yes, but, you know, I still have the same problem."

"What's that?"

"I'm still not sure I believe enough."

"I wonder if you don't believe you deserve to be forgiven. The thing is, there's nothing we can do to deserve salvation. It's a free gift."

"Yes, I know that, and I believe that. But still we have to say a prayer, and saying a prayer seems like an action, and so the gift doesn't really seem to be free. If it were free, really, I mean, no strings attached—there would be no action required. That's what *free* means, right? Everyone says that God loves us unconditionally, but it seems like there's actually a pretty clear condition." I realize what I've just said could sound blasphemous to God, and Bethanie's furrowed brow suggests she would agree, so I anxiously try to clarify. "I mean, that's just how it seems to me. I know I'm wrong. I'm not saying I'm right. I'm just saying that's how it feels."

"Sometimes it's hard to accept free gifts. My husband Scott gave me a ruby pendant once for Valentine's Day, and I kept saying, 'It's too much. I can't accept that.'"

"But that's what I mean. If it's so hard to accept, maybe I haven't fully accepted it. Maybe I haven't fully accepted Jesus."

"Scott said I could return the pendant. He said he didn't want me to be uncomfortable, but I decided to accept his gift. It really is a beautiful necklace. I only wear it on special occasions."

What is she talking about? My head starts to burn, my mind churns, and I get that sickly feeling in my stomach. "I'm feeling really anxious, Bethanie. I'm feeling like the prayer might not have worked. What if . . . ?"

"Snap it."

"What?"

"Snap the rubber band." I obediently stretch the band, but before I can even release it, Bethanie, motivated by what appears to be real emotion, grabs my hand and looks me in the eye.

"Maggie, listen to me. I'm here. I heard your prayer. I am your witness. And I'm telling you, you are a Christian. So you can let that go. You don't need to worry about your salvation ever again. Done." Bethanie has no logic to back up her assertion, no philosophical argument or empirical evidence. But it is clear. Bethanie is not at all worried about the sincerity of my faith. She's heard my doubts, and she's not worried. And for the very first time I think . . . Bethanie's not so bad. I warm a little, even to the floral blouses and insipid lace collars she cinches up to her throat every morning.

This budding fuzzy feeling of camaraderie, however, is immediately interrupted by Bethanie's chipper delivery of, "Next time we meet we can start to dig into what's really going on. Have you heard of chipmunk cheeks?"

"Chipmunk cheeks?"

"It's when the parotid glands in your face swell as a result of excessive vomiting. It makes your face look like a chipmunk. We call it *chipmunk cheeks.*"

My hands instinctively clasp my face.

"Don't worry." Bethanie smiles. "You don't have it yet. And you won't. That's why you're here."

I immediately have a bad thought about Bethanie and snap the rubber band.

CHAPTER NINE: **UNHOLY DESIRES**

"WE'RE GOING TO WORK on exploring our 'unholy desires,' Bethanie says, placing a stack of old magazines and newspapers with several pairs of child-sized scissors in the center of our circle. "Cut out an image that represents something you desire but also know is not in the Lord's will for you."

I pick up the *Chicago Sun-Times* and start searching. I look through pictures of handsome white people in "cranberry" and "dust gray" crew-neck sweaters. I see a picture of a marijuana joint. A dark-haired woman in a backless gown entering a casino. Bottles of beer, beaded with condensation and stashed in a tin ice-bucket on the shore of a lake. *Good things come to those who wait*, promises the beer ad, a slogan which strikes me as unintentionally Christian, one the four gospel writers would surely endorse.

Then the words *Girls you care to see naked!* catch my eye in an ad for a strip club called *Lookers*. I look underneath the text at a blond wrapped around a pole who stares boldly back out at me. Along the lighted runway, beneath the blond's stiletto heels, there's an invitation I find disconcertingly attractive: *Amateur Night. Every Thursday. 9 P.M. No experience necessary.*

"Girls you care to see naked" seems a pretty low bar for participation, and I imagine myself at the audition, dancing freely, boldly staring out from the lighted stage into the darkness. I wouldn't be able to see the men perched by the bar or sitting along the wall—just their eyes glinting and the ends of cigarettes marking their faces. I'm not sure why I find the fantasy so compelling, but I certainly know it's not *in the Lord's plan for me*, so I cut out the ad.

I'm the last one to finish, and when I put down my scissors, Bethanie begins.

"Mickey, what have you found to share with us?" Mickey presents a yellow smiley-face figure with oversized white clown feet holding up a sign that proclaims, *Smile and the world smiles with you.*

"I'm confused," Bethanie says. "What is it you desire that you feel is against God's will?"

"What do you mean?"

"Well, the assignment was to cut out a picture of something you desire, but you know is against God's will. Unholy desires. How does this fit in with that?"

"I don't have any unholy desires. Just like 1 Peter 1:16 says: *Be holy because I'm holy.*"

"Okay, that's what we strive for. But we all fall short of the glory of God. We all have something we desire that we shouldn't, and that's okay. I want you to think this week about how you might fall short, okay, Mickey?"

Mickey salutes. "Aye, aye, captain!"

Next Quinn shows the group her picture—an advertisement for Spam. The ad features a mom holding out a plate of sandwiches to her kids with the caption, *Wake up soldiers and report for Spam.* Quinn quickly says, laughing, "I don't desire Spam. I cut this out because of the kids. I would love a kitchen full of children to feed. I mean, I wouldn't feed them Spam." Quinn can't quite cover her feelings with a second forced laugh, though, so she stops trying and begins to tear up. "I mean that's what I really want, but I know it's not God's will for me."

Bethanie furrows her brow. "How do you know that?"

"Because I'm not able to have children, and no adoption agency will approve my husband and me."

"Why not?"

"Because I'm so crazy—I mean, because of my history with mental illness."

Bethanie falters for a moment before concluding the discussion with, "That's a shame. Thank you, Quinn." And then she turns to Petra.

Quinn inhales and opens her mouth to say something more, but seeing that Bethanie has moved on, she folds her hands in her lap, right over left. Then she switches hands, left over right. I try to make eye contact with her, but her eyes are elsewhere, focused toward the center of the circle to see something private, a thousand miles away.

"What did you come up with, Petra?" Bethanie asks brightly, unaware of Quinn's distress.

Petra's cutout is of a bronzed couple in barely present bathing suits intertwined on a beach, like Burt Lancaster and Deborah Kerr in *From Here to Eternity*—but sexier and with more skin. Petra says she chose this image because she misses having sex with Anthony, even though she knows it was a sin.

"What about your husband?"

"Rick and I don't have sex anymore."

"A wife's duty is to have sex with her husband."

"Well, it's not my choice."

Bethanie looks at her quizzically, and Petra explains, "Rick just isn't into it anymore, you know?"

"Have you two ever gone to counseling?"

This cracks Petra up for some reason. "Yeah," she laughs, nodding. "Total bust. I got Rick to go to our church pastor, Pastor Crandall—a felon and a perv, by the way, felt up women when he baptized them—anyway, 'nother story for 'nother day. During one session, Pervy Pastor asks Rick, 'Why have you not wanted to be intimate with Petra?' And Rick goes, 'Well, I hate to say this, but if I'm being honest, it's because Petra's body is not the same as when we got married.' Then Pervy Pastor goes, 'What's not the same?' And while I'm thinking, *How is this helpful?* Rick says, 'I don't know. I guess it's that cottage cheesy thing that women get. I know it's not her fault.' And I go, 'Cottage cheese? You mean cellulite?' And Rick goes, 'Yeah, cellulite. It's gross.'"

I must look shocked because when Petra catches my eye, she shrugs. "Aw, jeez guys, he's said so much worse. One time he told me my boobs were like sloppy joes, and I go, 'What are sloppy joes?'"

Mickey cheerfully offers, "Oh, they're delicious. They're a sandwich with ground beef with this terrific sauce—"

Bethanie silences Mickey with a look that surprises me. I didn't know she could be so fierce.

"Yeah, like that," Petra says, snapping her nails. "So not a compliment. Rick said he was just trying to make me laugh and then complained, 'You used to have a sense of humor. What happened?'"

Bethanie asks, "How did that make you feel when your husband told you your breasts resembled sloppy joes, Petra?"

"Uh, how would it make *you* feel?"

In a remarkable display of insensitivity, Bethanie responds with, "My husband would never say something like that."

I am stunned, but Petra just twirls one of her bracelets around her wrist with a *Well, lucky for you* expression and says, "I see. Well, it didn't make me feel great, when my husband said my breasts looked like beef sandwiches soaked in runny barbecue sauce, all right?"

"Not great?"

"Yeah, it made me feel like shit—"

"Whoa. Whoa." Bethanie's hands shoot up as if she were protecting a child from running into traffic. "Okay, no need for language. What's a feeling word you can use?"

"I don't know, *bad*, all right? It made me feel bad. What else do you want me to say?"

"Do you feel your husband's attitude was related to your affair?"

Petra gives Bethanie a stare that says *obviously*, and she twirls her bracelet with increasing aggression. Then, her defiant expression crumbling, she lets her bracelet clang against the others and breaks into tears. "Anthony used to call me *bella donna*," she whispers. "He said I was a beautiful woman. That I was beautiful inside and out—"

Bethanie, assuming Petra is crying because of guilt over the affair, says soothingly, "God tells us if we confess our sins, He is faithful and just to forgive us those sins and cleanse us from all unrighteousness. Pretty great news, huh?"

Petra, with tears streaming down and hydrating her sunbaked face, gags out, "Yeah, really great."

"Great," Bethanie echoes, and she turns to Dwayne. "What have we got here?"

Dwayne's habitually confused and vacant expression clears a little, and his lips press together slightly, but he says nothing. His eyes remain focused on a random point in the air.

"Dwayne?" Bethanie tries again, raising her voice. "I see you have a picture for us."

"Right." He blinks into focus and then presents a cigarette ad.

"Tell us about this, Dwayne."

"Smoking," he says. "I used to smoke. Now I can't."

"Well, that's good news, isn't it? When did you quit?"

"Last year."

"Congratulations," Bethanie cheers, giving Dwayne a little round of applause. "How do you feel now?"

"I feel like life isn't worth living."

Dwayne's expression is completely flat. I can't tell whether he is joking or not. Bethanie decides he is and peeps out a little laugh. "Oh, Dwayne. You are too much. Now tell me. What might be a healthy desire that can replace your unhealthy desire for cigarettes?"

"There's nothing like cigarettes."

"How 'bout a delicious piece of chocolate cake? A picnic on a sunny day, maybe with an old friend?"

"Sure, if I could have a cigarette."

Bethanie moves on to the twins. Ron tentatively holds up a picture of a sexy young Latina girl in a bikini eating a churro—an undeniably sexual image.

"I just cut this out because I know I'm not supposed to like girls until I'm married. And I like that girl."

"I can understand the feeling. It's hard to wait for your wedding day," Bethanie says intimately, making both of the boys squirm. "But imagine how wonderful sex will be when you're married."

Mickey bares his camel teeth and adds, "I like that churro. That's the real temptation, if you ask me."

"Mmm, I agree," Bethanie murmurs in support. "I love churros." Then she turns to Jon. "What have you got to show us?" Jon grimly lifts up a picture of a bunch of exuberant teenagers hanging out on the back of a pickup truck.

"Tell us about this, Jon."

"I picked it because they just look so normal. And I guess normal just seems really great."

"Normal is something you desire?"

Jon nods a hurried *yes* and looks down, clearly hoping to end his turn.

"But why do you feel that 'normal' is something you shouldn't desire? Why do you think it's not in God's will for you?"

"I guess because it's something I won't ever have. So I better not."

"Better not what?"

"Better not desire it."

Bethanie interlaces her fingers. "I'd like to tell you something, Jon. You can desire anything you want as long as you desire the right thing. Psalms 103 says, *God satisfies us with all good things so that our youth is renewed like an eagle.* Jon, how does this make you feel?"

Jon looks to Ron. Ron mouths *good*, and a split second later Jon says, "Makes me feel good."

"Good," Bethanie says, satisfied, and she turns to me.

I really don't want to share the strip club ad, especially with Bethanie, but I'm convinced I must go to difficult places, to bare my soul, if I want to get better. So I show the clipping to the group and quickly begin, "Okay, I know it probably seems weird I would choose this picture, but you know that I'm an actress, or I wanted to be one, and in college I played some roles that maybe I shouldn't have, I mean, maybe not, maybe an artist can praise Jesus through the quality of their work, I'm not sure . . . but the truth is I really enjoyed them."

Bethanie is perplexed. "What does that have to do with this . . . thing that you're showing us now?"

"All right," I say, "well, okay, probably my favorite role that I ever played was Maryanne from this play called *I Stand Before You Naked* by Joyce Carol Oates, which was never a very successful play and is probably something even Joyce Carol Oates isn't very proud of, but I loved it. Maryanne

is a stripper—or she *was* a stripper because in the play she's already dead—she's been murdered by one of her regular customers—but she comes back to life to valiantly dance at her old haunt, even though she has fresh strangulation marks and blood pooling in her eyes."

I tell the group how I loved playing zombie-stripper Maryanne in my black tube dress and strappy pumps with my special-effects bruise makeup that I made sure highlighted my cheekbones. How I loved growling my lines in a horrible attempt at Brooklyn dialect, twisting around an imaginary pole, twirling and tossing my hair. The pole kept shifting locations, but who cared? I was setting fires and wearing a fantastic dress!

The group looks at me with various takes on astonishment, at my sudden flood of words, I guess, more than anything, since I can't tell if they understand what I'm saying.

"Maryanne's not a victim," I continue, feeling the need to come to her defense. "She's triumphant. She even forgives the regular who strangled her, despite the fact that the regular never even apologized."

Bethanie shakes her head. "I don't understand."

"Yeah, forget the Maryanne example," I say, regretting my decision to try to explain something so complicated and weird, and instead I tap the ad with my finger. "My point is, whenever I see women like this, I think they look cool, and I know I shouldn't think that. Like it may be cool in a play or a story, but not in real life."

Bethanie betrays no understanding.

"And maybe it's not even cool in a play. Like playing the part of Maryanne might have been a sin. I don't know. I justified it by telling myself maybe God wanted me to do the role to show people what horrible things happen to you if you pursue a life of sin. You know, like you get strangled and things."

Bethanie's blankness increases my anxiety, and I hear a slight tone of pleading in my voice, which I can't seem to stop. "Yeah, I've always had this problem, even when I was a kid in Sunday school and they would tell Bible stories. When they would put up figures of Mary Magdalene or Delilah or Jezebel or Bathsheba, you know, the harlots or prostitutes—those were the ones I wanted to look at. Those were ones I found myself attracted to.

"I thought Mary Magdalene was the coolest of all. She got to wear amazing outfits with more colors than anybody else, and Jesus loved her. She got to pour perfume on Jesus's feet and then dry them with her actual hair, which seems very rock 'n' roll when I think it about it now."

I look to Quinn for support, but she's already saying, "It's true. Very Led Zeppelin, I'd say."

"No cross talk," Bethanie barks, wagging a finger.

But I smile at Quinn before continuing, "Also Magdalene is the one who Jesus always chooses and defends; even when she pours a bottle of perfume worth a year's wages on his feet, he defends her. I understand now that it can be read as metaphor. It's just hard to know what is a metaphor and literal. It all seems to be mixed up together, which would be fine if I didn't think my literary-interpretation skills impacted my eternal fate."

The certainty in Bethanie's face returns, fossilizing into the expression I recognize. "Ah, you found yourself attracted to these women, women like Maryanne, like the one in that advertisement, like Mary Magdalene. You're attracted to women. That's what you're saying."

"Oh no," I jump in to clarify, "I don't mean attracted like *that*. I just mean I had an affinity for them; I thought they were appealing. I was interested in them."

"When did you first recognize this attraction?"

"Oh, but it's not an attraction, like what you're saying, it's—"

"You said, Maggie, that you found yourself *attracted* to the women on the storyboards. That's the word you chose."

I feel my face getting hot.

"Now we know that inclination and action are not the same thing. You can have inclination to do something and still not do it—"

"No, but I really don't incline toward women. I'm really in love with my boyfriend." A wave of sadness hits me. "Not that he's my boyfriend anymore."

"Because of your attraction to women?"

"Seriously, Bethanie—"

"Sometimes it's difficult to acknowledge shameful sexual desires. It's easier to deny them."

"But I'm not denying anything. I don't mind talking about my desires—"

"Ah, so you have them. That's the point, Maggie."

"But it's not like you're saying. I don't have desires like that—"

"Sounds a lot like denial to me."

I see Quinn gesturing to me to drop it. I sigh, knowing she's right.

I stop speaking and simply nod.

"Okay, well, something to think about," Bethanie concludes, and interlacing her fingers as if she's about to do "here's the church and here's the steeple," she smiles her most satisfied smile.

I sit cross-legged on my bed after dinner, staring at the watercolor of the little boy on his beach gazing up at the sky. I wrap the pink velour blanket my grandmother gave me around my shoulders and feel the soft fabric. My fingers find the hole I burned in the threads with my cigarette, and they circle and circle. It's been a month since I've seen Cooper, and I wish he were here so we could talk about whether the boy in the painting is peaceful or terrified, or if he can be both at the same time, and if it's just a coincidence that all other land and sea creatures seem to be hiding beneath rocks or under waves at the same time.

But I can't talk to Cooper, so I just fold my knees into my chest, wrapping the blanket more tightly around my shoulders, and I give myself permission to have a good cry. Not a single tear falls, though, which feels unfair. Considering what I've been going through, it seems like I could at least have that. But I'm completely dry, so I pretzel my limbs around each other and squeeze myself into a protective ball.

I think how different my life has become after seeing *Dreams* and am reminded of the saddest song I know . . . John Cougar's "Jack and Diane," with its most heartbreaking lyric: *Oh, yeah, life goes on. Long after the thrill of living is gone.* Even when I was twelve, this line punched a hole in my heart.

That lyric runs through my mind now and feels especially true. I know I will keep living. I will still enjoy slipping into a hot bath with eucalyptus bubbles. I will still enjoy bacon chilidogs at Franks for the Memories (assuming I get my appetite back). And I will still enjoy the moment, right before falling asleep, when I rub my feet together and the world gets all fuzzy and smooth at the same time.

But the other stuff? Gone. I can't imagine ever finding love. Dating or marrying anyone after Cooper would be horrific. And theater! My life as an actress, blazing fires of truth throughout the world, now seems so fraught and dangerous as to be impossible. How many roles out there could be appropriate for a truly Christian actress? Certainly not the ones I'm excited to play. Like Cavale in *Cowboy Mouth* and her *rock 'n' roll savior*, or dear, brave Maryanne, dancing onstage postmortem, forgiving the world.

CHAPTER TEN: **FAMILY AND FRIENDS**

AT THE START OF MY THIRD WEEK, Bethanie tells us that Saturday is Family and Friends Day, when our family members will get the opportunity to go *one-on-one* with Bethanie, when she will update them on our progress, discuss our struggles, and let them know how they can be of support. My stomach knots. Only trouble can come of this. It will be like a parent-teacher conference guaranteed to accomplish nothing except make my parents feel confused and guilty. I don't want Bethanie going *one-on-one* with my parents. I don't want her telling them any of her thoughts or sharing any of her unsubstantiated theories. I know she'll inform them I'm bulimic and Mom will worry that it's her fault because she fed me too many sweets as a child, or not enough sweets, it doesn't matter which—she'll find a way to blame herself.

My parents are used to appointments where authority figures praise my work ethic, my willingness to learn and set myself to a task, my attention to detail, my lack of cavities due to a committed flossing and brushing routine—praise that reflects on them, praise they deserve. They do not deserve Bethanie. But there's no way to avoid it. Family and Friends Day barrels toward us with increasing, unrelenting speed. Bethanie has contacted my parents, and they will be here on Saturday.

On Saturday I'm in "God, Help Me Stop" group when I look past

Mickey's shoulders through the crack in the open door and I see a sliver of my parents. I see Mom's shoulders are hunched, her arms wrapped around her chest as if she needs to keep warm despite the dry Chicago heat. I see Dad's unusually erect spine, straight as a soldier's, both feet planted firmly on the floor, reminding me of the old photos of him in basic training for the Air Force.

At the end of group, I go to meet my parents in the waiting room, my overnight bag packed. Since there are no activities on Sunday, I'll be going home for the remainder of the weekend. My parents emerge from Bethanie's office with eyes fixed and jaws set, looking as if they've weathered an unexpected storm and are still a little seasick.

When Dad sees me, he raises his eyebrows, adjusts his face into a smile, and says with excessive energy, "Hey, kid."

I stand up and match his attempt at enthusiasm, "Hey, guys! I can't believe you guys are really here. Wow!"

On the car ride back to our house, Mom lets me sit in the front seat because when I was young I used to get carsick and now . . . that's just what she does. A small, everyday kindness. There is a silence in the car until I ask, "Did it go okay with Bethanie?"

"Yup, went great," my Dad answers quickly, and grips the steering wheel tightly.

"It went just fine," Mom adds unconvincingly. "She . . . *Bethanie* said that at first you two clashed . . . was that word? *Clashed*?" She reaches up from the back and touches my dad on his shoulder.

Dad nods, keeping his eyes fixed on the road. "Yes, *clashed* is what she said."

Mom returns her hand to her lap. "She said you clashed at first but now you're starting to be open to recovery."

I've always been open to recovery, I think. *Why else would I be here? Why is Bethanie the authority on my internal experience?* Then I answer my own question: *because I've given her the authority*. I've put myself in her care. This is "free will."

There is another silence until my mom pokes her head forward again between the seats and says in a truly impressive attempt at cheer, "So we thought we'd go to Red Lobster for dinner. We'll pick up Trisha and then head on over. How does that sound?"

Red Lobster was where my family always went to celebrate victories: my sister's and my dance recitals, stellar report cards, the one softball game when I managed not to strike out or get injured by a ball. This time we certainly don't have anything to celebrate, but both my mom and my dad proceed as if there were.

"Think you can go for some Cheddar Bay biscuits?" My dad asks as he takes familiar turns through my hometown. "What's your record? Four? Five?"

"Five . . . and *a half*," I correct him.

Dad parks the car in our driveway, and as we walk in the house I call, "Dibs on the toilet." Mom calls second dibs—another family tradition.

My sister, now thirteen, still a good foot shorter than me, runs up, flings her arms around my waist, and launches into information she's clearly been sitting on. "Did Mom and Dad tell you I changed the guinea pig's name from Flower to Rodent because I found out that guinea pigs are rodents? I call him Rodie for short. He seems to like it, but it's hard to tell. What play are you doing at camp? Can I come?" My parents have clearly not explained where I've been, so Trisha has apparently concluded I've been at theater camp like I was the previous summer, and she's anxious to hear tales I wish I could tell.

"I know what I'm going to wear. My new yellow dress with the duck on the front—"

Dad interrupts, "Okay, let Maggie go pee."

"I'll be out in a second, kid."

Trisha reluctantly lets go, and I walk down the hall. Passing my grandmother's room, I poke my head in. There she is, sitting there in that same rocking chair staring at that same blank television. I turn up the dimmer on the light and walk in. "Hey, Grandma, how's it going?"

"I reckon it's all right." Her eyes drift over me as if no time has passed at all. "Do you think there's a cold Budweiser in that there refrigerator?" After I come out of the bathroom, I get her a beer and she drinks it greedily, dribbling a little on her stained housecoat like always. Another tradition.

I turn around to find Trisha right there behind me. "Did Mom and Dad tell you we're going to Red Lobster? We can say hello to Barry." Trisha and I used to name the lobsters in the tank there, and Barry was the name we'd always give to the biggest lobster. We'd watch Barry while we waited for a table, and before we left, we would always check to see if he was still there. If he was, we would cheer Barry's good fortune. If not, I would bow my head and dramatically hum "Taps." Most times this would make Trisha laugh, but once she cried, spilling tears for a particular Barry that had somehow touched her heart. A small crowd of patrons gathered around to witness Trisha's emotional display that time, I'm sure making that particular lobster's death one of the most individually honored lobster deaths in history.

We drive to the restaurant and push our way through the heavy wooden door. Trisha grabs my hand, yanking me over to the lobster tank, until both our faces are splatted up against the glass. The glass is covered with waxy, mucus-like algae, streaking the sides, infesting the corners, clogging up the filter. We peer into the overcrowded tank and watch the lobsters pushing and shoving their way into the corners, frantically hiding behind rocks, insuring their own safety by using their claws to send their fellow captives up toward the surface where the waitresses' hands plumb. I notice that one very small lobster, a child-lobster maybe, is trying to hide in the muck behind a plastic lighthouse, his face and pinchers planted in the gravel at the base of the structure, his tail jutting up, still as stone.

My sister's eyeballs are almost touching the glass. Her fingerprints are everywhere. "Do you think that's Barry?" Trisha asks, pointing to a bloated lobster floating near the top, seemingly too fat to battle the more aggressive youngsters. "Not a new Barry. The same Barry from last time. I can tell by the expression on his face. Look. Don't you think it's the same Barry?"

My sister looks up at me expectantly. I know she doesn't really think it's the same lobster from three months ago, but I also know she wants me to say I think it is, and so I do.

A hostess with a phlegmy cough shows us to a booth with dark mottled stains on the shiny red leather seats. I think of how many people have sat in this booth, flopping onto the leather with their leaks and spills, for how many years. Trisha bounds in ahead of me. "I want to sit next to Maggie." She pats the discolored leather next to her, insistent.

A waitress comes by, carrying a red plastic basket with the famous Cheddar Bay biscuits, and plops it on the table. The biscuits are blanketed by a double layer of yellow grease-soaked napkins, which look to me like urine-stained sheets. My mother pushes the unappetizing basket toward me, clearly anxious to see me eat, but I hesitate, nauseous. My sister, however, dives her hand in without delay, clamps onto a biscuit, and swoops it directly into her mouth. While she chews, she asks, "What play are you doing at theater camp? Can I come see? Is it appropriate for thirteen-year-olds?" Before I can answer, she continues, "What's your costume like?"

Dad interrupts gently. "Why don't you let Maggie eat a little something before you give her the fifth degree?" Mom pulls back the yellow grease-soaked napkins, revealing the three remaining yellow globs. My parents look at me expectantly as I reach in the basket and extract my pick. Trisha continues eating and talking at the same time: "I'm gonna do plays when I'm older too. Remember that one play *Tell Me That You Love Me, Junie Moon*, where you yelled at the guy in the wheelchair? You were like, 'Walk! Walk! I know you're paralyzed but you can walk anyway. Walk!'"

I bite into my biscuit. I see the lines in my mother's forehead smooth as she watches me eat, and so I take another bite.

"You were so mean in that play, but I knew you weren't *really* mean. You're just a really good actress. If other people thought you were mean, I would be like, 'No, that's my sister. She's not mean. And she doesn't normally wear clothes like that—*that's because it's a play.*'"

I look down at my Cheddar Bay biscuit, which seems to get more yellow and waxy by the second.

"Remember your costume? The one with the white silk top and the long black lace skirt that went down to your ankles? That was my favorite costume. Have you seen your costume for the play you're in now?"

I split the biscuit into bits. "Uh, no. No I haven't. Not yet." I put small morsels in my mouth, wishing our dog Nicholas were here so I could feed the rest to him under the table, and that I could explain at least some of my life to Trisha.

"Remember that play *Dirty Work at the Crossroads*, where the mean guy put the pretty girl on the railroad tracks, and the mean guy was like, 'You have to pay the rent,' and the pretty girl was like, 'But I don't have any money for the rent,' and the lights made it look like a train was coming? Then the *whooohooo* sound got louder like the train was coming closer and closer. Remember?"

I swallow with effort. "Yes, I remember."

"And we got to throw popcorn at the mean guy, and I threw some and I hit him in the face. Is the play you're doing going to be like that, where I can throw popcorn?"

I give up trying to eat the biscuit and start thinking about the simplicity of melodramas when my Dad says, "I don't think Maggie knows."

Trisha looks at my plate and asks, "If you're not going to eat your biscuit, can I have it?" and she reaches her hand out.

My mother shakes her head more furiously than she intends and snaps, "No!"

Trisha pulls her hand back as if she's just been slapped; the corners of her mouth curl down. "Sorry. I was just asking."

I wrap my arm around my sister's shoulders. She looks up at me, her eyes filled with admiration. She still thinks I'm the sister she used to have.

That night I call my friend Sophie. She tells me she's gotten a summer waitressing job at a theme restaurant called the 94th Aero Squadron, that she's learned the menu and the routine completely, and that the wait staff is a big incestuous family she'd love me to meet. The following morning I take my parents' car and drive over to visit her during Sunday brunch. The walls of the restaurant are covered with World War II memorabilia, rifles, shell casings, service medals, and pictures of Rosie the Riveter. A vintage Boeing aircraft hangs from the ceiling.

I arrive at the height of lunch hour. I see Sophie is busy, so I take a seat by myself in the bar area. I order a Coke and watch the waiters and waitresses, clothed in military blues with USO caps, weave among the tables. They are all in their late teens and early twenties with skin fresh and smooth, preparing to go to college in the fall or home for summer break.

Restaurant work will not be their career, so they can take it lightly. They don't seem to feel the weight of their trays, the itch of their uniforms, the pinch of their shoes. The bark of a disgruntled customer bounces off them, and they walk to the next table with smiles, smiles that don't yet wrinkle or fold the cheeks of their perfect skin.

I am struck by how efficient they all are, with their balanced trays and smiles. And Sophie is one of them. She is an element of the mechanism, a part of the reliable rhythm of this restaurant: I watch her deliver a crock of French onion soup and a slab of prime rib to a table, then settle a child into a booster seat. I light a cigarette, pull the ashtray close, and imagine what I would look like in one of the server uniforms. I notice one waitress with lipstick dramatically painted over her lip line like Betty Grable and decide that if I worked here, I would wear my lipstick just like hers.

When Sophie sees me, she waves her hand high above her head, runs over, and hugs me. She turns to the husky bartender, the kind of guy you can be sure has a great handshake, and says, "John, this is my best friend, Maggie. We met on the playground in second grade."

John delivers on his great handshake and replies, "Wow, that kind of loyalty deserves a bowl of overly salty Chex Mix designed to make you thirsty so you purchase more beverages." He walks over and plops a wooden bowl in front of me.

I smile. "Finally. I knew I would be rewarded someday."

Sophie sits down on a stool and pulls it close to mine. When John walks back behind the bar, she whispers, "Okay, so, important gossip. John the Bartender loves Denise the Waitress." Sophie points to a blond in a pencil skirt with a lively ponytail that bounces enthusiastically as she walks. "But Denise the Waitress loves James the Cook, who everyone thinks is gay because he always leaves with . . ." Sophie indicates a lanky, bright-eyed Hispanic teenager, "Jaime the Busboy."

I think about how different Sophie's summer is from mine as I smile and say, "Wow. Who knew the 94th Aero Squadron housed such a soap opera?" Sophie sees an older woman at a table across from us raise her hand, and she pops up and squeezes my arm. "Gotta go. I'll be back." She turns to John. "Take care of my friend, okay?"

John salutes. "Got it. I know a VIP when I see one."

Sophie jumps back out into the swirl of waitstaff around customers, travelling from table to table to the kitchen to the bar and back. I feel the movement of the system, the steady easy rhythm. I pick out a pretzel from the salty mix in front of me and put it in my mouth, wishing I was spending the summer here with Sophie, wearing a USO cap with a pencil skirt and dramatic lipstick, gossiping, pondering nothing heavier than which table needed the A.1. Sauce and which was ready for dessert.

CHAPTER ELEVEN: **SCRUPULOSITY**

I GO TO DR. LAKHANI'S OFFICE for my first visit. Dr. Lakhani is a stout Indian woman, sharply dressed, with handsome features, a broad nose, and dark, focused eyes. She reminds me of a bank manager, the kind who deals with important accounts. I am grateful for her directness, her refusal to be sweet, and her seeming lack of need to please anybody, including me. I appreciate the chance to talk to someone unconcerned with being "nice," someone like Sophie's mother, who is willing to throw rocks at squirrels if that's what gets the job done, to hell what the neighbors think. Dr. Lakhani means business, and business is something I can understand.

Dr. Lakhani closes a folder she has been reading and asks me how things are going with Bethanie. Not wanting to be disagreeable in any way, I say too brightly for the occasion, "Good. I'm really happy about this rubber band she gave me. It makes a lot of sense. Like training a dog. Saying, 'Bad dog. No, don't do that.' I get that!"

Dr. Lakhani studies me as she flips a pen around her fingers. Uncomfortable with the silence and with being so clearly scrutinized by someone just two feet away, I plow on. "I think God really did answer my prayers by sending me to this place."

Dr. Lakhani tilts her head, as if wanting to observe me from another angle, her pen still whirling. Suddenly she slaps the pen down on the table. "Bethanie believes you are struggling with body-image issues."

This again. "I know she does. But really, I don't care very much about my physical appearance at this point. It's really the least of my worries."

"So why do you vomit?"

"It's just I get so anxious, so terrified. Throwing up is the only thing that . . ."

"Right, of course. I will talk to Bethanie. Very often bulimics deny their body-image issues, and that's what Bethanie thought you were doing."

"I know. I kept trying to tell her my situation was different."

Dr. Lakhani continues, unapologetic for what seems to be Bethanie's clear obstinacy, "The word for what you are experiencing is somatization, a physical manifestation of a psychological experience. We will be treating the underlying issues causing the somatization here with therapy and Bible counseling, but we can also work from another front: we can start with the body. I want you to see Dr. Benton, our psychopharmacologist. He can prescribe you some medication—"

I stop her before she can even entertain the idea. "No, I don't want to be on medication."

"It's just something to consider. Many psychotropic drugs have an anti-nausea effect while simultaneously tackling the neurons in the brain—"

"No, definitely, no. Thank you, but no."

I cross my arms over my chest and press my lips into a small tight line and hope that I've clearly expressed my position. Medication could lead me to believe I'm saved when I'm really not, could allay my fears when I possibly *should be* afraid. I can't have anything messing with my neurons, clouding my judgment. I'd rather be scared and anxious for the rest of my life than risk damnation by quieting a voice I shouldn't be quieting.

Dr. Lakhani persists. "I think it's at least worth meeting with Dr. Benton. Just to talk about options."

I know I won't like the options. "Actually my nausea has been better," I conclude the discussion. "I'm gonna try not to throw up anymore. Some of it's a matter of willpower."

"Okay, well, if you ever want to meet with Dr. Benton, he's here," Dr. Lakhani says as she picks up her pen again and resumes twirling. "Bethanie tells me you have accepted Jesus into your heart but that you don't think you're saved."

"Well, it's not that I don't think I'm saved. I mean, if I had to bet, I would bet the prayer 'worked.' It's just that I can't be sure."

"Ah." Dr. Lakhani nods. "Do you confess your sins repeatedly?"

"Yes, because I need to be sure I've confessed my sins *sincerely*. I know God forgives all sins, but only if the apology is authentic."

"Do you worry about sins that are very small?"

"Yes," I say, oddly excited. "Last semester I forgot to capitalize the *G* in *God* in a paper for my theater lit class. I confessed to God immediately and submitted a revised copy to my professor, but I worried it might have been more than a mistake. It might have been an unconscious display of my disrespect for God."

"Mmhmm. And you feel Christ's sacrifice on the cross wouldn't cover this?"

"No, I know it does. But only if I'm sincere. If I sincerely believe. But how do you measure 'sincere'? I don't feel I'm completely sincere about anything."

Dr. Lakhani leans forward. "Have you heard the term *scrupulosity*?"

"Like *scruples*? Being moral?"

"Yes, but scrupulosity, religious scrupulosity, is on the excessive end—you could say it's being *pathologically* moral."

I like that there might be a name for what I have. I try saying it out loud. "Scrupulosity?"

"Yes, people who suffer from scrupulosity have an excessive fear of sinning, of divine retribution, of being guilty before God. It's a condition that has cropped up throughout history in different places at different times. It was very common amongst Christians in the Middle Ages but also is prevalent in Hasidic Jewish communities and certain Islamic sects. It's called by different names. Sometimes the 'doubting disease.' Sometimes 'tender conscience.' It's a preoccupation that prevents a healthy relationship with God."

Scrupulosity. A condition with a name seems like it would be easier to solve than an unnamed one. Just like it's easier to hit a target you can see than one you can't.

"The term comes from the Latin *scrupulum*, a sharp stone, implying a stabbing pain on the conscience."

Yes, it does feel like a stabbing.

"I counseled a young Catholic man once," Dr. Lakhani shares, leaning over her impressive desk, "who knew that fasting was required for an hour before communion, and this young man was extremely concerned about what *fasting* meant. What if he had a piece of food lodged in his tooth and he tried to spit it out but accidentally swallowed it? What about ChapStick, especially the flavored kind? What about cough drops he sucked on so he wouldn't cough in church and disrupt the congregation?"

If I had grown up with this prohibition, I would have worried about the same thing. *What is the difference between a cough drop and a meal,* I'm sure I would think, *beside proportion? Isn't a bit of ChapStick just a very small lunch?*

"Scrupulosity," Dr. Lakhani explains, "involves a groundless fear of sinning."

"But how do I know for sure it's groundless? Couldn't it be the Holy Spirit convicting me of my sin?"

"That concern is a common feature of scrupulosity."

"I like that there is anything common about my experience, but I feel the fasting Catholic guy's situation is different. It's easier, after all, to control actions than thoughts. If I were worried about eating before communion, I could just keep my mouth closed for an hour. Easy. I could lay off the ChapStick. But I don't have that kind of jurisdiction over my internal dialogue. Like I know God is Love and I'm supposed to praise Him for being so loving. But I keep thinking cutting people off and burning them without letting them die can't be loving, or at least not according to the definition of *love* I'm familiar with. So how can I bank on anything? Should I change what I think the meaning of the word *love* is? What would love be if the concept of love included scalding most people in the world eternally, without reprieve?"

"Well, there's justice."

I keep talking, even though I know I probably shouldn't. "But even if God's punishment is justice, it's justice that neither instructs nor corrects, right? So that's vindictive justice, seeking damages without care for the offending party, *vindictive* meaning 'action solely taken as retribution for a wrong done,' *vindictive* meaning 'in NO WAY LOVING.' Right?"

Dr. Lakhani doesn't agree or disagree.

I continue. "Maybe *vindictive* means something different in God's world. But then language becomes useless, doesn't it? I feel like I don't know what words mean anymore."

I stop and attempt to gauge Dr. Lakhani's response. But it's hard; she is professional, unrattled, focused. "I want you to try to disengage from these sorts of ruminations," she says, and then she points to my wrist. "I'm sure Bethanie explained to you the logic of the rubber band."

"She just said to snap it anytime I have a bad thought."

Dr. Lakhani's lip curls slightly. "Let's say an *unwanted* thought or a *false thought*. Rather than a *bad* thought. These thoughts about you going to hell are *false* thoughts. You've accepted Jesus Christ as your personal savior, so you are saved. You are a Christian, Maggie. You are going to heaven. That is a fact."

I love hearing her say these words. I wish she would say them again and then a thousand more times and I could record them; maybe that would cure all these doubts.

"Any thoughts that you are not Christian, that God has not kept His promise, are simply not true. They are from Satan. So each time Satan comes into your mind to say, 'You're not saved. God hasn't forgiven you,' you're going to snap that rubber band and then shift your focus to something else. Try a funny joke. The point is to replace the thought with something else. Does that make sense?"

"Yes, completely. I'm on it. I'm good with assignments. I'll think of ten jokes."

Dr. Lakhani is not impressed with my desire to overachieve. "Any joke will work. Just report to Bethanie and let her know how it's going. I'll be curious to hear." Dr. Lakhani stands up.

"Oh, Dr. Lakhani. One more thing."

"Yes."

"Bethanie thinks I'm a lesbian."

Dr. Lakhani matter-of-factly asks, "Are you?"

"No, I'm really not. Bethanie thinks I am because I said I was attracted to women I knew I shouldn't be. But I didn't mean attracted to like *that*, I just meant attracted to them, like I want to *be like* them. But when I tried to explain that, she kept saying I was in denial."

Dr. Lakhani's lip curls again with displeasure. "I'll talk to Bethanie."

That night I go out to the courtyard to have a cigarette. It's my favorite type of night: crazy filthy hot. I love brutally hot nights that others would find oppressively warm and humid, where there's not the slash of direct sunlight, just the warm cozy blanket of darkness. Several stars are hung in the darkening sky, and there is a gentle breeze swaying the birch tree above me. The yellow gardenias are a deep orange color now, their stems barely visible, making the spread of petals look like small floating suns.

My cigarette tastes fantastic, one of those cigarettes that makes you feel like you're finally catching your breath. Non-smokers don't understand the infinite varieties of the smoking experience, but I appreciate each unique manifestation. All snowflakes. And I am actually feeling hopeful for the first time in a long while. I have a diagnosis. *Scrupulosity*: a condition I now know others suffer from—which means I am part of nature. I am not an aberration. My problem has a history and history of its sufferers being cured. And now I have a prescription: a tool and a plan. I take a big long inhale of the cigarette. It seems like a long time since I breathed all the way in.

I stand out in the courtyard for a while as the night darkens into an almost-perfect blackness, the last pool of light on the pavement drying up. I'm still standing when the wind surrenders, as if satisfied with a day well spent. I take a deep drag on the last bit of my cigarette and feel a bit of calm, which maybe is the Holy Spirit, maybe the nicotine, maybe the embrace of the thick night air.

I walk back through the halls to my room, careful not to wake anyone already in bed, and as I pass by Mickey's door, I'm startled to hear him playing a harmonica. I stand for a minute before recognizing the melody he's playing—a song called "Do Lord." *I've got a home in glory land that outshines the sun / Way beyond the blue / Do Lord, O, do lord, O do remember me / Do Lord, O, do Lord, O do remember me / Way beyond the blue.*

I smile as I think that even without Patti Smith and Marianne Faithfull, there can still be art and beauty for me to enjoy in life. Poetry isn't confined to the lyrics of iconic rebellious rock singers that I've recently discovered in a liberal arts college. It can pop up in very unexpected, very Christian places. Like plucky little Mickey playing the harmonica, bending notes and sending them soaring on a warm summer night when he thinks no one can hear him. I stand outside his door, listening. And, for the first time in a long while, I think it is possible that I just might be okay.

CHAPTER TWELVE: **JUNIOR GOD BADGE**

MY TOOL ISN'T WORKING. I've spent the last two weeks praying and whacking my wrists with such dedication that I now look like I'm wearing two red puffy bracelets, and still, I am not better. In fact, I'm worse. The dull ache in my stomach is sharpening into slicing stabs, and my time is running out. I only have three weeks before I'm hoping to return to school, and my rubber band tool, which was supposed to fix everything, has failed.

It's not like I didn't try. I tried as if my life . . . well, actually as if my *eternal* life depended on it. If I had disturbing thoughts about hell, I was to flick the rubber band and shift my focus to "something else." Dr. Lakhani had suggested shifting my focus to a joke.

I found that I couldn't control my thoughts, couldn't dispel their arrival through force of will. "I" couldn't stop "me" from thinking anything. "I" could consciously *add* something to my range of attention, to my beehive of thoughts. I could add a joke to the buzzing; I could add, "A man walked into a bar. Ouch." But I couldn't *subtract* anything from the swarm.

And the more I tried, the more aggressively I attempted to shut out the thoughts, to avoid that imp of my mind and shove him in a corner the more that imp came chasing after me screaming, "Bad fruit! Bad fruit! Ha-ha, you can't catch me!" It's as if there were a part of my brain that wanted to screw with another part of my brain, like when I would hold my sister's hand and slap it against her face and say, "Stop hitting yourself. Stop hitting yourself." I was hitting myself. There was a brawl going on in the ring of my rattled head.

But I still acted normally, talked normally. I didn't stare off into space, my pupils fluttering back into my skull like the patients at Garden Grove. I remembered to close my mouth when I chewed my food, unlike my grandmother, who always put her meal on full display. I became facile at functioning on several levels at once. I was able to fully participate in social interactions while running theological arguments in my head *and* maintaining my rubber band regimen like a real champ.

At dinner one night, our little group was seated together at our regular table in the building's cafeteria, a table that was always available due to its proximity to the bathroom. We ate every meal at this table, purposely segregating ourselves from the functional working members of corporate society, who would never choose a seat so far from the salad bar. I wondered what the others thought of us as they walked by, the ladies with their pumps click-clicking on the linoleum, proudly announcing the spending power that enabled their purchase; the men in neckties yanked up to the strangulation point, twisting their glinting watches not to see the time, but rather to display the flash of the gold. A glowing, gilded, functional, useful, click-clacking system, heading to the toilets. Probably not to vomit, I guessed.

Then there was our little Grace Point ragtag crew, reliably found downwind of the ladies' facilities, upwind of the men's. It's not like any of us on our own would look crazy. None of us were drooling or slobbering or twitching. Any one of us by ourselves, I was sure, would go unnoticed, the typical odd bird in any corporate dining flock. But together as a group, our general unhinged "we've got bigger things to worry about than our appearance" vibe was surely amplified. Well, except Petra; she could pass. Petra dressed in short fitted skirts that displayed her lean, sun-roasted legs and pricey-looking sandals that reliably matched the color of her fitted blouse and dangly earrings.

I am able to swallow down small chunks of Salisbury steak with big gulps of water, like oversized, unwieldy capsules, WHILE participating in dinner conversation AND simultaneously keeping up the theological arguments going on in my head AND snapping the band when called for. It is a tour de force. As Petra squeezes lotion out of a thin silver tube and says, "It's placenta cream. Human placenta. I get it shipped from Iceland," I think of the word *womb*, which makes me think of the verse *I knew you before you were in your mother's womb*, which makes me think, *If God loves us so much, if He knew us before we were in our mother's womb, why would He ever say* too late *and* Depart from me. I do not know you?

But without pausing I say, "Iceland? That's funny. I don't associate Iceland with placenta. Why Iceland, do you think?"

Timbo is shocked by the placenta revelation, struggling to compute and form an objection at the same time. "Placenta? Isn't that like . . . ?"

Petra stares back at him, digging her shiny heels into the linoleum, challenging, "Yeah, afterbirth."

I think of the verse *Before you were conceived, God had numbered all the hairs on your head*, which makes me think, *Why is it such a great thing that all the hairs on my head are numbered if God will allow those numbered hairs to be singed in eternal fire? Why would I care if God were clued in to my hair count?* The number of hairs on my head and God's awareness of that number seems absolutely, entirely beside the point. I whack my wrist.

Timbo strokes his beard, which seems to somehow become redder with each tug, and eyes Petra warily. "So you are telling me you put afterbirth on your face?"

Petra re-crosses her legs and jabs a heel into the floor. "Yeah, you got a problem with that?"

"I might. Whose placenta is it?"

"I don't know the lady personally."

Timbo shakes his head in disgust. "So ladies just give up their placentas these days? For nothing? Nothing at all?"

Timbo seems so upset about the "for nothing" part that I add, "Well, maybe they get paid for it."

Timbo erupts, "That's even worse! They *sell their placentas*? *For money*?"

I look over at Quinn, who has been silent this whole time and is now swirling her fork in a leftover puddle of gravy on her plate. I remember her talking about not being able to have children and wonder if this placenta discussion is upsetting while also wondering if there is anything I could care about less than somebody knowing the number of hairs I have on my head.

"If you've got placenta on your face," Timbo's chest heaves with frustration, "I don't want to be touching it."

"Fine with me," Petra spits back, and she clicks her nails.

Forget about my hair-count, I think. *Just be nice to me and don't threaten me with eternal retribution for something that may or may not be in my control.* This is decidedly a bad thought, and I whack my rubber band.

I head to individual therapy prepared to tell Bethanie that the rubber band is not working, that I need to try something else. Anything else. Except drugs. I've seen what my grandmother looked like on drugs. So definitely no drugs.

"Look who's here," Bethanie says flatly when I enter, not looking up. Bethanie has been acting weird around me ever since my meeting with Dr. Lakhani. I'm guessing that Dr. Lakhani reprimanded her for her clumsy textbook diagnosis of me and general lack of insight—a pattern I suspect has been persistent. Ever since, Bethanie has stopped mentioning bulimia or lesbianism but has begun regarding me with icy eyes, wary and suspect, as if I'm a sneaky opponent who she's learned doesn't always play fair.

During my session I explain to Bethanie that I've followed the instructions with the rubber band, but that it's not working. "When I have a thought about my salvation, I say, *Stop.* I snap the rubber band. Then I think of a joke."

"A joke?"

"Yeah, like the one I thought of is: 'A man walked into a bar. *Ouch.*'"

Bethanie is delighted with this joke: "Oh that's wonderful! A man walked into a bar? Like a bar he hits his head on, not a bar that serves alcohol. That's too much!"

Once she settles down, I continue, "So I can add that thought, that joke, the-man-walked-into-the-bar joke, to the mess of my thoughts, but that doesn't stop me from thinking the original thoughts that I'm trying to avoid. In fact, it seems to make it worse. It's like the thoughts gather more fuel, and that scares me, and then I have more thoughts."

Bethanie shakes her head and asks her favorite rhetorical question: "You sure like to make things complicated, don't you?"

But this time I rear a bit and counter, "I don't know that I *like* to make things complicated. It's just that that's the way things seem to me. It's not my preference. I'd love to see things simply. I really would."

Bethanie assures me, without irony, "One day you'll get there."

Now that bulimia and lesbianism are off the table, Bethanie has alighted on a new theory, one whose truth she is utterly convinced of without ever having tested it. This is the theory: there was a traumatic event in my childhood, perhaps one I feel guilty for, that I've repressed, and this repressed memory is now leading to all my troubles.

I have no problem with this. I'd love if there were some psychological nugget lodged in my unconscious that I could locate and cough up, allowing me to start breathing normally again. Like in *Ordinary People* when Timothy Hutton remembers his brother drowning in the lake and thinking it was his fault, sobs in Judd Hirsch's lap, and is cured. Or like in the final episode of *M*A*S*H** when Hawkeye recalls a refugee woman holding a squawking chicken and silencing the chicken so as not to be discovered by the enemy, and then remembers that the squawking chicken was actually a crying baby that she smothered. I'd be overjoyed if I could remember a drowning brother or a chicken that was a really a baby, but nothing is coming to me.

"Tell me why you might feel you deserve to be punished."

"I really don't think I *do* deserve to be punished."

"Think back."

"I've tried. I really can't think of anything. I think I'm a pretty decent person. Not the greatest. But then I've been given so many advantages it's hard to tell how I would measure up. It's like that verse Luke 12:48, *To whom much has been given, much will be required.* I've been given a lot, so I should be a good person."

"What do you mean you *should* be a good person?"

"Well, like I've been given every opportunity to be a good person, a healthy supportive environment, no physical or emotional abuse, no deprivation, no trauma." I lean forward in my chair. "I read this article once that said all recorded serial killers have suffered at least one of three traumas: they were either molested, abandoned by one of their parents, or dropped on their heads as infants. I was not molested, abandoned, or dropped on my head as an infant, so what pride can I take in not being a serial killer? I'm certainly not worthy of being rewarded for that.

"And why should a serial killer feel guilty? If I had Jeffrey Dahmer's genes and I was raised in his same environment, wouldn't I have behaved exactly as he did? Stocking human parts in my freezer for upcoming meals? And if Jeffrey Dahmer had my genes and environment, wouldn't he be here in a born-again psychiatric facility explaining why he isn't any better than a serial-killer cannibal?"

Bethanie's eyes glow, a diagnosis forming. "You feel like a serial-killer cannibal?"

"No, no!" I protest in exasperation, "I'm just saying . . . everyone is good or bad on some sort of scale, and then you have to add in genetics and environment—so it seems sort of impossible to know how God will judge people."

"Think back. Anything you might have done way back when that's making you worry now about where you'll fit in?"

"I really wish there were."

"Let's play a game. You tell me the worst thing you've ever done." What Bethanie is suggesting bears no resemblance to a *game*. There's no competition. No back-and-forth play or volley. Just a demand that I tell a woman in a prairie skirt the worst thing I've ever done—when she doesn't have to tell me *her* worst thing.

"I can't really think of anything."

"Have you ever killed an animal?"

I am horrified. "No! I would never kill an animal. Never." But then I pause, remembering . . .

"Well, I did have these two gerbils named Munchkin and Mischief when I was seven. One day I forgot to feed them, and the next day Munch-kin was dead. But my mom and dad said they were both really old and that going without food for a day wouldn't have done Munchkin in. And I certainly didn't intend to kill him."

"How did you feel when you saw Mischief had died?"

"*Munchkin*," I say, enjoying a petty thrill in correcting her. "Mischief lived for another month."

"How did you feel when Munchkin died?"

"I felt sad, but then, I think I just kind of moved on. I mean I was in seventh grade and I had a crush on this boy named James Kane, which meant a lot of time curling my hair and planning out funny things to say about *Far Side* cartoons."

"But still . . . you feel like you might be a serial killer?"

I throw up my hands in exasperation. "Bethanie, I don't feel like I might be a serial killer. I was just using the serial killer example to say I don't know if I can feel proud of being a good person because my environment has been so supportive and without trauma."

"So you feel you deserve to be punished for your supportive upbringing?"

"No, I don't. I really don't feel like I deserve to be punished. I don't feel like anyone *deserves* to be punished. And certainly not eternally." I stop myself, knowing I'm tiptoeing into blasphemy territory. I consider my words carefully. "I mean I know some people deserve to be punished eternally because the Bible says they do. But I have trouble *feeling* like they do. The word *deserve* is so tricky. It seems everyone behaves according to their genetics and environment."

Bethanie shoots up straight in her seat as if I've just goosed her. "So we're robots? That's all we are? Robots just following some programming?"

"No, we're not robots. I'm just saying . . ." Seeing the fire in Bethanie's eyes, I decide to bail. "Never mind. Let's just keep going. Let me see if I can think of something else." Then I have an idea. "For a while when I was nine, after my grandmother had her break, after she moved in with us, there was this group of boys who lived down the block. Sometimes when I walked by the boys, I would lift up my little T-shirt and flash them. Even though my breasts looked just like theirs, they always cheered."

"Good. This is good. Now, did your parents know about your activities?"

"Well, they found out eventually and told me not to do it anymore.

But they weren't really that upset. They tried not to let on, but I could tell they found it kind of amusing."

"Amusing? What could be amusing?"

"Well, I guess it was amusing because I was so young. They knew I sported the same little squirty nipples the boys did. I might as well have flashed my knees or my elbows."

"But you didn't flash them your knees or your elbows. You exposed your breasts. This is good. I think we've got a lot to talk about."

Bethanie beams, giddy off the scent of the exposed-breast track. I can't wait to meet with Dr. Lakhani again next week and tell her how Bethanie has misunderstood me again, believing I might be a serial killer: a bulimic lesbian serial-killer cannibal with repressed guilty memories of flashing my undeveloped breasts. Dr. Lakhani will set Bethanie straight.

"And Maggie, you don't have to make everything so complicated. Leave the complicated stuff to the Guy Upstairs." The corners of Bethanie's mouth start to rise, and I can tell she's quite pleased with what is about to come out of her lips. She lets loose her gem: "I think it's time you took off your Junior God badge. God is doing just fine on His own."

CHAPTER THIRTEEN: **GOD PICTURE**

IT'S AMAZING HOW "STRANGE" becomes "usual" so quickly. I've been here for just five weeks and already my days are starting to seem normal. To the point that sometimes I forget that this is not how every nineteen-year-old spends her summer. Even our daily group walk around the block together, which had at first seemed mortifying, like we were "loonies on display," now just seems like a matter of fact. It is our walk around the block. That's all. That's what me and my people do at ten A.M.

I've grown accustomed also to daily Bible study and the size of Sed's nose and how he begins every session with, "Thank You, Lord, for giving us Your inerrant Word to guide and instruct us. *It is truly a lamp unto our feet.* Bless our time together today." Today Sed blinks his little caper eyes open and asks us if any of us know the parable of the "friend at night." The room is silent. I raise my hand—this is an easy one.

I notice my *Flashdance* sweatshirt is hanging off my shoulder, and I pull it straight before addressing the group. "It's from Luke chapter 11. A man has unexpected visitors show up on his doorstep in the middle of the night. The man doesn't have enough food to feed them, so he goes to his downstairs neighbor and knocks on his neighbor's door and says, 'Friend! Could I have some bread? I had unexpected visitors show up in the middle of the night.' The neighbor barks back, 'No, I'm sleeping,' but the man doesn't give up. He keeps knocking and knocking until his neighbor can no longer stand the racket and so gets up and gives him the bread. I think Jesus compares this to the necessity of persistence in prayer. *Pray without ceasing.*"

Sed says genially, "Nice work, Maggie. I better watch out. You could take my job," and then laughs significantly louder than necessary. "Yes, that's right—*pray without ceasing.* This is a parable about perseverance. If the man in this story had given up after knocking once at his neighbor's door, he wouldn't have gotten the bread. But the man didn't give up. He pressed. Knock. Knock. I'm still knocking. Here I am, *knocking, knocking, knocking.* Can you imagine that neighbor?" Sed does an awkward impression of a frustrated neighbor, stamping his feet, tearing at the tufts of gray hair above his ears, like an impassioned community-theater star. "Okay! Enough, already! I'll give you your dang bread. I'm up! I'm up!"

Mickey laughs and slaps his knee, shaking his head as if to say, *Oh man, this is too good.* The color of Timbo's face, however, darkens, and he starts snapping his neck from one side to the other and tugs at his beard. "Why didn't the neighbor just give the man some food? What the fu—" Timbo quickly revises, "What the *heck*? Why would he be such a jerk? Look, that dude is no kind of neighbor I want."

Sed welcomes the chance for lively group dialogue. "Well, Timbo, it was the middle of the night. Do you like to be woken up in the middle of the night?"

"No, but if I was, I wouldn't be a sissy about it. I'd get out of bed and help my neighbor."

Petra crosses her bronzed legs, hooking them at her ankles. "I think *sissy* is a nasty word. I work with a lot of men at the salon, and they don't like the word *sissy.*"

Timbo's grip on his beard tightens. "Sure, no *sissy* likes being called *sissy*—"

Sed has had enough of the lively discussion so abruptly cuts it off. "Okay, I think we're getting off track. The parable is showing us the importance of prayer and not giving up on God. In the next verse, Jesus says, *Knock and the door shall be opened unto you.*"

I think, *Yes, but apparently knocking once is not enough. You have to keep knocking over and over again if you want God to get out of His heavenly bed and open the door.* This pestering aspect of prayer has always bothered me. I understand the praise aspect—celebrating the glory of God; the thanksgiving aspect—expressing gratitude for the continual wonders of this life; the confession element of acknowledging mistakes and resolving to start anew. And I understand request-making, when it involves cultivating attitudes or emotional states. Like a gymnast picturing herself nailing a routine, asking for focus, summoning confidence and ease.

What I don't get is praying in an attempt to get God to do things He may or may not already be planning. Why in the world would my requests bear weight in the cosmic decision-making process? And why does God want me to keep submitting my request over and over and over? If I tell my dad I'm hungry and I want something to eat, he doesn't make me ask over and over until I finally wear him out.

This kind of prayer seems like telling God what to do, suggesting how He could do better—like clenching a fist at the heavens and shaking it instead of opening a hand, spreading a palm. I don't have the big picture, but God does. It seems like my job should be accepting life circumstances as they come and reacting to them in the most open and loving way possible. But I don't know. I'm nineteen. I'm not a theologian. I'm not a doctor. I'm not a saint. I'm a terrified liberal arts college student who misses her boyfriend and acting in plays with stripper poles and dead crows. Who currently lives in a psychiatric facility. Not the best qualifications to run for expert on life. Maybe Bethanie's right. Maybe I should take off my Junior God badge.

Bethanie begins activity therapy by posing the question: "How can we learn about God?"

Mickey's hand shoots up, and unable to contain himself until Bethanie calls on him, he blurts out, "The Bible. We find out about God from the Bible!"

"That's right, Mickey. We can learn about God from His Word." Bethanie looks around the room. "How else do we learn about God?"

Quinn offers, "From His creation, from the world around us."

"That's right. Like we can learn about an artist from his or her work, we can learn about God from His creation. From looking at a beautiful rainbow. Or a flowing stream in a meadow, or a babbling brook." *Yes, I think, we can look at these things, they're very nice things, but we can also look at war and stillborn babies and Jeffrey Dahmer's freezer.* It seems to me that trying to deduce God's nature from His massive "everything in the world" oeuvre is a ludicrous endeavor. Like trying to figure out from his plays whether Shakespeare was a nice guy, but far more challenging.

Petra removes a small bottle from her purse, squirts cream on her hands, and rubs it between her palms. The scent seems to arrive immediately at my nostrils, more pungent than the placenta cream, a sharp lavender or maybe eucalyptus.

Bethanie repeats her question, "How else can we learn about God?" then notices that Petra is slowly spreading her fingers wide and then crunching them into a fist, more absorbed in studying the freshly moisturized skin on the backs of her hands than in the conversation. "Petra, what's going on?"

Petra blushes, reddening her already-rouged cheeks. "Oh, sorry. I was just trying to figure out the best way to hold my hands so they don't look all scary-old-lady-like."

This seems like it might be a comment worth exploring, but Bethanie doesn't think so. "Okay. Well, try to stay focused. The question was, how do we learn about God?"

"Right." Petra places her hands on her lap, in a way I'm guessing she has determined from her recent experiment is the least *scary-old-lady-like*. "Okay, um, how 'bout . . . like from our conscience? When we feel guilty about things we've done? Bad things. Like that?"

"That's right. Good. We can learn about God from our conscience. What else?"

Bethanie looks around the room. Everyone is quiet. Mickey's eyebrows slam together, as if trying to push an answer out from his brain. Ron and Jon stare at their feet, plunged in thought. Timbo cracks his neck back and forth—but then he suddenly snaps it back upright, his eyes ablaze. It is clear: Timbo's got something.

"From visitations."

Bethanie falters, her voice uncertain. "Visitations?" I can see the bind Bethanie is in. On the one hand, *visitations* is textbook schizophrenia language, and Bethanie loves her textbooks. But . . . she doesn't want to deny a genuine apparition, deny God appearing on earth, because that's treading into blasphemy land. Bethanie, more fretful than I've seen her, bites her lip. "Did these visitations seem . . . real?"

Timbo's eyes burn. "Totally real. *God spoke directly to me.*"

I'm sure Bethanie knows that the sentiment "God spoke directly to me" has prompted the strapping of many a straightjacket on many a frothing-at-the-mouth delusional imbecile. But she also knows "God spoke directly to me" has been uttered by scores of saints and prophets. Bethanie looks up at the ceiling, as if feeling God's scrutiny, the stern teacher looking over her shoulder, judging her work, and then . . . decides to bail on the whole thing: "Right, okay, that would probably come under the category of personal experience. What else?"

Timbo, offended by what he properly feels is a dismissal, glowers, and the room falls silent except for the sound of Petra clicking her nails. Finally Bethanie shares the answer she's been waiting for: "How about from other Christians? A pastor, or a therapist?"

Mickey bangs his thigh with his fist. "Of course! From other Christians!"

Bethanie sweeps her eyes over the group and says, "Our activity today is to draw a picture of God. A picture of praise, celebrating God from everything you know about Him—from the Bible, from creation, from your personal experience, and from what you've learned from other Christians."

Bethanie walks to the center of the room and places an array of art supplies on the floor: a stack of white construction paper, a sixty-four pack of Crayola crayons, a box of felt-tip Magic Markers, and an array of fluorescent highlighters. Once Bethanie has laid out the supplies, she hops out of the way with far more urgency than is required, seemingly afraid we'll all savagely descend on the materials and trample her in the process. Only Mickey pops up immediately. The rest of us trail behind, politely standing in line and allowing Mickey to have first choice of markers and crayons.

I plop back in my seat with my selection of crayons and markers, wishing I could pass on this exercise. I'm terrible at drawing and certainly don't think I can come up with a piece of art that would in any way be flattering to God. I stare at my blank sheet of paper and wonder about God's insistence on being praised. It can't be because He needs the assurance. Maybe we praise Him to remind ourselves that He *is* great and wonderful and all the things we're supposed to remember to tell Him all the time. Regardless, I don't know what in the world to draw on this stupid piece of paper with these stupid crayons. But I'm going to come up with something. This place is my chance at recovery, my silver bullet, and I'm not going to blow it just because I don't want to draw a picture on a piece of construction paper.

I look over and see Dwayne gliding his crayon over the paper and for the first time notice how slight his fingers are, how supple and feminine almost. His hands strike me as artist's hands, with intelligent fingers working together, having cooperated often. Dwayne's stillness seems to make more sense when he's holding a crayon in those fingers, when his eyes are fixed on the paper, even and undistracted.

Next to Dwayne, Timbo is attacking his sheet with a red marker, vengefully rendering his image.

Ron and Jon have not started at all. They have taken neither paper nor crayons nor markers. I figure they feel the same way I feel—they don't know what to draw or don't think they're good at drawing—but then I notice it's something more. Jon's lower lip is shaking and he looks up at his brother, agonized. Ron raises his hand. "Bethanie, um, I, well, Jon and I would rather not do—we'd rather not participate in this activity."

Bethanie peers at them both, bewildered. "Why not?"

"Well, in our religion—"

Bethanie's hands fly up and clutch her cheeks. "In *your religion*? What religion is that?"

"I mean in our church . . ." Ron hastens to add. "*Christian* church. In our Christian church, we don't believe in representing God with any images. There's that verse, *Thou shalt not make unto thee any graven image of the Lord.* Our church is really big on that verse. It's like their favorite verse, I guess you could say."

I had never heard of this prohibition before. Why not picture God? Isn't that what we're supposed to be doing, keeping His holy visage always in mind?

Bethanie narrows her eyes, somehow managing to pin one on each twin. "I'm not asking you to make a graven image. I'm asking you to draw a picture."

Jon, spooked, looks to Ron, who continues to speak for them both. "Me and my brother would rather not participate—if it's okay."

"Fine, but I don't understand this. *Graven* means *false*. I'm not asking you to draw a false picture. I'm asking you to draw a true picture." I'm pretty sure *graven* does not mean *false*. I'm pretty sure it derives from *engraved*. But I'm not 100 percent sure.

Ron tightens his jaw. "We'd rather not." Jon's eyes are panicked, skittish, like those of a horse about to bolt.

"So in your church there are no pictures? None at all?"

"Well, no pictures of God," Ron explains. "There are pictures of nature and stuff. Trees. Flowers. Lakes, oceans, and stuff."

Dwayne, unexpectedly roused, sits forward in his seat. "I can understand that. Every representation is a reduction of reality."

Bethanie whips around. "What?" Dwayne, surprisingly lifelike, continues, "There's the saying, 'If you see the Buddha on the road, kill him.'"

Bethanie bristles at the word *Buddha* and rubs her hands together as if disinfecting them from the pollution of Eastern religions before responding, "Well, Buddhism can be a very violent religion. I don't even know why we're talking about it."

Dwayne persists, unconcerned with Bethanie's clearly ruffled feathers. "It's not about being violent. It's about ideas getting in the way of reality. It's about the danger of reducing a vast God to a containable image." I think of Georgeanne telling me that one day I'll find out God is bigger than I think.

Bethanie's shoulders rise up and squeeze around her ears. "Okay, well, Jon and Ron, if you want to sit out this exercise, that's up to you. Your recovery is your responsibility." Then the two brothers, as if they've come to a previous understanding, both sit on their hands in unison and resume staring at their shoes and occasionally snapping the bands on their wrists.

I'm struggling to come up with something to draw, something that would require little to no visual artistic skill. Then I have an idea. I remember one night when Sophie and I were lying out on the grass in her backyard, looking up at the stars. It was a warm night—thick and heavy, with no breeze at all, where you feel a little sweaty but it might just be the humidity settling like dew on your skin. We lay on our backs on the grass, our arms and legs splayed like starfish, in halter-tops and short shorts, our limbs having recently sprouted like the weeds around us.

The sky was my grandmother's favorite color, periwinkle blue, a color she called "blue and purple with a little magic." There was a yellow moon that rested easily in the periwinkle sky, as if it would never have anywhere else to go. That's how I felt. Like I had nowhere else to go. Like this sky was taking care of me so I could just lay back and be a part of this night, with the stars and my friend, an easy breeze blowing inside me. It was an odd and wonderful feeling that I've never quite had again. I take a blue crayon and a purple crayon and color a periwinkle sky, then draw two girls lying on a lawn beneath who look like they're making snow angels without the snow.

When it's time to show our drawings, Bethanie pops up, claps her hands, and twerps, "It's showtime, folks!" Timbo goes first. His furious drawing is of a very psychedelic-looking Jesus with hands reaching out like trippy beams of light, perfect for an acid rock album cover.

It is a rock 'n' roll savior, I think.

Bethanie coos, "Ooh, I love it. Tell me about this."

"This is what God looked like when He visited me."

Bethanie, still uncomfortable with the term *visit*, asks warily, "When did God . . . *visit* you?"

Timbo launches into a tale I can tell he's told many times before, his words pouring out easily. "Getting high or drunk was the only thing I thought about. I drank to drown my problems, but damn if my problems didn't learn to swim. Plus I kept getting fired." Timbo's tone tilts away from self-recrimination and back toward his more-standard outrage. "My boss had a real stick up his ass about me drinking on the job. But the thing was, the drinking made me do my job better. I mean, you don't have to be Mr. Sober to stand in a line and put a metal coil in some shit and then screw a top on the fuck—" Timbo corrects himself, "a top on the *honking* thing." Then his shoulders wilt a bit. "But still, I did have a problem. And I knew it.

"I got evicted from my place so I started staying with whatever chick would let me, and then one night I woke up in this bitch—woke up in this *young lady's* bed. And this particular young lady had vomited on her pillow and instead of cleaning it up, she just put a towel down and rolled over to go back to sleep. She had two kids screaming in the other room so I went in to tell them to be quiet, and the one kid screamed that I wasn't his dad, so I screamed back, 'You're right! I'm not! Lucky for both of us!' And I grabbed my bag and took off.

"There's nothing like tearing off for nowhere with nothing in your rearview mirror, so that's what I did. I stopped for the night at this cockroach hotel and I smoked this stuff called angel crack. It's not really crack. Crack is . . ." Timbo stops himself from elaborating. "The point is I looked outside to the street, outside my window to all the lights, out to the flashing neon Budweiser and Old Style signs at the liquor store, and the All-You-Can-Eat-Ribs sign at Ponderosa and 'Girls Girls Girls!' And then all the lights came together and they formed a cross in the sky. They came together, and it was as clear as the hair on my arms, which were standing up, and that's the truth. I knew this glowing cross was guiding me out of the darkness, out of the sorry mess I'd made of my life."

Timbo pauses for effect. He spreads his arms, an electrified prophet, almost knocking Mickey in the face, but Mickey ducks just in time. "And then I heard a voice, and I can't tell you how, but I knew it was the voice of the Lord. The voice was booming inside and outside of me at the same time: 'Have you had enough? Have you had enough of chasing one high after another? Of women? Of pounding?'" (I still don't know what *pounding* is and am happy to maintain my ignorance.)

Timbo's face is glowing. "The cross shone down, lighting my way out, my way up. Everything was on fire."

Mickey moves his chair away from Timbo's.

Timbo does not notice because he is soaring. "The voice said, 'Do you want to end up like your dad?'" And hell no, I did not want to end up like my dad. My dad was a classic grade A bum who died drunk in a pool of his urine in the liquor aisle of A&P with a bottle of whiskey in his hand. Some cashier chick held him while he vomited himself to death." Timbo cracks his already-inflamed knuckles. "Yeah, that's not what I wanted. My whole life changed after that. That visitation saved my life." Timbo collapses back into his seat, winded from his tale.

Bethanie crosses her arms and squints her eyes, a look she often employs to convey the depth of her thought. "Well, that is quite a story." But then, she juts out her chin, suspicious. "Are you saying you were on drugs when this 'visitation' happened?"

"Yeah, angel crack. But it's not really crack, like I was going to say. It's just a strain of meth."

Bethanie twists her mouth to the side. Timbo does NOT like this expression, not at all. "What's with the face? Why are you making a funny face?"

Bethanie keeps her mouth contorted to the side and replies with a very funny-looking face indeed, "I just don't want you to misconstrue an experience you had on drugs as a genuine spiritual revelation. The Bible clearly condemns the use of narcotics."

Timbo flares. "What's the verse that says God's against narcotics? Where's the verse that says God can't use drugs to communicate with us? Where's that verse?" Bethanie looks to me, aware of my Bible verse–memorization pedigree.

I am pleased with the opportunity to not offer any assistance and shrug my shoulders as I reply, "I don't know any Bible verses about drugs. There's the one about not getting drunk because it leads to debauchery, but other than that . . . yeah, I don't really know."

Although I have to admit, I do see Bethanie's point. It does seem odd that God would choose to appear to Timbo when he was whacked out of his mind on angel crack, but maybe altering the chemistry of the brain can lead you to see God. I know the psychologist William James had his initial mystical experiences while on nitrous oxide, a drug that resulted in seminal texts on the religious experience. Should we disregard James's theophanies because he had them while tweaked on Whip-its? I don't know. Maybe. But I do know I will never do drugs, either recreational or prescribed. Drugs seem far more likely to lead you away from God than toward Him.

Timbo's rage continues rising. "Look, I'm off the drugs now. I'm working the steps. All the damn steps. I'm letting go and letting God. I'm taking one day at a fucking time. All because of that night. Are you telling me that night was bullshit? The whole thing was bullshit? I should just go back to doing what I was before? Well, I mean, fuck this. And fuck everybody telling me how I should fucking talk."

I see Bethanie is uneasy with the situation. She seems to recognize her position of responsibility and for the first time actually feel its weight. "No, no, I'm sorry, Timbo. That was a mistake. I shouldn't have said that. I'm unfamiliar with drugs, and so sometimes I misspeak." Then she adds, "My brother-in-law accepted Jesus into his heart while he was in prison then got a tattoo of a dove on his inner thigh. And he was on drugs then, I'm sure of it."

I agree. An inner-thigh dove tattoo by an inmate seems very likely to be a narcotic-fueled decision.

Timbo is pacified by what seems like her genuine show of regret, especially when she follows it with, "I like your drawing very much. It's very vivid." Timbo, soothed by the praise, and unburdened by the repeated telling of his tale, sits back into his chair.

Dwayne shows his picture next, and it's stunning. The image is segmented into four parts, each drawn in a different, clearly practiced, adept style. The first quadrant looks like something you might see in a life-drawing class, the second is made up of clusters of crayon dots, the third appears Tibetan with a yin-yang-y vibe, and the fourth is splashed in luxurious tropical colors.

Bethanie is agog. "Oh my goodness, Dwayne. That is just beautiful. I never knew you had such talent. Has anyone ever told you you have talent as an artist?"

From the expression on Dwayne's face, I can tell that yes, he has been told he has talent as an artist and that Bethanie's opinion of his talent is of no more importance to him than her opinion of the chair he's sitting on. I'm liking Dwayne even more.

"Because what you did right here shows real promise. Have you thought about taking art classes?"

"Yes," he replies, "well, I was an art professor at a community college for twenty years."

Whoa, wooden Indian Dwayne was an art professor!

"Well," Bethanie pronounces, "you should be an artist *yourself*. It appears you can do more than just teach." I think I detect a wince escape Dwayne's mouth, but I can't be sure. Bethanie continues, oblivious to her possible offense. "You are very, very talented. I can't believe all the colors you came up with to use. So creative." Bethanie gives Dwayne a little round of applause as he stares back at her, wooden.

It occurs to me that Bethanie would have made a wonderful preschool teacher. Her tone, her manner, her mentality—all of it would be perfect when dealing with toddlers or others of limited intelligence—maybe Alzheimer's patients or dogs. But human adults in the in-between years are complicated. I see now, however, that she is really trying, trying to do a job unsuited to her disposition, and I have a fleeting moment of sympathy.

Bethanie leans over Dwayne's drawing, clasping her hands to her breast, and gushes, "Well, now that we've gotten over singing your praises, tell me more about what we have here."

Dwayne, immune to the flattery, replies simply, "It's hard to reduce God to one image. As Jon and Ron have pointed out. So I tried to break open the one image—pointing out the fact that God may be many things."

Bethanie purrs, "Oooh, tell me more," in a way I imagine a preschooler or a dog might go gaga for.

But not Dwayne. His brief puff of animation collapses, like a toy that's been shut off. "That's it," he says. "You can move on." The focus of Dwayne's eyes fuzzes, and he settles back into his seat and his uncanny stillness.

Bethanie feels the dead end of the Dwayne discussion and so turns to Mickey. "Let's see what you've got." I expect Mickey to reveal a picture as sunshiny as his disposition, but instead, he turns his paper over to display a man-beast creature with red eyes, pointy ears, and a nose that curls under to touch its snarling lip, a creature resembling a devil more than a god.

Bethanie fingers the cross around her neck, as if protecting herself from Mickey's rendering. "Hmm, is this how you see God? Pretty scary."

Timbo mutters with an unsettling satisfaction, "I like Mickey's drawing. Mickey's right. Everyone will get theirs in the end."

Mickey stands up as he displays his picture, even though we can all see it perfectly well with him sitting down. "Sometimes I think we forget to fear God. *The fear of the Lord is a fountain of life, to depart from the snares of death.* We must not forget to fear Him."

I think, *Well, I'm good with God on the "being afraid of Him" front. At least I've got that going for me. I'm pretty much constantly fearing Him, so I'm certainly in the way-upper percentile of fearing Him, so off the charts I must be seriously blowing the curve of terror.*

Mickey looks at his drawing again and is frightened all of sudden, seemingly spooked by his own creation. He quickly sits back down, pulls out a folder, and puts his drawing in a random spot amongst a stack of handouts, a spot, I'm gathering, in which he hopes the drawing will soon be lost. Then he slaps his hands together. "Enough about me. I'm no artist. Let's see Dwayne's picture again."

Dwayne's eyes remained focused straight ahead, as if he's all of a sudden become hard of hearing. Bethanie, rightly assessing his lack of enthusiasm, jumps in. "Dwayne's had his chance. Let's hear from Maggie."

I was hoping a tornado or something would strike and I wouldn't have to take my turn, but the winds outside are still and mute, and I have signed up to be here. "Okay, so this is weird. It's very abstract. I'm a terrible artist." I look over at Dwayne and say, "I'd love to take your class." Dwayne nods almost imperceptibly as I continue, "So . . . the idea behind this—I was just thinking of one night with my best friend that I felt peaceful. I'm an anxious person, as you all know . . ."

I look around the group. Quinn laughs immediately and says, "Oh yes, we know." Petra nods and smiles. The twins both manage to lift their eyes from their laps to meet mine. For a brief moment, this odd group of people I've been thrown together with really does feel like "the gang."

"Right," I continue, buoyed by the recognition, "you guys know. So this night, it was really rare. I wasn't anxious at all. For once I felt like it was safe to relax." I point to the top of the paper. "The color of the sky was periwinkle blue, which my grandmother used to say was blue and purple with a little bit of magic." Bethanie looks back at me with an expression I have trouble reading, but I keep going nonetheless. "I don't know. I'm just thinking God has something to do with that experience somehow."

After a moment, Bethanie's inscrutable expression brightens into a clear smile. "Well, that's lovely, Maggie. I like that you thought outside the box." I like that my turn is over and am glad to be moving on.

"Okay, so who do we have next? Petra?"

Petra shares her picture of Jesus on a cross, with a loincloth hanging below very pronounced musculature, all pecs and biceps and triceps and the excessive abs of an underwear model. Her savior's mouth is twisted in an expression of either agony or ecstasy, and as she runs her nails over the picture, she says, "So this is my Guy. We've been in a relationship for thirteen years. Every other guy I've been with has let me down, but not this Guy." "My Guy" has the ring of romantic endearment, and "been with" seems an odd, sexually charged phrase to describe a relationship with God's son. I half expect Petra to plant her lips on the naked Jesus, but I'm pleased to see she somehow restrains herself.

Quinn's next. On her paper, she has drawn a beatific, kind, clearly . . . *female* face. When Bethanie sees the image, she instantly recoils, then gets very serious, as if she's just found out there's a bomb in the room and we all need to work together to disarm it. "Okay, what . . . is . . . that?"

Quinn explains that since she was molested by her father, she finds it complicated to picture God as a father, that she can understand God's love more if she envisions a female, the women in her life having been so much more loving than the men.

"Quinn," Bethanie's voice drops an octave, "in the Bible, which is God's inerrant Word, God is clearly described as male. Do you know that this is true?"

"Yes, but I've been working with Dr. Benton, and we've been talking about how the masculine imagery might be getting in the way of me understanding God's love. When I picture a father, I get frightened, and I don't think that's what God would want for me."

"Yes, but God is not a woman."

"Yeah, that's one thing for sure," Timbo jumps in. "God's no sissy." Petra rolls her eyes at Timbo's apparent fascination with who is and who is not a "sissy."

"Let's stop talking about sissies." Bethanie's voice is pitched high and wild. "Sissies have nothing to do with anything. God is not a sissy or a woman. I did not expect this exercise to be so hard for everybody. Quinn, I'd like you to put that picture away."

All of my pent-up aggression toward Bethanie breaks, and I rush to Quinn's defense in a way I never could for my own. "I think Quinn should be able to picture God in whatever way works for her."

Bethanie is stunned for a second but then shoots back, "Not if her picture directly contradicts the Bible."

"But the Bible says God is Love; that seems to be main thing, before gender. I mean, wouldn't God be genderless? Isn't saying God is a father just pointing to His protective nature, since men at the time were more in the role of protectors?"

Dwayne, who has been studying Quinn's picture, adds, seemingly oblivious to Bethanie's and my disagreement, "I find the image lovely. It reminds me of early Tibetan drawings of Kwan Yin."

Bethanie pins her arms to her side and fixes her pupils, as if to stop them from rolling back into her head. "*Who is Kwan Yin?*"

"Kwan Yin is the goddess of compassion in the Buddhist tradition."

"*Buddhist tradition?*" Bethanie shoots to her feet and proclaims, "I will not have false idols discussed in this group. I won't have it." Then she points to Quinn's drawing as if it were a loaded weapon. "I'm going to need you to put that away. *Right now.*" Buddhism has reared its ugly Eastern head twice today, and it's sending Bethanie into a tizzy.

I expect Quinn to stand up to Bethanie, but instead, she gently folds her picture and places it obediently under her seat. I wonder about images of God, which ones are appropriate, and if it's dangerous to picture God at all. Is a representation automatically a reduction? *In the Bible, God is pictured as all sorts of things*, I think—*a dove, a great light, thunder, spirit*—so *why not a woman?* If the image of a woman for some people communicates more deeply God's kindness or love, why not use it?

I think back to Push Hands Eric and his three identical pictures of Mary Cassatt's *Mother and Child*. Maybe that was his God picture. Maybe Eric's God was a mother, holding her child. Maybe Eric had those three identical prints on his walls so everywhere he looked he could see Her.

CHAPTER FOURTEEN: **UNPARDONABLE**

I HAVE A DREAM ABOUT COOPER. We sit on his red sleeping bag and I open the locket he gave me for Christmas. I take out the scrunched-up little piece of paper, which still manages to display, despite its weak, faded ink, *Will you marry me?* and I hand it to him. But before he can take it, the paper bursts into flames between my fingers. Instinctively I throw the burning paper away, where it lands on Cooper's lap and instantly engulfs him in flames. I wake up with a start.

It takes me a moment to piece together my circumstances. Where am I? I feel my pink blanket gripped tightly in my hands. My fingers bypass any cognition, searching for the singed ring, until finally they find the little charred nub and can circle it over and over and over. Now I can think. I look up at the picture of the boy at the beach and then slowly I penetrate the mystery: I am here. Grace Point. It's been over a month. My parents found this place. God led them here. I am lucky. It's important that I not forget how lucky I am. That would be unforgivable.

I shudder underneath the pink velour blanket I've now anxiously pulled around my shoulders and remember a terrifying concept I've somehow managed to ignore until right this moment . . . *the unpardonable sin.* How could I have forgotten about the one sin that cannot be forgiven? I have no explanation, except that I forget all kinds of things I shouldn't.

I'm distracted. I'm led astray. I pull the blanket even tighter. But this is an especially grave oversight.

I first heard about the unpardonable sin when I was ten. Pastor Womac mentioned it offhandedly in one of his Sunday sermons: "God can pardon all sins but one—blasphemy against the Holy Spirit." I sat up stiff in the pew, electrified with fear, as Pastor Womac dully continued a sermon he himself seemed to hope would be over soon. *What sin can be unpardonable? What does that mean?* I'd never heard a single thing about this ever. *What is "blasphemy against the Holy Spirit?"* Why had I never been informed of this clear exception to the rule of God's unconditional forgiveness? *This is a criminal omission of information*, I thought, *like forgetting to tell a toddler not to touch a hot stove or warn her not to insert bobby pins in an electrical outlet.* The invisible claws stabbed into my scalp even more savagely than during the Antichrist sermon where Pastor Womac talked about the beast coming out of the water with its sprouting slimy heads and eyes all over.

The choir stood up and began the closing hymn: *What a friend we have in Jesus. All our griefs and sins to bear.* Why weren't they shaking? How were none of them worried about the unpardonable sin? Didn't they hear the sermon I just heard? They could be as guilty as me and it could be *unpardonable.* How were they lifting their hymnals, locating the appropriate page, and singing in four-part harmony? As soon they intoned the final lines, *In His arms He'll take and shield Thee / Thou wilt find solace there*, I bolted out of the pew, tore down the aisle, and slammed through the sanctuary doors. I had to find out from Pastor Womac, from his own mouth, what this unpardonable sin was, and acquire the information necessary to make sure I never committed it.

So after the service I headed straight to the Afterglow, an oddly sexual name for what just meant coffee, donut holes, and small talk in the church gym. I got to the gym before anyone else and waited alone under the basketball net, determined to be the first person to nab Pastor Womac. But I was too late. When the pastor walked in, he was already three deep in old ladies and deacons. I waited in the corner, watching adults fill their coffee cups and joke about their need for it be "leaded," watching kids cram post-limit donut holes in their mouths when their parents weren't looking, waiting for the crowd to thin out, waiting for my chance. I waited until there was only one chatterer remaining, but this chatterer was a doozy: Merrick McKee, a garrulous, spindly man my family referred to as the Supertalker. The Supertalker was gifted with heroic powers to trap anyone, young or old, in conversation, deftly forestalling the possibility of excusing oneself through his steady, insistent monologue.

I became increasingly desperate as Supertalker continued to display his power. I knew my parents would be ready to go home soon. The Afterglow was winding down; adults and children sufficiently jacked on caffeine and sugar were making their way out of the gym, the heavy wooden double doors swinging behind them. But then miraculously, Mr. McKee interrupted his own aggressive barrage of boredom and excused himself to go to the bathroom.

I leapt in without a second's delay and spat out, "Pastor Womac, can you tell me more about the unpardonable sin? I want to make sure I don't commit it. I thought God forgave all sins if you confessed them. I didn't know about the exception. I'm scared I've already committed it. If I'd known about the exception, I'd have been more careful."

Pastor Womac put his hand gently on my shoulder. "Maggie, you definitely have not committed the unpardonable sin. And you never will. I promise you. It's impossible to commit the unpardonable sin if you're worried about it. Anyone who is blaspheming the Holy Spirit does it deliberately and is glad to be doing it." He squatted down, which wasn't easy for him, but he made the journey, landing his butt on his heels so he could look directly into my eyes. "And that is definitely not you, Miss Rowe." I heard a snap in one of Pastor Womac's knees. Then he placed one hand against the floor and shoved himself back up, bracing and balancing with the opposite foot, avoiding pressure on his snapping knee—without spilling the contents of his Styrofoam cup.

Beyond Pastor Womac's shoulder, I saw my parents coming. I didn't have long. "But maybe I do blaspheme deliberately, Pastor Womac. Deliberate and accidental are hard to tell apart when it comes to thoughts, especially when you're the one who's thinking them and especially when you're having a lot of bad thoughts, like thinking that God is unfair, like even that He's mean. Thinking that God is mean, that could be the unpardonable sin."

Pastor Womac shook his head with confidence, without any sense of alarm. "Let me tell you the context of the verse. Jesus had just exorcised demons from several possessed men, sending their spirits into swine. The Pharisees, who were the big religious leaders at the time, said that it wasn't the power of God that enabled Jesus to perform this exorcism, but the power of Satan. The Pharisees were accusing God of being Satan. I'm sure you'll never do that, Maggie."

I saw my Mom's eyes scanning the room for me and Mr. McKee returning from the bathroom, chatting away even before he was within hearing distance, so I quickly thanked Pastor Womac and ran after my family. I was glad I'd asked. I'd acquired valuable information. I just needed to make sure I didn't attribute any act of *God* to *Satan*. I figured I should just avoid making any judgments at all about what comes from Satan and what's from God. Period. The good news was, I couldn't remember a time when I'd had occasion to make such a judgment. So that was hopeful. I just had to make sure that if this opportunity came up in the future, *I was very careful.*

But now as I sit on my bed, swaddling myself in the blanket, hoping the restraint of my limbs will calm me, I wonder if I've already committed the unpardonable sin. I keep thinking that God is cruel, horrible, like Satan. Isn't that the same thing as calling Him Satan? Could I be blaspheming the Holy Spirit? I start whacking the rubber band against my wrist furiously. Stop. Stop. Why can't I just stop it?

And then that "stop hitting yourself" phenomenon grips me more savagely than ever before. I split in two: subject and object, persecutor and persecuted—in the war zone of my mind. A part of me forbids the thought that God is cruel, which causes the other part to rise and say, "But God *is* cruel. Sadistic. Worse than the worst human being." The first part responds with equal intensity, "Stop. Stop. You're going to blaspheme, and blasphemy is the one sin that cannot be forgiven."

Then in spite of myself, or *to* spite myself, I start shooting out the words in my head: *blaspheme blaspheme blaspheme.* The insistent thorns in my scalp dig in deeper, warning me of a danger of which I'm already acutely aware. I am under assault from within, unable to quell the insurrection. I blast out, "I blaspheme the Holy Spirit. I blaspheme you, Holy Spirit."

"Oh my God, why am I doing this? Forgive me, Father. I know not what I do. Please. I believe. Help now, my unbelief." Stop. Whack. I go to the bathroom and vomit. My stomach heaves up like a wave, and at its crest, the opponents in the battleground of my mind give up their quarrel. I enjoy for a moment what I know is only a temporary truce before I replace the top of the toilet seat.

As I exit the bathroom, I hear a crash from Mickey's room. I pass by his open door and see Mickey, red-faced, huffing, staring down at something beyond my field of vision. I peek in to see the object of his gaze. The pull-up bar that was hooked on the doorframe has been heaved into the corner and now Mickey is towering over it, gloating, like a boxer standing over his pummeled opponent.

At morning check-in, we all stick to what have become our standard answers. We all vary a little, but the exercise has become similar to calling out our names.

Me: Anxious.
Twins: Scared.
Quinn: Sad.
Petra: Heartbroken.
Dwayne: Numb.
Timbo: Frustrated.

Mickey, when it's his turn, usually replies, "Good," or "Joyful," or "Overwhelmed with happiness by God's grace." But this time when Mickey says, "Good," he sounds angry and defiant, like he's hocking out a wad of bile at a bully.

Bethanie takes in Mickey's agitation, pulls her shoulders back, and asks with skepticism that she makes sure the whole gang picks up on, "Are you sure you feel 'good'? You don't sound like you feel good."

Mickey's eyes dart around the room. "I'm good. I feel GOOD. The joy of the Lord is my strength!"

"Okay, Mickey. What else are you feeling besides *good*?"

Mickey bites his already-inflamed lip and replies, with skittish, crazed eyes, "This is the day that the Lord has made. Let us rejoice and be glad in it."

"That's right," Bethanie says, consulting the file folder sitting on her lap. Then she spots something. She closes the file and looks up. "Dr. Lakhani noted in your file that you lost your mother this year. That must have been very difficult."

When Mickey hears the word *mother*, his face seems to dissolve into a sea of unrecognizable features. All the grooves melt away until I only see his eyes, which look young and sad and searching, reminding me of the boy in the watercolor above my bed. Bethanie alters her voice, elongating her vowels, probably aping a professor from a psychology class. "Tell meee about yoo-ur mother."

Mickey states solemnly, as if under oath, "My mother was wonderful. When people say their mother was a saint, I never believe them. Because they never met my mother. They don't know about mothers." I can imagine Mickey exiting the witness stand, his testimony complete; he's said his piece, it's true, and he can rest well.

But then he continues, "My father married my mother when she was pregnant with me. She had been living in sin with a saxophonist who took off when he found out she was going to have a baby. But my dad married her even in that unfavorable condition, so my mom did everything she could to make it up to him. She cooked and cleaned up and put up with his moonshine, what he called 'joy juice.'"

"Did your father drink quite a bit?"

"No one could beat him." Mickey shakes his head, in what could be either disappointment or pride. "Wooden leg? He had wooden legs, arms, and a wine barrel of a torso. Sometimes my dad would get so high on joy juice," Mickey says, his eyes darkening, "that he would stomp his feet in celebration, before gesturing for my mother to follow him up to their bedroom." Mickey clangs his knees together and locks them before continuing, "I remember once Mom and I were playing cat's cradle, sitting together on the living room floor. I was about to scoop the cat's cradle from my mother's hands into 'fish on a dish' by pulling the outside strings up and around, but my dad finished off his joy juice and stumbled up the stairs. He yelled at my mother without looking behind him, and my mother let the string between our fingers go and she said, 'We'll do more tomorrow.' Then she went up the stairs. I knew what they were going to do and I knew she didn't want to do it. But I understood she had to. For me. I was her prize. She always said so."

Bethanie speaks simply and kindly: "I'm sure you were."

"She taught me about music," Mickey says. "She bought me a banjo for my birthday. A banjo that sounded good even when you pressed the wrong fret or plucked the wrong string. You couldn't mess up with that banjo." *A forgiving banjo*, I think.

Mickey's eyes dart around at the group, searching, but finding nowhere to land. "Then my dad smashed it against the wall one day when he was full of joy juice. He hated the sound of that banjo, he said, and he wasn't going to tolerate the racket anymore. It was his house, and some little runt was not going to mess it up." Mickey bounces both of his knees with increasing speed, staring at a spot between them. "Then the next thing my banjo was was just a whole bunch of wood chips, a thousand wood chips. They were flying everywhere. My mother squeezed me so tight I couldn't cry, whispering into the top of my head that she was sorry. She got me a harmonica after that. That day, she went out and got it."

Bethanie places her hand on her heart. "Well, I hope it's a comfort to know that one day you will see your mother in heaven."

Mickey looks sick, the type of sick I feel when only running to the toilet to vomit can help. But Mickey doesn't vomit. Instead, he swallows hard before choking out dryly, "No, I will not see my mother in heaven."

"But you said your mother was a saint."

"To me, she was. But not to God."

"What do you mean?"

Mickey says nothing.

"Mickey? Tell me what's going on inside of you. I can see the outside. But sometimes the outside is mislead—"

Mickey slices through her probing. "My mother was Jewish and she never gave up her faith. It was the one thing she wouldn't give up for my dad. So that's why she's not in heaven."

The entire room freezes, suspended for a moment with shared focus. Bethanie's jaw falls open, but no sound escapes. I wait for her to come up with something reassuring, some form of comfort. Mickey waits also, expectant, but I can see also prepared for inevitable disappointment. He knows there's no comfort. How could there be? Mickey believes God has denied his mother peace in the afterlife, that despite her kindness and her motherly sainthood, He has rejected her for all eternity and now it's *too late*.

"I'm sorry to hear that, Mickey," is all Bethanie has to offer.

"I tried to get her to accept Jesus so many times," Mickey continues with a voice stripped of its usual cheer, "but it was the one thing she wouldn't do. Her grandmother had been in the Holocaust, and so my mother inherited a kind of phobia of Christ and crucifixes, I guess you could say, but maybe *phobia* is not the word. She never shoved her faith in my father's face, she never went to synagogue or talked to her friends about the Ten Commandments or anything like that, but at night she'd whisper her prayers. I'd hear her. She called God 'Adonai.'"

I have a thought that I want to snap away, a terrible thought, which is that . . . I hate Christians. I wish I didn't have to be one. I don't like being part of this group who thinks all other groups will lose out in the end. Christians supposedly sympathize with the sick and the hungry, supposedly mourn for the suffering, the rejected, the downtrodden, the abandoned. They feel bad when they hear about genocide or children with cancer or mistreatment of puppies. But in comparison to eternity, who cares?

Who cares about these little finite peanuts of pain? They will all die and find relief in some sort of oblivion. There is mercy for them. People can always say, "at least they're not suffering now." But that one comfort is denied the "out" group according to traditional Christianity, denied all those who called God by the wrong name, like Mickey's mother saying "Adonai."

I know plenty of people at Hope Valley Baptist who have loved ones that have died unrepentant. They have agnostic children and grandchildren being raised Jewish because of a wayward son; they have mothers and fathers who denied the Word, who rejected the one condition of the unconditional gift, who now are presumably shut out from light, into darkness, denied any sort of mercy, small or large, for ever and ever and ever and ever, with no hope of deliverance. *World without end. Amen. Amen.*

I want to ask, *How? How are you able to stand up, bearing the burden of this knowledge? Why aren't your knees buckling? Why are you not wailing and bawling and howling at the horror? Why don't you need to be sedated? How are your internal organs still functioning? Your liver. Your stomach. Your bowels. Your spleen. Why aren't you running to the bathroom? Why aren't you puddling into to a weeping, quivering mess that needs to be carried out on a stretcher? How can you stand up? How?*

And why in the world if you're a Christian would you ever have a child? You are risking bringing a being into the world that may or may not accept Jesus Christ as his or her personal savior. You don't know what your kid is going to do. Plenty of Christian families have children who reject Jesus. *The path is narrow and few shall find it.* Why would you risk dangling your offspring over the eternal pit, even if there is a possibility for paradise? It's still only a possibility. I wonder how Pascal would feel about the wager of procreation, but whatever he thinks, I know I will never . . . *never* have children. I will never place a being of my own creation in that sort of jeopardy. I will never trust God with my son or daughter. It is not worth the wager.

Mickey's eyes droop with tears for a moment but then quickly blink themselves dry. He steels himself but is unable to fully steady his voice. "I prayed without ceasing for my mother. I tried to get her to repent over and over and over again. But God did nothing. Like always. Like . . . like how I got a pull-up bar and hung from it every night and prayed for length without *ceasing*. And how I am not one inch taller? *Not one inch!*"

"Pull-up bar?" Bethanie wrinkles her nose.

"I've been working on my height," Mickey relays simply. "The spine can be lengthened up to three inches with dedicated stretching."

"Where did you read that?"

Mickey lashes out, the energy of his cheerfulness lasering into a sharp bitterness. "It doesn't matter where I read it. It's true. But God didn't answer my prayers. I did my part. I prayed without *ceasing*. And NOTH-ING! No inches and . . ." Mickey manages to crack out despite his faltering voice, "and my mother . . . my mother was a *saint*."

I've never met Mickey's mother who calls God "Adonai," but I want to rush to her defense. I want to ask God, *Why?* But more than that, I want to yell at Him, scold Him, to plead with Him, *What about Mickey's mother? Is it really too late?*

I arrive for my fifth visit with Dr. Lakhani. As soon as I enter her office and see her seated nobly behind her impressive desk, my shoulders relax. Dr. Lakhani, I've come to see, is on my side. She understands how Bethanie can be dead wrong and is not afraid say it. She puts my struggles in con-text. I'm not the only one who worries about unforgiven sins. There are Hasids and Muslims and the kid with the ChapStick before communion. She is, to me, a beacon of rationality and logic in the messy, emotional sea of Grace Point.

I sit down, adjusting my *Flashdance* sweatshirt, which keeps falling off one shoulder, and excitedly launch into what I've been waiting to talk to her about: blasphemy, the unpardonable sin, and the puzzle of how Chris-tians can stand up.

Dr. Lakhani interrupts with a directness I instantly cease to appreci-ate. "We can talk about this later, but right now . . . I want to talk about your dress."

"My dress? I'm not wearing a dress."

"Your choice in clothing."

I look down at my slobby, stained mess of an outfit: puffy comforting socks blanketing feet stuffed into orthopedic-looking slipper-shoes, over-sized sweatpants with a stretch elastic waist, and the same grimy *Flash-dance* sweatshirt I've been wearing for the last three days, which has fallen off my shoulder. Again.

Dr. Lakhani's face is stoic. "In a coed environment you need to be aware of the temptation you present."

My mind feels dull, unable to process what I know should be simple information.

"I don't understand."

"There are men in this program who are trying to work on their spiritual issues, and having a sexualized environment can be a hindrance."

"Sexualized environment?"

Dr. Lakhani continues blithely with no discernable discomfort. "It is possible to see down your shirt when you lean over."

I quickly center my already-centered sweatshirt. "What? When do I lean over?"

"Bethanie said—"

"Bethanie said what?"

"Bethanie said you dropped your notebook in activity therapy, and when you leaned down to pick it up, the group could see your entire bra."

Dr. Lakhani continues, immune to my obvious distress, "As supervisor here, I'm responsible for the group." Her words fade away as I try to picture the details of the incident, an investigator in my own transgression. The oversized neck hole of my sweatshirt could definitely have flopped open, I conclude, but normally I put my hand on the fabric at my chest to keep that exact thing from happening. But maybe I don't always do that. Maybe I forget.

Dr. Lakhani continues evenly, ". . . so things need to change around here, dress-wise."

I manage to stammer out an apology. "I'm sorry. Okay, I wasn't thinking . . ." But the more I apologize, the more betrayed I feel. Dr. Lakhani was my ally. She was the one who immediately knew I wasn't bulimic, who understood the concept of somatization, who agreed Bethanie was wrong, that I wasn't trying to be a size six, that I threw up because I was literally having trouble stomaching things. But now, I know, Dr. Lakhani is not on my side, a glaring truth I somehow missed, like many other glaring, obvious truths. She's all business. I was right about that. As she continues talking at me, referring to "mutual understanding," employing the words *policy* and *coed* more than could possibly be necessary to make her point, I realize that my initial assessment of her as a bank manager was correct.

My outrage blooms as I think, *And it's not like I was wearing a bikini or hot pants. Or even anything like what Petra wears every day. Did you see last Friday's ensemble of tube top, romper-culottes, and cowboy boots?* I want to ask Bethanie, *And you're talking to* me?

But I know it's not worth the fight. I only have three more weeks before I need to be back in school, so I answer robotically, "I. Will. Make better clothing choices."

"Great," Dr. Lakhani replies, as if her inappropriate scolding had just vanished into thin air and my apology was not completely rote. "Now . . . how's everything else going?"

But I can't let go. *The men's recovery?* I think. *What about* my *recovery?* But then the other part of my brain rises up, ready to throw down with equal force. *Why do I keep thinking things I shouldn't? I can't control myself. What if I force myself to commit the unpardonable sin?* The old familiar panicky claws in my head dig in, causing that same prickly burning I felt when I first heard about "too late." I reach up and jab my fingers into my scalp, so I'm feeling something real and not imagined.

Dr. Lakhani observes my fingers entwined in my hair, manically massaging my scalp, then says, "I think you should at least talk to Dr. Benton about medication."

I know I'm not going on medication. I need to remain vigilant. I must never again fall asleep at the spiritual wheel. I can't even afford to be drowsy. Not for one moment.

But at least Dr. Benton will be someone else to talk to, I think, s*omeone who is not Dr. Lakhani and not Bethanie.* Plus, I just need to get out of here, out of the thick stale air of this office, and out into the courtyard where the air actually moves so I can have a cigarette and I can breathe.

"Okay, I'll talk to Dr. Benton."

I lie in bed that night waiting for the tide of sleep to pull me away from the shores of consciousness, out to where my mind will still circle, but far-less viciously. All I can think, however, is *How dare she?* I jolt up and sit crossed-legged in my bed, rocking back and forth. How dare she listen to Bethanie? How dare she tell me how to dress and what to do when I lean over? She's the one who told me *scrupulosity* meant "stabbing of conscience," and now she's the one twisting the knife.

But then outrage gives way to a more-familiar terror as I start wondering, Was *my attire inappropriate?* Was *it a sin?* Was *that bad fruit? Did Dr. Lakhani uncover evidence of my lukewarm heart for Christ? Have I done something truly horrible? Unpardonable, even?*

No. No, I have not, I decide. I have done nothing wrong. Dr. Lakhani's indictment does not mean I have committed a crime. It only points to a flaw in my accuser. Just like Bethanie's judgment of Quinn's picture is not evidence of Quinn's sin, but rather, of Bethanie's limitation.

I lie back and listen to Mickey playing his harmonica. It's tune is still troubled, but it's bolder than the night before.

PART THREE

CHAPTER FIFTEEN: **FEAST**

THE NEXT DAY ON THE WAY to morning check-in, I notice that Mickey's door is open. I peek in and see that all of his belongings are gone. The room is bare, silent. No dust. No footprints. Nothing except the ragged indentation in the wall where Mickey had hurled the pull-up bar.

At check-in, Bethanie explains that Mickey is no longer with us. For a moment, I think Mickey's dead and am relieved when Bethanie continues with, "He left a note saying he wishes you all the best and he will be praying for you without ceasing." *A note? Why would he take off like that? Why not just wait a little and say goodbye?* It's spooky. I remember how the rooms here once stuck me as murder-mystery rooms, and now I think of *Ten Little Indians* and how the guests mysteriously disappear, one by one.

After check-in I see Quinn standing outside her room with several suitcases packed. I panic. My friend is leaving. We're all being knocked off, one little Indian at a time. I run up to her. "Where are you going? Why didn't you tell me?"

"Oh, sweetheart!" I am surprised and pleased to hear her call me sweetheart. "I'm not leaving the program. I just can't stay here anymore, the horrible bed, the whole sharing-a-bathroom thing. Jack, my husband, found me a furnished apartment right down the street, across from the strip mall. I'm gonna stay there at night and come here during the day. I cleared it with Dr. Lakhani and everything. You should stay with me sometime."

I'm relieved I haven't lost her. "Yes, that would great."

I walk to my appointment with Dr. Benton prepared to tell him I want to be on medication only for nausea, nothing that will affect my judgment. I plan to tell him chemicals are too risky, given the stakes I'm dealing with. I'm ready to explain the burden of eternity, the gap between finite and infinite. I open the door and see a tall man with severe facial asymmetry, the features on the left crashing down far below those on the right. His tilted wire-rim glasses struggle to hold the thick lenses, lenses that magnify his skewed eyes, making him look not unlike a lopsided snail. Despite these severe personal-appearance obstacles, Dr. Benton still manages to be handsome.

He gestures to a chair across from his desk and starts looking through my file. I sit down and look over his shoulder at an old family portrait on the wall behind him. The portrait looks like it's been taken right in the middle of the dust bowl, the dusty children standing even more stiffly than their erect gray parents, bracing themselves against the cruel, dusty wind.

"Let's she."

She? It must be his accent.

"I like your accent. Where are you from?"

Dr. Benton looks up, confused. "My accent?"

"Yeah, you said, 'let's she.' Instead of 'let's see,' which is how I would say it."

The corners of Dr. Benton's lips lift asymmetrically, further toppling his glasses to the right. "I think what you're noticing is my speech impediment." Dr. Benton continues, amused and seemingly not at all angry, "I'd rather sound like I have an accent than sound like I've had a head injury, which is what one patient thought."

I laugh, grateful to be let off the hook so adeptly.

"The patient very politely asked me if I'd thought about taking a little more time off before coming back to work."

"A more egregious sin than mine, I guess."

"By far. And I can say that officially because I am a professional." Dr. Benton slaps my file shut and leans in. "Okay, I've talked to Dr. Lakhani. I've read the notes. Now you tell me what's going on."

"Well, first off, I don't want to go on any medication that would alter my thinking or perception of anything. Just maybe something for the nausea—"

"Whoa, whoa there. Let's wait to talk about medication. Dr. Lakhani tells me you came here after having a panic episode during a film." Dr. Benton stops for a moment, genuinely curious.

"It was called *Dreams*. Akira Kurosawa."

"No kidding. The *Rashomon* guy, right?"

"Yeah, that's him. *Dreams* is the—"

"Oh, yeah, the one with the kid standing below the rainbow."

"Right. That's the picture on the poster."

"Was there something with white-faced people with pointy ears that whipped their heads around in a freaky—"

"Yeah, that's the foxes. They're mad because this boy saw their wedding ceremony so now the boy has to get their forgiveness or his mom is gonna make him kill himself."

"Wow, that's some tough-love parenting. As a professional, I could recommend some viable alternatives to that mother, maybe no dessert after dinner. Okay, back on track."

I like how Dr. Benton says funny things but doesn't wait for me to laugh. It's a nice change from Bethanie, who would put a klieg light on herself after a joke while she held for applause, if she could.

"Basically I'm terrified because I feel like I can't be certain that I've actually been born again."

"Makes sense."

Dr. Benton is the first person here to tell me what I'm feeling makes sense, something I've longed for but now am not so sure I want to hear. "It makes sense that I'm worried?"

"Completely. God doesn't mail you a conversion certificate. You're talking about an internal change that can't be measured in concrete external terms. Who even knows what 'born again' means? Is it a one-time thing? Something that happens every day? Every second?"

"Right. Exactly. And I'm trying to give it over to God and not worry about it. Bethanie says I should take off my Junior God badge—"

"Ooof, that's an unpleasant phrase."

"I know. Bethanie can be . . ."

"Yes, I know."

I laugh as Dr. Benton's eyes fall to my wrists. "How's the rubber band working?"

"I feel like it just makes things worse. The more I try not to think something, the more I think it. It's like I'm making myself think what I don't want to think. Like I'm forcing myself."

"Makes sense."

"It does?"

"Sure. It's like trying to not think about pink elephants on the wall. The effort to negate creates."

I like this phrase. So I repeat it in my head: *The effort to negate creates.* It makes me think of Push Hands, about not combating force with force, about accepting and redirecting energy.

"You can't do it." Dr. Benton's glasses have slipped down his nose, revealing a raw spot on the bridge. "It's like trying to still water with the palm of your hand." He pushes the frames back up as I look past him to the dust bowl family. Then I look closer. There's something strange about the faces of the children. No, not just the children. The adults too. Something's weird. I peer deeper.

"Are those monkeys?" I ask suddenly.

Dr. Benton looks behind him and grins. "Yeah, aren't they great? Some things only make you laugh the first couple times you see 'em, but these guys get me every time."

"Don't you get in trouble for that?"

"In trouble?"

"Well, I don't know. Everyone else has crosses on their walls and pictures of Jesus. Also, with the whole evolution thing, having monkeys standing up and all . . ."

"Ha, I hadn't thought about that. No, I just have always been a sucker for animals dressing like people. When I was boy, I always put glasses on my dog and scarves on my cat. Managed to get a hat on a duck once. Big ol' mallard sailing down the river with my beat-up Boston Red Sox hat. Worth losing the hat, I'll tell you that."

I ask without really knowing why, maybe just enjoying the ease of the chat, "Are you from Boston?"

"No, I told you, I have a speech impediment." Dr. Benton does not pause for my laugh but continues without a breath, "Now, can I see that rubber band?"

"You want me to take it off?"

"Yeah, hand it over."

I hesitate, feeling like I'm disobeying Bethanie and Dr. Lakhani, and possibly giving up a tool that could save me.

"If you miss it, we'll get you another one. Promise."

I slip the band off and place it in Dr. Benton's outstretched palm.

"I know the perfect place for this." I follow his sightline to a garbage can with a basketball net attached to the top. Dr. Benton pulls the rubber band back over his finger and lets it go. It sails right to the sweet spot on the backboard and banks down through the net, swishing into the trash.

"Sorry, I just always wanted to do that. And the rubber band's not working for you. It's creating a double bind."

"What's a double bind?"

Dr. Benton looks sincerely happy to be able to explain. "Well, when you try not to think about something, that right there is creating the thought. You're in a feedback loop, where point A is sending you back to point B and over and over." Dr. Benton stops and cocks his head, interested in his own side-note. "That's all anxiety is, you know. Feedback. Fear of fear. It self-perpetuates." Then he's back on track. He slaps his hands on the desk. "Okay, I've got a new plan for you."

"Great." I like plans and I like Dr. Benton.

"You go into arguments in your head about whether or not you're forgiven."

"Yes, Dr. Lakhani mentioned the term *scrupulosity*. I guess it was popular in the Middle Ages, but now not so much. I'm old-school, I suppose."

Dr. Benton smiles. "I would say a particular brand of scrupulosity. Something that has been called 'soul weighing,' a questioning of whether grace is sufficient." Dr. Benton cocks his head again. "More of a Protestant problem than a Catholic one. Once Martin Luther came out with salvation coming from grace, there was a lot of soul weighing, including by Martin Luther himself—" He cuts himself off and snaps his head back to center.

"Yes, that's right—I'm weighing my soul, but it's worse than that. Sometimes I make myself say things I know are sinful. Like I know there's one sin God can never pardon and that's blaspheming the Holy Spirit, so sometimes I make myself do it."

I wait to see panic form in Dr. Benton's eyes, but it never arrives. He appears to not be bothered at all by my flagrant admission. "Eh, I think the Holy Spirit can take it. Here, I'll do it too." Dr. Benton looks dramatically up and jabs his finger toward the ceiling. "Hey, Holy Spirit, I think you're . . . the least popular of the Trinity. No one even knows who you are. The Father, Son, and the Who? I forgot."

I laugh, grateful for his silliness, but more for his implication of himself in my sin. Dr. Benton, spurred by my appreciation, continues, "You're lame, Holy Spirit! You're a loser! Why don't you take a long walk off a short pier and . . . drown? Everyone would be better off, and nobody would even notice. There, I said it."

Dr. Benton looks up at the clock on his wall. "Here's what I want you to do: give yourself a half hour a day to go into your arguments, to weigh your soul, and the rest of the time just watch what your mind does, where it goes, what it worries about. When thoughts come up, acknowledge them. They're not going to frighten God, and they don't need to frighten you. Acknowledge the thoughts, then let them go. Save your arguments for that one half hour: any calculations you want to make about your soul, its weight, worth, destiny, you can do it then. Otherwise just watch."

I do not want this session to end. This is what I was hoping for when I first arrived.

"Before you go, let's talk about medication."

"Oh, right, well, I get nauseous sometimes—"

"Explain to me your fear of medication."

"I don't want it to compromise my judgment. I've got to take care of . . ."

"Your soul—" Dr. Benton completes my thought.

"Right, my soul."

"Well, do you know what compromises mental acuity more than any other chemical? More than alcohol or marijuana or almost any prescription drug?"

"What?"

"Cortisol. Cortisol released in the brain from stress or anxiety. Rational thinking is compromised by an excess of cortisol."

"How can I tell I have an excess of cortisol?"

"Well, I can't be sure, but I'm guessing you do, because you're hyperventilating. I've been counting your inhale-exhales per minute and marking it here." Dr. Benton gestures to a pad of paper with a bunch of tiny slashes all over, a smattering of little stars. "You are taking twenty full inhale-exhale cycles within a minute."

"That's not normal?"

"Well, it's normal if a crazed elephant were attacking you, or if you were a shell-shocked claustrophobic vet getting an MRI, something like that . . ." Dr. Benton stops his joking and looks at me kindly. "It's possible anti-anxiety medication could increase rather compromise your clarity of thought."

He reaches over, grabs a prescription pad, and begins scribbling. "No pressure. Do what you want. I'm writing a prescription for BuSpar and Anafranil, which will take a while to kick in, and a low-dose Klonopin, which is a faster-acting kind of thing." He whips off the prescription and hands it to me.

Bethanie is too slow. And he's a little too fast. But I trust this man, with his screwy face, his bulging snail eyes, and his strange speech impediment. He extends the prescription toward me, his arm knifing through my view of the apes' family portrait. I take the paper, fold it, and put it in my pocket.

I leave and go straight to the courtyard to have a cigarette, my thoughts swarming. The light is soft and welcoming, falling through the branches of the tree, speckling the stones with delicate shadows. I think about my time with Dr. Benton and remember a documentary I once saw about a boy incapable of speech, who made sounds, some guttural, some high and airy, but no one understood him. No one except for his mother. When he spoke to her, he would pat her knee over and over, as if he were getting her attention and thanking her at the same time.

The mother explained that it wasn't just simple ideas her son was able to communicate, like "I'm hungry" or "I'm sleepy," but also ones far subtler. She said that he had once told her he often feels like his mind is locked in a room and the more he struggles to get out, the smaller the room gets. He said communicating with his mother felt like flinging open the door and being bathed in light. That is how I feel now, after talking with Dr. Benton. The room my mind dwells in has become more spacious, my language has been understood, and I feel flooded with light.

I look at the prescription in my hand and without ever deciding to, I start walking to the pharmacy in the strip mall next to Sunny and Shears. Images of my grandmother after her shock treatments come unbidden, images of her slumped in her chair, eating the ZERO Bars I brought her at Christmas, her mouth open, displaying the churning of white chocolate and caramel against her gums and lips. To avoid the thoughts, I focus instead on the insistent rhythm of my footsteps, a rhythm more determined and courageous than I feel.

But new images arise. Now I see myself at that same hospital, my pupils floating in the milky white sea of my eyes, untethered, bobbing without focus. I am slumped in a chair like my grandmother's, slack-jawed, absorbed in the task of holding the weight of my head up and balancing it on top of my neck. I have a milkshake in front of me that I try to drink, but I can't manage to aim the hole of my mouth down over the straw, so the straw keeps poking me in the face. A Christian hospital volunteer comes over and tries to tell me about Jesus, but I don't understand.

I know this vision is ludicrous. I know that everyone else at Grace Point is on medication, including Quinn, and that they can all hold their heads up and drink with straws just fine. I know if I start feeling my judgment becoming impaired, then I can just stop taking the medication. But, if my judgment is impaired, I argue, how will I be able to assess whether or not my judgment is impaired? But then again, maybe my judgment is already impaired. Maybe like Dr. Benton said, cortisol is already compromising my perception, maybe even more than the drugs written on the paper in my hand will.

• • •

I walk back from the drugstore with a small plastic bag full of pills, Jack returning home with his magic beans. I don't really know what these magic beans will do, what roots will take hold inside, what stalks they'll sprout, leading to what visions or what giants.

Each night I give myself a half hour to fully go into all the arguments in my head. The first night, sitting on my bed, my pink blanket on my lap like an agreeable pet, at exactly nine P.M., I start off with: *If God loves everyone, why doesn't He save everyone?* Then I think, *Well, maybe He can't. Maybe God is doing the best He can, but because of people's free will, His best isn't all that successful.*

I think of my chemistry teacher Mr. Pershatte, Fat Pershatte, who prided himself in failing over 80 percent of his students. Chemistry was difficult, of course, but Fat Pershatte's aggressively boring teaching manner made it even more tedious, his voice alternating between two flat sour notes, his watery fish eyes seeming to suffocate whatever life there was beneath the surface, his overall manner suggestive of his having drunk too much Robitussin. Fat Pershatte blamed the students' high failure rate on the siren appeal of athletics, specifically on the charismatic gym teacher Mr. Crow, who inspired students to "shot-put their lives away on sports." Was God like Mr. Pershatte: ineffectual, helpless, hapless, failing to win souls from the more captivating Satan, i.e. Mr. Crow? I look up at the clock and suddenly it's 9:32. When I try to cut off the thoughts, a part of me screams, a baby furious at being weaned.

The next night, again at nine o'clock, I think about what I've been postponing all day. How can God ask us to forgive our brothers seven times seventy-seven times like it says in Matthew 18:24, but fall short of his own requirement? How can God be more petty, less generous, than what He expects of man? How can God not meet His own benchmark? Again the time leaks away. And again I don't want to let my ruminations go; they could lead to resolution. I want to rigorously challenge my eternal standing, probe its possible weaknesses until I can finally prove, once and for all, that it is solid.

But I try not to. Outside of that half hour, I try not to go into the arguments. I try to watch my thoughts. I find that my anxiety spikes initially when I delay rumination, that there's a relief in dedicating a discrete portion of the day to actively considering my fate and refraining the rest of the time. I still feel like there's a cage match going on in my head, but at least now the combatants sometimes get a time-out and can retreat into their corners for a breather before heading back into the fray.

I don't notice any effects from the medication for about a week, but then one day before lunch, I feel a fluttering in my stomach. My mind wanders to Papapolis's Perpetual Pies, thin-crust pizza with nuggets of sausage nestled in never-ending mozzarella and feta cheese. Then I start thinking about the sweet-and-sour chicken my family used to get at Kim's Chop Suey, and how we used to ask for the sweet-and-sour sauce on the side, so the chicken would stay crispy and we could pour the sauce on right before we ate it. The weird quivering in my stomach continues for another minute before I finally solve the mystery of what is going on with me . . . *I am hungry.* That is exactly what is happening. I remember this feeling. I am hungry! This is a sign of health, of some sort of resurrection. This is good.

Plus, today is Friday. On Fridays, the gang goes out to lunch. Past excursions have included Burger King, Hardee's, Long John Silver's, and Ponderosa. At each of these outings, I haven't had an appetite, but today I am famished, and today our destination is McDonald's.

When we walk under the golden arches, I inhale deeply, the scent of salty meat and greasy bread piquing my already-raging appetite. For years I took for granted the glory of McDonald's, but now as I stand in front of the golden menu, my chin raised, my eyes scrolling through the panoply of options, I think how blessed I am. Hamburger. Cheeseburger. Big Mac. Chicken McNuggets. Chicken sandwiches. Fish sandwiches. Fries. Of all sizes. I can have anything I want. Surely goodness and mercy shall follow me all the days of my life.

I walk up to the cashier. "I'd like an order of Chicken McNuggets."

The cashier, wearing a nametag that reads, *McDonald's Mandy*, asks flatly, "Six-piece, nine-piece, or twelve-piece?"

"Twelve-piece."

I half expect McDonald's Mandy to be shocked by the audacity of my order. After all, I haven't been able to eat for weeks, and now I've just ordered the largest option.

Mandy is unfazed. "Sauces?"

"Sauces?" I parrot back awkwardly, still gazing up at the menu, unable to pry my attention from the lavish spread of options.

"Barbecue, honey mustard, or sweet-and-sour?"

"Oh, they all sound good . . ."

"I can give you one of each."

"Thank you. I'd really like that," I say with complete sincerity.

"Anything else?"

"I'd like an order of fries."

"What size?"

"Large?"

"You mean jumbo?"

"Yes, jumbo."

"Anything else?"

"Yes, uh . . . a jumbo Coke."

"There's no jumbo Coke. You mean large?"

"Yes. Large."

"Is that it?"

"Yes, that's it."

In a miraculously short amount of time, in a veritable twinkling of an eye, Mandy hands me my sack. It is warm and heavy. I take my sack back to the table where the gang is sitting, then reverently spread its bounty before me. I open and place the three different sauces in front of the nuggets; I squeeze the ketchup into a little puddle in front of the fries. And then in a world of my own, the sounds of everyone else eating around me blurring together, my vision narrows to the feast before me and I begin.

I eat like every prostitute in every romantic comedy, from *Pretty Woman* to *Mighty Aphrodite* to *Taxi Driver*—the peculiarly famished sex worker who orders pancakes with butter and some extra pancakes. I scarf down my food like it's my first meal post–hunger strike, sending crumbs flying and grease slinging. I dip the nuggets, making sure to hit all of the sauces, evenly spreading my attention like I used to do with my stuffed animals. Barbecue. Honey mustard. Sweet-and-sour. Just like I did with Booboo, Dragon, and NingNong. I take out two fries at a time and plunge them twice each in the ketchup. Then I shake up the pattern and begin dipping the fries in the three different sauces, and treating the nuggets to the ketchup. I pull out one exceptional fry from the pack, a fry that is taller, meatier, and sturdier than the others, the NBA star of fries. I eat the NBA fry, naked, no sauce. It is pure warm salty grease, and it is a miracle.

I think of a Bible verse as I continue the assault on my rapidly diminishing food: *The lions may grow weak and hungry, but those who seek the Lord hunger for no good thing.* I laugh as I think of the Psalmist illuminated by golden arches, scribbling on parchment smudged with barbecue sauce, then I go back up to McDonald's Mandy and order another six-piece. While I'm there, I ask for a cherry pie. Again, Mandy's speed in materializing my order is astounding. When I return to our table, I impatiently rip the bag open and bite into the sweet heat of the cherry pie. I dip the nuggets into the cherry lava goo without care for fast-food protocol and can't remember when life felt so sweet. *Those who seek the Lord hunger for no good thing.*

I look up for a moment, finally sated, to see Quinn laughing.

"This is so good," is all I can say. "I never knew McDonald's was so good."

"Well, two billion served. Sometimes the masses are right."

I look down at the dregs of my meal, fries fossilizing, sauces congealing in their plastic rooms, and the last bite of cherry pie hardening into stone. I pop the cherry pie in my mouth before it's too late.

CHAPTER SIXTEEN: **GIRLS' NIGHT**

WHEN I WALK INTO BETHANIE'S office, she immediately notices my naked wrists and asks sharply, "Where is your rubber band?"

"Dr. Benton suggested I not wear it."

"Why would he suggest that? I don't understand. Did he talk to Dr. Lakhani?"

"I don't know—"

"I don't understand why Frank would—" Bethanie slaps her hand over her mouth, as if she's just let out a national secret and jeopardized worldwide security by exposing Dr. Benton's first name, a name readily available on all promotional material. "Please forget I said that. I don't understand why *Dr. Benton* would do this."

"He said it was creating a double bind."

Bethanie is unable to hide the agitation in her voice. "I don't know what a double bind is. I've never heard of anything like that."

"I think it's where trying not to do something causes you to do that very—"

Bethanie snorts air out her nose, impatient. "You don't know whether he talked to Dr. Lakhani or not?"

"No, no idea."

"Using a rubber band to treat patients presenting obsessive thoughts is standard practice. It's . . . it's textbook!"

Exactly, I think. *And I am a live person standing in front of you.*

Saturday night, I go with Quinn to her new apartment, a small, simple space with a balcony that overlooks the street. It smells warm and clean, like biscuits and laundry detergent. Quinn drops her keys on the counter, then walks directly to the kitchen cabinet and pulls out a bottle of red wine and two glasses. "Join me?"

"Oh, no, I . . . can't," I immediately reply as I longingly watch her fill the first glass. "I'd love to, but I think it might be a sin."

Quinn takes a sip that quickly turns into a gulp. "Why? Jesus drank wine."

I watch her indulgence, envious. "Yeah, but the Bible says not to get drunk to intoxication, and drinking any alcohol at all will lead to some level of intoxication. Plus I'm not twenty-one. So it's illegal."

Quinn studies me, sympathetic, her lips turning downward into a warm, kind frown. "I bet it's rough being in your head sometimes." Her eyes rest on me gently, familiar, like she's known me since I was child. I fight the impulse to run over to her like a little girl who's been hurt on a playground, but I'm no longer little, my hurt is unseen, and I've only known this woman for two months.

"I really don't think God would mind if you had a glass of wine. You're dealing with so much for your age. I doubt God's the stickler you think He is."

I look at the empty glass beside Quinn's full one. "You think?"

"Yes, I think." Quinn fills the second glass without hesitation and hands it to me. I take a sip, holding the wine in my mouth for several moments before swallowing.

"C'mon, let's go out on the balcony. We can have a smoke."

I follow Quinn out to the small slab of cement and we sit on a pair of tattered lawn chairs, the bottle of wine balanced between us on a three-legged table. The outside lamp is broken so the only light comes from the moon, a full globe suspended in the star-filled night. A car sails across the street in front of us every minute or so. Sometimes there's a truck. Quinn and I sit in silence, drinking our wine, smoking our cigarettes, our eyes following the arrival of headlights and the departure of taillights, and then the space in between.

Quinn puts out her cigarette, lights another, and asks as she exhales, "What is Cooper like?"

I had talked about Cooper in group therapy, about the unequal yoke, but only briefly. I am surprised Quinn remembers his name.

"Thanks for asking. That's nice." I say sincerely. Then I curl up my legs and fold them underneath me. "I would say he's like me, but male. But I know everyone says that when they're in love; everyone talks about the feeling that they've found their other half, the one they've been separated from like a twin, since birth." Smiling, I add, "That and he's got a really big jaw. He can stick his fist in his mouth."

Quinn laughs. "Impressive." We watch as two trucks come in and out of view.

"Do you think," Quinn asks without looking over at me, "that you want to have kids?"

I shake my head. "No, I don't think I could do it. I'd be too scared they wouldn't accept Jesus."

Quinn frowns again, that same frown that warms me; it's comforting, like the soft smell of her apartment. Then she looks up at the sky, at the clouds, which seem to be suspended lower than normal, forming a canopy above us.

"I can't have kids because of damage from the abuse," she says as she dabs the corner of her right eye on her shoulder and continues with just a hint of a waver in her voice, "from my father. There's damage. That's a big part of my depression."

I say what I'm thinking: "Oh, but you sure would be such a great mother." And I immediately know it was the wrong thing to say.

"Yeah, I think I would be," Quinn says simply, "I really do."

The road is empty for a while. We sit and watch the moonlit stretch of cement. I've seen people sit on their front porches in my parents' hometown in North Carolina, rocking back and forth on creaking chairs for hours and hours, watching nothing go by. I never understood how they weren't desperately bored. But as I sit here with Quinn, I begin to understand.

There is a long silence before Quinn says, "A boy or a girl. I think about it a lot," and then she refills our glasses. I do not object. When both glasses are full, she continues easily, "I was at a wedding with Jack last fall and I saw this woman on the dance floor. When the song ended, she looked back to her table. And there were her two kids, one boy and one girl. Both wore glasses—the girl's were pink and wiry; the boy's were thick like Buddy Holly's. The woman squatted down right in the middle of the dance floor, spreading out her arms. She was wearing a shawl that she held on to with her hands, so when she stretched out her arms, it looked like she had wings. Big angel wings. The kids ran up to her and she swooped the shawl around them and all you could see of them was four little feet."

Quinn lets a pause settle in the night.

Several moments trickle by. Then I ask, "Have you thought about adopting?"

"We can't. With my history of depression, no agency will take me." Quinn abruptly sits up in her chair and claps her hands together, clearly signaling her desire for a change in topic. "Are you and Cooper broken up?"

I pour the first bit of the second glass of wine down my throat. "Sort of. We kind of put everything on hold. We stopped having sex because I knew that was wrong. And I'm still trying to figure out this unequal-yoke thing. I don't want to risk going to hell."

Quinn turns and looks directly at me, at once fierce and gentle. "Maggie, I promise you, God is not like that. You're a Christian, and nothing you can do will change that. Who you marry has nothing to do with it."

"But some people think you can lose your salvation."

Quinn's eyes turn flinty, her jaw set. "I am not one of those people. God makes a covenant with his children, not a contract. I heard that in a sermon once and I believe it."

"What's the difference?"

"A covenant is a promise that doesn't require any action on the part of the recipient. A contract involves an obligation."

Another car passes.

We hear a siren in the distance. Quinn's eyes widen almost imperceptibly with concern. I can't help but picture her as a mother.

"Have you tried . . . other methods? You know, to get pregnant? Like in vitro or anything like that?"

The moonlight sifts over Quinn's face, highlighting the weariness of her features, as she replies, "I guess I . . . I just don't think it's right."

"Not right? What do you mean?"

"If God wanted me to be pregnant, I think I'd be pregnant."

"Yeah, but couldn't it be like that old joke, the one where the guy is trapped on a cliff and a bunch of different people try to help him, but he refuses help because he's waiting for God? Couldn't in vitro be a way God helps?"

"I'd sure like to believe that."

"Maybe you can. Is there anyone you trust that you could talk to about this?"

"You know, maybe I could . . . maybe I should write . . . Oral Roberts."

Oral Roberts is not what I expect to hear. *Oral Roberts* makes me think of sex and scandal and syrupy thick Southern snake oil.

"Oral Roberts?" I ask, attempting to strip my voice of judgment.

"Yeah, Jack went to Oral Roberts University. And he says Pastor Roberts answers every piece of mail he receives. He tells his congregation to ask him anything." Quinn's eyes glisten even in the dark of the night. "Do you think I should write him?"

I feel like there must be someone better to ask than Oral Roberts, but . . . then again, maybe not. I don't know. "Sure," I say, "you could ask several people. Maybe start with Oral Roberts."

Quinn rushes inside and retrieves a pad of paper and a pen with an enthusiasm that reminds me of when I first got my rubber band. Together we compose a letter to Oral Roberts, explaining Quinn's situation, all the circumstances, and asking for Roberts's Biblical learned perspective on the ethics of in vitro. Quinn puts the letter in an envelope, hopeful, and licks from end to end.

We watch the waves of traffic for a while until Quinn says, "When Jack told my nephew Roland that he went to Oral Roberts, Roland asked, 'When did you decide you wanted to be a dentist?'" Quinn laughs, unabashedly proud of her nephew's peculiarity. "He's a funny kid. Such a funny kid." Then with a wine-infused voice, she adds, "I think I'd want a boy. No, a girl. I don't know. It's so hard to decide. Especially if you haven't been given a choice."

I sleep on the pullout bed on Quinn's couch. I feel the springs through the thin mattress, corkscrewing into my back, but still, I sleep easily under the low-hanging clouds.

Once a week, Sed leads the "God, Help Me Stop" group. It follows a more-Christian version of the Twelve Steps, a version where the Higher Power is narrowed down to a Christian God and all other conceptions are dismissed. Well, more than dismissed. Sed tells us explicitly, "If your Higher Power is not a Christian God, the steps will do no good." Timbo loves "God, Help Me Stop" group, prides himself on being the recovery expert, delights in being the only one in our gang to have completed the twelve steps. He barrels through the initial Serenity Prayer louder and faster than anyone else, reliably finishing first, spurting out the concluding phrase, "wisdom to know the difference," as the rest of us trail amateurishly behind. Then Timbo waits with patience, his race run, but happy to cheer on his competitors.

After the Serenity Prayer, Sed launches into his prepared lesson. "There are many kinds of compulsions. Drugs and alcohol are just one example. But there are others, including compulsive thoughts." Sed pins his focus on the twins, who look especially squirrelly today, their eyes darting around all over the place but landing nowhere. Then I notice that each boy is balancing an upturned baseball cap in his lap, each squeezing its brim far harder than necessary to hold it in place.

"Ron and Jon are going to do an exercise today. With the group here for support." Ron and Jon look up at Sed, helpless, as if he's about to throw them into a deep pool before they've learned to swim. "Ron and Jon struggle with compulsive thoughts. Ron and Jon's individual therapist wants them to share some of the thoughts they're trying to give over to God with the group. So they've . . ." Sed stops himself. "Well, why don't you guys tell us what you've got cooked up?"

Jon looks up, desperately, at Ron. Ron, clearly uneasy in his role of the strong one in a weak pair, tightens his grip on the brim of his baseball cap before reluctantly answering, "We've written down thoughts we have about our mother that we're trying to give over to God on pieces of paper, and we've put them in a hat. And now we're going to pick ones out at random and read them."

"And why are you doing this?" Sed focuses his eyes on Jon.

Ron nudges Jon with his shoulder until Jon answers, "We are doing this because when you say something out loud, you can let it go."

Sed nods. "Great. All right, who wants to go first?"

I imagine the two boys walking a plank, being pushed to the edge by a force they don't dare resist or even turn around to see. Ron takes a big breath and holds the air in as he squeaks out, "I will. I'll go first." Then he reaches into his hat and pulls out a scrunched-up little piece of paper.

Ron flattens the paper and reads, his voice vibrating with courage, "Okay, um, this one . . . is having intercourse with my mother in an oral manner. She's bent over the . . . in the kitchen . . . there's an island, where she's bent over, exposing herself from behind . . . and I'm squatting down . . . That's it." Ron's face turns painfully red. He looks as if he'd be hot to the touch.

"Okay, good. I know that was difficult. Jon?"

Jon plunges a hand into his cap as if expecting to be bit by something poisonous and quickly removes a balled-up piece of paper, his face reddening just as Ron's flush begins to fade. He unballs the piece of paper and reads, "Mom peeing on the sidewalk."

I feel a laugh kick in my chest. I try to breathe through it, knowing how absolutely horrible it would be to laugh at this moment, how destructive and deeply unkind. But then I picture a middle-aged woman squatting on a suburban sidewalk, next to where kids are playing hopscotch, holding up her skirt, her urine darkening the cement around her. I tell myself, *Breathe. This isn't funny.* But I can't stop it. The transgressive laugh rumbles up through me, and the only thing I can do is turn it into a cough, a loud hack. Sed, along with the rest of the group, turns and looks at me, but thankfully, in a moment of grace, no one seems to suspect my secret insensitivity. I cough again, cementing my cover, narrowly escaping judgment.

Ron and Jon go back and forth uncrinkling little pieces of paper and reading their illicit contents out loud, exposing thoughts they've been stashing for years: thoughts of their mother scrubbing the floor topless, her breasts pendulous and soapy; of their mother emerging from a cake, frosted; of her dancing with two men in tuxedos, naked in red platform heels. After this last share, Sed asks Ron, "Is one of those dancing men your father?" Ron adamantly shakes his head and barely gets out, "No," before Jon quickly adds, "No, there's no father."

"Okay, well then," Sed probes, "who are the men dancing with your mother?"

"They're friends," Jon snaps out. "They're just friends."

His mother's lack of clothing, I think, seems to indicate her dance partners might be more than platonic. Sed is also suspicious. "Friends?"

Jon panics. Air spits in and out of his lungs like a frantic bellows, until he finally heaves out, "Yeah, my mom has a lot of friends. Sometimes they're men. And sometimes they help her out. They give her money. There's nothing wrong with that."

Whoa. It seems like Jon is building up to have an *Ordinary People* moment. I expect him to recall, in fits and spurts, walking in on his mother *in flagrante* with one of the male friends who gives her money. But Ron places his hand on his brother's shoulder, Jon's breathing slows down with the added weight, and Sed backs off.

"No, there's not. There's certainly not."

Jon concludes his defense of the honor of a woman he can't help defiling in his head with "Our mom is nice lady."

I wonder if the boys' obsessions about their mother are fueled by their desire to give them up. I wonder if asking God to take away their thoughts is like trying to not think about pink elephants on the wall. I wonder if Ron and Jon should allow their thoughts and watch them like Dr. Benton told me to do, like Quinn and I watched the traffic. Or maybe Dr. Benton is wrong. Maybe I should be asking God to take away my thoughts, like the twins. Maybe I shouldn't have given up my rubber band.

I resolve to simply watch for now, as instructed, as the fears appear and disappear, coming and going like the headlights and taillights on the street in front of Quinn's apartment. But there's a part that forces me to think about my worst fears despite my best efforts. When I try to sweep my mind clean, I purposely dirty it up. It's not just that pink elephants pop up; it's that I goad myself into creating the elephants, lifting them up, deliberately cluttering the walls of my mind.

The following week I meet with Dr. Benton again. I tell him about the feast, about the chicken nuggets and the fries and the ketchup and the sauces, about the lava-hot cherry pies, and how my tongue is still partly numb, but I don't mind. I tell him I'd forgotten how good food is. I report that I've been trying to "watch the show," like watching traffic on an open road, but that sometimes I can't do it, and sometimes I foil my own plans. It infuriates me, I say, that "I" make "myself" disrupt the show, that I'm the one unsettling my own peace.

Dr. Benton's eyes alight, not so much with sympathy but with interest, a quality I find I much prefer in a listener. "I've always been fascinated by what people mean when they use the word *I.*" He presses his finger on the bridge of his glasses and slides them back up his nose, aggravating the raw spot. "I think it might be helpful for you to think of 'I' as just another thought."

"What do you mean?"

"It might be helpful to think of the whole construction of 'I.' 'I' do this. 'I' think that. To think of the 'I' as just part of the show. Not the originator of the show, but a product of it. A thought among other thoughts."

"But 'I'm' not just a thought."

"Your body, your organism is not just a thought. But maybe what you perceive as the controlling principle of your organism is. When most people say 'I,' it seems like they're talking about the sensation of a solid nugget of consciousness somewhere halfway between their ears, behind their eyes . . . some little guy in the cockpit of the cranium steering their body's way through the world."

"Well, not necessarily located there, but *someone's* clearly choosing to think about things."

"Or maybe's there's choice, without anyone who decides. Maybe the 'decider' is just a thought."

Dr. Benton looks like he's having fun, as if uncertainty, something outside his grasp, gives him some sort of buzz. "My favorite phrase, which is also my bumper sticker, is 'Don't believe everything you think.'"

"But there's got to be an 'I.' That's the soul, right? I mean, all of Christianity is based on having a soul." I look past him to the portrait of the monkeys, with their buttoned-up collars and fitted coats and skirts, hairy but sophisticated. "Otherwise, we'd just be like animals or robots, just the product of our programming. I mean, we've got free will, right?"

"I don't know. Maybe. I guess it depends on the definition of *free will*. Maybe it's not that simple."

I am so happy to hear him say this that, completely out of context, I bust out with, "I told Bethanie that I read this article about how all serial killers have experienced one of three childhood traumas, they were either abused, abandoned, or dropped on their heads. I told her it seems ridiculous to feel superior to a serial killer really, because none of those three things happened to me."

Dr. Benton asks, with a hint of delight, "How'd that go over?"

"Not very well. Not very well at all. She said I was calling her a . . ."

Dr. Benton says "robot" at the exact same time I do.

"I guess *robot* is worse than *monkey*." I look at the simian matriarch in the portrait behind Dr. Benton, one of her four fingers extended as if she were holding a teacup, elegant and aware, and continue, "But if we were just a product of our genetics and our environment just like animals, if there was no separate nugget of a soul, wouldn't it be unfair for God to judge us? You can't send a monkey or a robot to hell."

Dr. Benton interlaces his fingers and flexes them out toward me. "I'd like to talk about the word *literally*."

I know where Dr. Benton is going and I want to answer what I'm sure will be his first points so we can continue. "I know hell might not be *literally* fire, literally burning, literally a bunch of singed souls, but it would still represent everlasting suffering. I'm not particularly scared of burning as a form of punishment. It's the *unrelenting* part. The 'Depart from me. I do not know you' part. The 'too late' part."

Dr. Benton fiddles with his glasses before finally taking them off, seemingly annoyed with the barrier they present. "What if everlasting abandonment was itself a symbol? Maybe a symbol of present-tense disconnection. What if heaven and hell were *here*? Like what you're feeling now? What if that were hell?" Dr. Benton replaces his glasses on the well-worn bridge of nose.

"You mean, nothing happens when we die?"

"I'm not saying that. I'm just asking the question. What if *hell* were a description, an evocation of the feeling of doubting God's grace? Maybe you're scared of what is already happening. Maybe hell is trying to not think of pink elephants on the wall and having them stampede you."

"But if there's no afterlife—"

"I didn't say there's no afterlife. Let's back up. I'm just talking about different ways that symbols can work."

"Okay, but if heaven and hell were here, then what would the meaning of life be?"

"I don't know. What's the meaning of a symphony? Does something need to go on and on to have value? Is a symphony's goal to arrive at the overture?"

"But there's the story," I object, "about Lazarus and the Rich Man, and the Rich Man asks for Lazarus to touch the tip of his tongue with the healing waters of heaven. And Lazarus refuses. God refuses. They turn their backs on the Rich Man, denying him even the slightest bit of relief."

"That's an interesting parable. And remember, parables themselves are symbolic stories. Notice that the Rich Man asks Lazarus to fetch him water to ease the burning of his tongue. Why do you think he'd do this?"

"Because he's really thirsty and is hoping someone will be nice to him."

"But," Dr. Benton cautions, "notice the use of *fetch*. The Rich Man is still thinking of Lazarus as his servant; he's asking Lazarus to fetch something. He's still suffering under the delusion that he is master, a very painful delusion, an isolating delusion that might feel like burning. Present tense."

The idea that heaven and hell could be here and now, well, that would be wonderful, but it's an extremely risky idea. Dr. Elkins is asking me to relax my guard, to weaken my vigilance, but I will not abandon my post until I've tested it and am sure the danger is passed.

"Yes," I argue, "but God clearly says, *Depart from me. I do not know you.*"

"Maybe that's a symbol too."

"But there's got to be justice, right? *Our God is a God of justice,* right?"

"Maybe justice is just a servant of love. Not an equal. Maybe love wins in the end. Maybe the Rich Man is invited into the kingdom when he's ready, and maybe even Satan eventually. I know that's a pretty radical idea. But Jesus is a pretty radical guy, ready to go past justice and proceed to love."

I have not cried since I've been here. My eyes are parched like the Rich Man's mouth, spidery, thirsty red veins popping up from dehydrated corneas. But now my tears flow freely, big fat slick tears, wet and oily. *Could the Rich Man really be welcomed into the kingdom? Could God not be cruel in the end? Could I have gotten it wrong?* I enjoy blinking through the flow, my eyelids windshield wipers happy to be able to do their job. I remember crying like this years ago into my oatmeal when Georgeanne suggested God might be bigger than I thought.

Seemingly more comfortable with messy thoughts than messy emotions, Dr. Benton suddenly realizes the time without looking at a watch or a clock, and he pops up to his feet. "Well, I could talk about this forever. But our time's up." While he's standing there, I notice it's not just Dr. Benton's face that is lopsided. His right shoulder also dives far below his left, sending his whole body listing, off-center but still somehow maintaining balance. It's a look that suits him.

After my session, I again walk straight to the courtyard to have a cigarette. It's almost dusk so the sun is surrendering and the light is easy. I sit on that same bench, beneath the same tree, with its constant branches and steady shade. A familiar place in an unfamiliar world. The journey of the smoke through my lungs, inhale and exhale, becomes as rhythmic as the breeze, and my shoulders fall a little bit away from my ears.

Then I hear the clang of the door, and there's Quinn.

"You wanna stay with me tonight? I got another bottle of wine."

"Yes," I say, pleased.

We walk together in the darkness past quiet houses, our cigarettes lighting the way.

CHAPTER SEVENTEEN: MORNING HAS BROKEN

I STAY WITH QUINN SEVERAL nights in a row and grow increasingly accustomed to the pullout bed, the goose-feather pillow, and the sun from the balcony window waking me up in the morning with its dependable streaks.

After we take turns in the shower, Quinn and I walk to breakfast before we are fully awake, sluggish, resistant to the coming day, but not alone. My nausea has decreased. My appetite is back. In the cafeteria after every meal, including breakfast, I have soft-serve ice cream, and lots of it. It reminds me of the snow cream my parents used to make for my sister and me with sugar, vanilla extract, milk, and large pans of freshly fallen snow.

I am able to add some distance, some bit of air between my thoughts. I don't know if this is a result of the medication or because I've given up the rubber band in favor of allowing the thoughts to arise, but I feel some space, some expansiveness. I get better at watching, as Dr. Benton has instructed, the formation and dissolution of the thoughts. I get better at watching the "thinker" too. I begin to observe the mechanism of obsession, the phenomenon of a feedback loop within my own head.

When I meet with Dr. Benton again, I tell him I feel more hopeful than I've felt in a while and that I've been eating a lot of ice cream. Dr. Benton smiles and asks me if I'm experiencing any side effects, besides the boon of renewed appetite from the medicine. I tell him that my mouth has been dry.

"You know what will help with that?"

"What?"

"Water."

I smile at his small joke. "Thanks."

"Always glad when my medical expertise can help. Anything else?"

"I notice my hands are shaking a little."

"I suspect that will go away in the next week or so. What else?"

"That's it, really."

"Good. Okay, so I want to ask you something." He scoots his chair toward me. "What do you like about being a Christian?"

"What do I like about it?"

"What are the good parts?"

"I'm not sure I know what you mean."

"Well, for example, here's what I like. I like that our leader was embodied on earth not as a king, but as a carpenter born in a manger, who washed people's feet. *Washed people's feet*. The radical nature of that? Can you imagine? God washing man's feet."

I try to think of what I like about being a Christian, what I would miss if I didn't have faith. It's a tough one. All I can think is that faith is the smart move, as Pascal would say, the best bet. "I feel like being Christian makes your life more difficult on earth, but it's worth it in the end."

"What about what it's worth now?"

Even tougher.

"I guess . . . I don't know, I guess I like having someone bigger than me in charge."

"Do you *really* like that?"

"Well, I certainly don't like someone being in charge of my eternal fate if that fate turns out badly for me. But I like that there's some guiding principle or reason."

"Why do you like there to be a guiding principle or reason?"

"I guess because I feel like there should be a reason."

"Because 'there should be' . . . uh-huh." Dr. Benton is clearly looking for something else. "Okay, can you maybe think of a time you were in church or a time you were praying, or even when you were thinking about God, that was good? Not because you felt it *should* be good, but just because it, in fact, seemed good."

I try to think: *something good.* What's good? There must be something good. Then I remember. "I went to an Easter sunrise service with my dad once," I tell Dr. Benton. "It was just the two of us."

My dad had heard about this annual outdoor gathering about an hour from our house, so we drove together in the dark to an out-of-the-way thicket where stone slabs were laid out on a hill to form a small amphitheater. I wore a new canary yellow dress that came with a matching jacket stuffed with two enormous shoulder pads and pantyhose, the kind that came out of the egg, smooth and silky and adult. I looked like a football player applying for a receptionist position, but I could not have been more pleased with my outfit. Or the alone time with my father.

There were fifty of us seated on the cold stone steps, but it was so dark we could barely see each other. We listened to a pastor talk about new beginnings, about daily resurrections of hope, and then when the orange glow of the sun started to peek over the horizon, we all sang "Morning Has Broken."

"Do you know it?" I ask, and I start to sing with no skill whatsoever: "*Morning has broken . . .*"

Dr. Benton joins in, even more off-key and rhythm-less than me, "*Like the first morning. Blackbird has spoken—*"

"*—like the first bird,*" our voices clash together.

"Yeah, that's the one. I remember feeling close to my dad and to everyone there that morning even though I'd never met them and knew I'd never see them again."

I realize the story I've been telling doesn't exactly answer Dr. Benton's question, but it's all I can think of and he doesn't seem to mind. "Interesting. I've wondered this before. And now I'm wondering it again. Maybe true connection with God can be defined as whatever inspires kindness, whatever makes your heart big. Maybe whatever softens our edges, brings us peace or health, maybe it's wise to keep going that way."

I want to say something but come up completely dry. Dr. Benton continues, not bothered by my lack of reply, fueled by his own interest. "If we didn't have the Bible, what would you think God was like?"

"I don't know . . ."

"'I don't know' is a great place to be. I would never discourage anyone from dwelling in that state. But for now, just, guess. What if the Bible didn't exist?"

"I guess I would think . . . well, that God is what is in best in us, the part that's decent and kind and generous, maybe like that verse about love from 1 Corinthians that they always read at weddings . . . that love is patient, love is kind, love keeps no record of wrongs."

"Makes sense."

"But we have the Bible, so why would it matter what I think? I mean the Bible says God *does* keep a record of wrongs. He has the Book of Life that He'll consult on Judgment Day, so clearly He does keep a very thorough record of wrongs. Shouldn't I trust the Bible before whatever instincts I might have?"

"I don't know," Dr. Benton shrugs. "Maybe the Bible is a guide to help us follow instincts we already have. Maybe we need to stand in our own, I like to call it, idiosyncratic authority. Maybe everything else is just mimicry."

I am silent as I try to puzzle out exactly what this could mean, but Dr. Benton barrels ahead. "I have a theory. It's just a theory, but I've wondered if it's even possible to change our own innate perception of God. Maybe our job is simply to be true to the God we already believe in, the God we sense before thoughts even come into our heads. Maybe we are given a spark, a perception of divinity, before language, before dogma, and all we can do is act according to that perception."

Dr. Benton becomes increasingly excited as he tries to grasp what seems even to him to be a slippery thought. "I'm not sure you can yank yourself, contort yourself, to believe something you don't, and if you could, whether that would even be beneficial. It might just make you really uncomfortable." I wonder if I am trying to contort myself as Dr. Benton continues, "The earliest Christians, before there was any sort of official New Testament, would sit together in meditation and allow their deepest selves to teach them about God. One of these mystics said, 'Be still and listen to God. Then listen also to the silence.'" I enjoy the paradox of this statement. Just like when Quinn said "It's hard to make a decision when you haven't been given a choice." Dr. Benton clears his throat and cuts through the silence: "Well, enough of my theories for the day. Thanks. I like talking about this stuff, and I don't often get the opportunity."

Bethanie begins group therapy on a mission, mercilessly lasering her attention on Quinn. "Quinn, your therapist tells me you've written a letter that she would like you to read to the group."

Quinn nods obediently, then shuffles through the papers in her folder. When she locates the letter, she lays it on top of her notebook, running her thumb back and forth over the crease in the middle. Then she looks up with a meekness I haven't seen before, a meekness of a much-younger, less-secure woman than the one I'd spent time with on the balcony.

"Should I just read it?"

"Yes, but first, why don't you explain to the group what you'll be reading? Give them some context."

"Well, as I've talked about before, I was a victim of abuse, sexual abuse. My father. His name . . . well, it doesn't matter what his name is." Quinn picks up the letter, bends it backward at the crease, and then flattens it again, her thumb returning to its repetitive task. "So my individual therapist thought it would be a good idea for me to write a letter to my father. Not to send it; just to express myself and my feelings about the abuse."

Bethanie's eyes widen and she claps her hands together as if she's the head cheerleader in charge of our sad pep rally. "Sounds great. Whenever you're ready, we're ready to hear."

Quinn lets her lips part, then mashes them together before beginning. "Okay, so . . . *Dear Dad.*" She tries to clear her throat, but it's dry, so only a futile wheezing escapes. "*Dear Dad,*" she presses on, "*It was a long time ago and I know you think I've probably forgotten. But I haven't. 'Our little secret,' you called it. Just between us. I want you to know I hurt for the little girl that I was who had to keep such a secret. I hurt for the adult woman I now am who remembers. How could you expect me to forget? How could you violate my trust so deeply? How could you be such a fucking monster—*"

Bethanie throws up her arms, like a referee declaring a foul: "Whoa, whoa! I don't think that sort of language is appropriate for the group."

Quinn instantly drops her head before quickly apologizing, "You're right. I'm sorry."

Bethanie settles herself. "It's okay. But this time, let's try it without the salty language." *Salty language?* Like Quinn is some swarthy sailor cursing in front of delicate ladies, instead of a victim expressing the trauma of molestation to her attacker, her father, in a letter he will never read, a letter for own recovery.

"Okay," Quinn looks meekly up at Bethanie, "so I'll just start from . . . okay, here . . . *How could you be such a . . .*" She falters. "I'll just say, *such a . . . jerk?*"

"That sounds fine."

Before I even decide to say something, I hear myself hurling out words at Bethanie. "I really don't think that's fair."

Bethanie's eyes narrow, her resentment coming to a point, her anger focusing into a solid, single, challenging beam. "Excuse me?"

I know I wouldn't be able to stand up for myself against Bethanie, but in defending Quinn, I am surprised to hear my own voice, strong and flinty. "It seems like the main concern here should be Quinn's recovery. Maybe she needs those 'salty' words to describe the extent of her pain. Maybe those 'salty' words are the only words that will work."

Bethanie's body quivers. "You mean, profanity? I don't believe people need to fall into the gutter to express themselves. The gutter is . . . is . . . *very dirty.*"

I want Dr. Benton to be here so he can reprimand Bethanie; I want somebody to step in and question her use of the word *dirty* and the metaphor of *gutter*, but there's nobody. Bethanie's in charge, and I am a patient. I walk out on a ledge of objection, unsure of my footing, but nonetheless manage to press, "Are you sure? Maybe language from the gutter is an appropriate response to behavior that is far below the level of gutter."

I'm impressed with my words as they echo back to me, and I wonder if like Dr. Benton said, I'm standing in my own "idiosyncratic authority." If I am, it's immediately challenged, as Bethanie picks up her Bible and holds it against her chest, girding herself for battle, and says with precision, "*Do not let any foul or unwholesome talk come out of your mouth.*"

I know the verse. "Yes," I say, "but that verse—Ephesians 4:29—might not necessarily mean swearing." And then, fueled by my session with Dr. Benton, I add, not even quite understanding what I mean, "And no matter what the Bible says, shouldn't we trust our hearts?"

Bethanie snaps back a Bible verse I know well: "*The heart is deceitful above all things.*"

"Yes, of course, Bethanie. Jeremiah 17. But maybe our *deeper* heart—"

"Our deeper heart? *Deeper than the Bible?* I'm not sure what that would be."

"Like maybe we can only be true to what we already know is right."

"I have no idea what you're talking about right now." Bethanie's mouth contorts and she spews out, with what even she must know is too much emotion for a professional, "Are you the therapist here, or am I?"

I remain calm, my voice even. "You are definitely the therapist, Bethanie. I was just expressing my opinion." Pretending to be innocent but fully aware of the barb I'm slinging, I continue, "I'm sorry. Maybe we should all just be silent and listen to you. I was thinking therapy was about discovering our voice, but maybe it's just about submitting to authority. I should work on that." Then I add, sarcastic, unable to stop myself, "Maybe we should just let you . . . speak for God."

Bethanie's whole body vibrates. "Maggie, this discussion is between myself and Quinn."

"Oh, then maybe you shouldn't have asked the group to weigh in. It gave me the impression you wanted the group to weigh in."

I hear my voice, a voice that is arch, with a spine I don't recognize. It's hard to tell if it's a voice that I like. It's definitely too fraught with emotion, jangling out of control, unsettling. But there's a health in it, some rigor, a fight that I like. But is it a good fight or a bad one? Who knows? Again, I wonder, how do people *know* things? When people at Hope Valley Baptist would testify that the Holy Spirit was speaking through them, how did they know it was the Holy Spirit? How did they know it wasn't a deep-seated desire to be heard, their desire to be spiritual, an ego flare instead of divine presence? How do people tease apart their own voices? *How is everyone so certain about everything?*

"Okay, I think we all need to calm down and remember what our jobs here are."

My heart is thumping harder than normal. It's not a sensation I completely dislike, this insistent rhythm, hammering up toward my collarbone, pounding out my own worries with *Bethanie's wrong. She's wrong. And I'm right. I'm right. I'm right.*

"I'm just saying I think Quinn should be the priority here."

I fail to notice that Quinn has become increasingly uncomfortable with the escalating tension until her voice cuts through our argument. "Thanks, Maggie. It's fine. I'll just read it without the cursing."

I feel like I've been yanked back from a schoolyard fight unfairly, by the very person I'm trying to defend. Bethanie is clearly wrong! Doesn't Quinn see that? I haven't been able to call Bethanie on her bullshit in the past, for *myself* I haven't been able to rise to the occasion, but now for Quinn, I can. The cause is righteous and I know I am right, but Quinn shakes her head.

I deflate.

Bethanie is triumphant. From the expression on her face, she is listening to a choir of angels swelling in a hallelujah chorus, celebrating her victory over me. I nurse my wounds, bitter, wanting back into the fray, my heartbeat not ready to surrender. *My impulse was sincere*, I think, and I watch as Bethanie basks in her glory so completely she seems in danger of losing consciousness altogether. Quinn takes advantage of Bethanie's lapse, catches my eye, and mouths *thank you*, before adding, *I'm sorry*.

Over the next few days I think about what Dr. Benton said: "Listen for the voice of God. And if you can't hear anything, then listen to the silence." I resolve to listen. On Monday I decide to spend the lunch break by myself in the courtyard, to practice this new technique. I go to the cafeteria, purchase *two* cheese sandwiches, then retreat to the solitude of the courtyard for . . . listening. The sun is bright, but the tree shields the bench with an easy shade that seems designed to comfort me.

As I sit under the tree I think about Jesus multiplying the fishes and the loaves, and I begin unwrapping the sandwiches from the wax paper, then spreading the four halves in front of me. I ask God to speak to me and to allow me to listen. Then I take a bite from one half of the sandwich, then another, then a third, happy to be eating with such ease. I think about Dr. Benton saying to trust the path that gives me peace, that softens me, that feels healthy.

I notice a small gray bird on a limb of the tree staring directly into my eyes, then at my sandwich, then back at me. After several moments, the bird flies down, settling in by my side as if I've extended an invitation. I accept its presence as if I had. Then I take another bite from my sandwich, enjoying the basic motion of appetite—hunger and satisfaction, hunger and satisfaction, hand to mouth again and again and again. The bird looks at me, his eyes all pupils.

I take a crust of the sandwich and put it in front of him. He pecks at the scrap, breaking it into small discrete portions, then sucking them into his beak. When he finishes, he looks back up, expectant but not demanding. I rip off a bigger piece of crust and place it in front of him. I continue peeling off bits of crust and setting them aside. For several minutes this small, unexceptional bird and I sit together and eat in silence. I think about God taking care of the sparrows and feel thankful to be breaking bread with this sympathetic creature.

CHAPTER EIGHTEEN: **SIN BRAVELY**

I HAVE TWO WEEKS LEFT before I'm hoping to go back to school, register for classes, and resume college life. Back on schedule. I've been taking my medication, watching my thoughts, and questioning the "I" of the thinker, and I've been eating. A lot.

We have just come back from lunch at Long John Silver's, where I scarfed down a barrel of hush puppies before attacking my Fisherman's Feast like a challenge, a challenge I undeniably won. Now I sit back in my chair waiting for group therapy to begin, my stomach puffed out with seafood and starch, satisfied, hopeful, imagining myself going back to school in the fall, with new wisdom, new tools, a desire to ingest food, and the chance to start again.

But then in group, Timbo says something unthinkable. He doesn't know it's unthinkable. He has no idea his small throwaway statement will be so upsetting, that it will hit me and knock me off-balance, slamming me back to the ground of my anxiety, pressing my face into the dirt of my fears. But that's exactly what happens.

Timbo is talking again about the vision of the cross he received when he was on angel crack, his favorite topic of all time: "When I had my vision, my heart just pulled me to God. There was nothing I could do. I knew I had to give up my old life, and not because I was scared of punishment. I mean, you can't just come back to God for . . . fire insurance." That last phrase, *You can't just come back to God for fire insurance*, ricochets through my head, angry and violent: *You can't just come back to God for fire insurance*. Isn't that exactly why I came back? Because I wanted an insurance policy against hellfire? Isn't that precisely what happened when I watched *Dreams*, then stumbled out of the theater, disoriented, into the brutal, unforgiving wind, and rededicated my life to God?

I look at Bethanie, assuming she must know Timbo's statement will set off a terrifying alarm inside me. I'm hoping that knowing my vulnerability, she will counter the idea and offer some assurance, tailor-made to my predicament based on the unprecedented access I've given her to my internal experience. She is my individual therapist. She should be able to deal with me individually.

But, no. Bethanie slaps her hands together and hoots, "Fire insurance. I love it!"

I hear almost nothing of what anyone says for the rest of group because I have begun a panicked reevaluation of my situation. Not waiting until my worry hour to weigh my soul, I set up the scales and immediately begin calculating. Could it be true that you can't come to God for fire insurance? But then, why would God tell us about the fire if He didn't want us to be scared and insure ourselves against it? Would He cut us off for responding to a fear tactic He Himself implemented? For preparing for a future He has fashioned?

I think about Aesop's fable of the ant and the grasshopper. I've always fiercely identified with the ant, who prepares for the winter, storing up nuts and seeds in the hollowed-out knob of a tree. And I've always judged the grasshopper, who whiles away his summer hours, singing and dancing in the sun, playing a concerto on a blade of grass, only to find he has no food when the winter frost hits.

I put great stock in an ounce of prevention. To prevent tooth decay, I brush my teeth for the dentist-recommended ninety seconds per quadrant. Every night. To prevent corneal irritation, I soak my contacts for a minimum of eight hours, even if that means not wearing them to morning check-in. I wash my hands before every meal, always digging my nails into the soap at the end, an added protection against the bacteria that might be lurking. I've always been this way. Before falling asleep, I used to review our home escape route in case of fire, an escape route which, because of the tininess of our home, consisted solely of: open window, jump out. I started doing breast self-examinations when I was eleven, before I'd even grown breasts, before there was a place for lumps to hide out.

Risk offers no thrill for me, at least in comparison to the heady rush of security. But is security the only reason I'm a Christian? If so, does that mean I'm not a Christian? I remember, *for those who are lukewarm, I will spit out of my mouth*, and my heart squeezes with a spasm of fear. Could it be true that I am now and have always been lukewarm? The room suddenly becomes suffocatingly hot, an oppressive angry heat. I grab the fabric of my T-shirt and repeatedly pull it away from my chest and back, in a futile attempt at ventilation. I need to get out of here. I need to talk to Dr. Benton.

Immediately after group, I burst through the door to Dr. Benton's office, hurling the words at him before my new mentor can hang up the phone, too distraught to be concerned with protocol, that . . . "I'm doomed! I came back to God for fire insurance and who am I to think I can fool God?" I explain what happened in group, my lower lip quivering, my arms crossed in front of my chest, each hand squeezing the opposite shoulder in support.

"Sit down."

I sit down. Dr. Benton looks at me, considering. "You think God is going to punish you for looking out for your eternal destiny?"

"Maybe. Yes. Who knows? I certainly wouldn't put it past Him."

Dr. Benton smiles at the phrase "put it past Him," then leans in. "How much do you know about Martin Luther?"

"Uh, Protestant Reformation. Ninety-five theses nailed to the church door."

"Excellent. Now, what do you know about his early life?"

"Nothing really."

"Okay, well, Martin Luther worried about his salvation. Probably more than even you worry about yours, a feat not to be scoffed at. He spent hours in confession every day, confessing every little act he felt was not up to the Lord's standards. He had marathon contrition sessions, splintering his sins into a thousand different components. In penance, he would whip himself, sleep out in the snow in his skivvies, eat the dirt under his fingernails for dinner, and still he wasn't sure he'd been forgiven."

"Scrupulosity."

"That's right. Finally Martin Luther had his big revelation. He came to the conclusion that doing good works wouldn't save him. Only God's grace was sufficient. And he posted those famous theses. After that, he came out with his most controversial doctrine, the doctrine of *pecca fortiter*, or the brave sin. Luther wrote, 'Sin bravely in order that you may know the forgiveness of God.'"

"What does that mean?"

"It means Martin Luther felt that the most important thing for a Christian to understand is that he is forgiven, even if that means sinning."

"Okay," I say, still holding myself tight. "I don't understand what this has to do with fire insurance."

"I think you should consider laying off the Bible for a while, lay off reading it, lay off doing what it says. Sin whatever sins you want, including coming to God for fire insurance. Don't try to change your motivation. I truly believe the most important thing for you now is to understand God's grace." This is the first time I've heard Dr. Benton say he believes something. Normally he just asks questions, proposes possibilities. "I think it's more important that you repair your relationship with God than that you follow the letter of the law."

"Well, I can't just start sinning."

"Why not? What would happen?"

"It would be wrong."

"And then what would happen?"

"I guess . . ." I hesitate, "people could be hurt."

"Do you think you'd do things to hurt people if the Bible didn't tell you not to? Do you think you'd murder someone?"

"No." I smile. "Probably not."

"Do you think you'd assault toddlers or the elderly?"

"No."

"Would you release a deadly gas on the subway when it had reached the maximum level of occupancy and could conceivably cause the most harm?"

"No."

"Would you run up to long-haired, scraggly men and yell, 'Dirty hippies!' or pin a note to the back of a fat woman that says, *blubber butt?*"

I laugh. "No, I wouldn't."

"Okay, well then, I think the world is safe from your sins."

"Yeah, but what about sins that don't hurt people?"

"If they were not prohibited in the Bible, what non-hurtful actions would you consider sins?"

I think about this for a moment. "I don't know, I guess, anything that doesn't hurt other people doesn't seem wrong. It might be unwise, but if the action doesn't cause harm, it doesn't seem like it would be wrong. Good and bad seem to be about loving or not loving."

"Okay, well, there you go then. That's your personal ethical code. Try to live up to it. Don't worry about the Bible."

I walk out of Dr. Benton's office off-kilter, ineptly putting one foot in front of the other, as if I hadn't been walking since I was two.

I walk to the courtyard, imagining what it might be like to not worry about the Bible, and see Dwayne seated on the bench puffing away on a cigarette. I remember that in group he'd said he quit smoking, so I ask, "Should I be discouraging you?"

"I'd rather you didn't."

Dwayne lights my cigarette.

"Hey, I wanted to tell you not to worry about that fire-insurance thing. I wanted to tell you before I leave tomorrow. People come to God in all different ways. Timbo came to Him on angel crack, for God's sake."

I'm surprised Dwayne noticed I was worried. Bethanie hadn't. "You're leaving?" I ask.

"Yeah, my ninety days are up."

"Why ninety days?"

"Because that's what the court says." Dwayne takes a drag and explains,

"Driving while intoxicated. Second offense. It was either jail or court-appointed rehab, and for some reason, this place was on the list. I'm no fan of born-agains, but they're better than junkies."

"You're not a Christian?"

"Not a *born-again*. Raised one. Literalism all the way. It's why I got married. I was in love with a boy, a boy from art school. I thought getting hitched would cure me. 'Better to marry than to burn,' as good ol' St. Paul says."

Dwayne stares past me, up to the top of the birch tree, up to the branches that rise and fall, swayed by the unseen wind. "Leave it to born-agains," he says, shaking his head, "to load the Bible with fear and shoot it like a gun."

I'm curious, so I ask, "Are you still gay?"

Dwayne smiles, amused rather than offended at my naïveté. "Yeah, it threw a bit of a screw in my marriage." Then more seriously, he says, "The whole thing wasn't very fair to my wife. But what's done is done."

Dwayne looks beyond me, up to the pocket of sky above us, before returning his eyes to mine. "You know Jesus said, 'The letter of the law kills, but the Spirit gives life.' Christians forget that. They forget it all the time."

Then Dwayne reaches down and, without guilt, plucks a gardenia. He rolls the stem between his fingers and examines the golden blossom.

That night I sleep over at Quinn's again. I've been waiting all day to talk to her about Martin Luther to see what she thinks. As soon as we're out on the balcony, before we can even sit and attempt to balance in our rickety lawn chairs, I explain what Dr. Benton told me, about not thinking about the Bible for a while and trusting that I'm forgiven, that it's more important that I repair my relationship with God than that I follow the letter of the law.

Quinn looks surprised, even shocked at the suggestion at first, her spine arching in her seat. "Sin. Bravely," she says, pronouncing each word distinctly, disturbed, it seems to me, by the pairing. But then after a moment she softens and places her hand over her heart as if she were pledging allegiance to me. "You know? I think that makes sense."

"Do you really?"

"Yeah, you're so scared all the time, Maggie. I bet you're becoming resentful of God." Quinn takes a sip of wine. "When Jack and I met at a Young Life retreat, I was a sophomore in college and he was a senior. When he graduated, I wanted to drop out so we could get married and start a life together. But Jack insisted I stay in school; he said I'd always resent him if I dropped out. I wonder if you'll resent God if you're constantly worried about being punished." Quinn looks at me, her eyes reminiscent of Sophie's mischievous cat eyes. "Like what would you want to do? Sinning-wise?"

"I'd get back together with Cooper," I say instantly, "but that's too big to think about now. I feel like I should start small, nothing too reckless, so I guess . . . maybe I'd swear."

"What sort of swears?"

I giggle, trying out words I haven't used in months. "Shit. Fuck. Mind-fuck. Fucked if I know."

"What else?"

"I guess maybe . . . maybe I'd gossip again," I say, but then amend, "if I were sure the gossip wouldn't get back to the person."

"Great." Quinn thrills at the idea. "Tell me some gossip. About anyone. Someone I don't know. I don't care."

I feel like I'm back in junior high at a slumber party. Who can I gossip about? Then I have an idea. "Okay. I've got one."

Quinn settles in and folds her legs up to her chest.

"So there's a couple I know from the theater department at school, Stella Clarke and Matt Mierding. Stella loved Matt Mierding from the moment she met him."

"What does he look like?"

"Like someone who would work as roofer or an amateur boxer. And . . . I can't speak from personal experience, but word around the dorm was that he was . . . well endowed."

"Big cock?" Quinn shocks me with the ease of her enquiry.

We giggle like Sophie and I once had in our sleeping bags. "Yeah, big cock."

"Go on."

"Well . . ." I stop myself, realizing that this story might be wrong to tell, the upcoming event not something that should be laughed at or taken lightly. But I remind myself—*sin bravely*—take a gulp of my wine, and forge ahead.

"Well, one day, I went over to Stella's dorm room. She was in bed, sleeping on a big blood stain."

"Period?"

"No, way more blood than that."

"Oh goodness."

"And Stella was faint, not totally conscious. She stammered, 'Matt and I made love. We love. Matt make love.'"

Quinn's hands shoot to her mouth. "Oh no."

"So I call an ambulance and go with her to the hospital. I wait several hours in the ER until finally a doctor comes out. The doctor asks me—I swear to God I'm not making this up, I'm not committing the sin of lying on top of everything else—he asks me . . ." I take a pause, hoping to give the doctor's statement the most bang, "'Did your friend have sex with someone who possesses an exceptionally lengthy penis?'"

Quinn howls with laughter. "'An exceptionally lengthy penis'?"

"I didn't know how to answer. I had no personal experience. Just dorm rumors."

"What did you say?"

"I said, 'Yes, I think so. His name is Matt Mierding.' I don't know why in the world I decided to give his name, as if that mattered at all. For some reason, I wanted the owner of the enlarged appendage to get credit."

I enjoy seeing Quinn almost choke on her wine.

"Then the doctor explained that Stella would be completely fine. Her uterus was punctured during intercourse, making a two-inch crescent-shaped rip."

"Okay, I've heard of big penises before, but long enough to reach your uterus?" Quinn presses her finger just below her belly button, and we both dissolve in fits of laughter.

I catch my breath long enough to cough out, "There's more."

"More?" Quinn giddily motions for me to continue.

"Okay, so then I go into Stella's room. She's all drugged up on something. And I sit down on the bed. I say, 'Hey, sweetheart, how are you feeling?' She moans, 'So good,' and then lifts herself up on her elbows and says, 'Oh, did you hear? I've got news. They said it was a crescent. Matt . . . *made a moon in me.*'"

"No."

"I swear I'm not lying. Isn't that crazy? *Matt made a moon in me.* How's that for a desire for romance? The symbol of a moon, literally inside you."

We laugh again, but Quinn's laugh becomes jangled, its pitch unsettling. I realize then that she is crying. She drops her head in her hands, her speech slightly slurred. "Sorry, I don't mean to ruin your sinning bravely. I just got to thinking about uteruses, damaged uteruses . . ."

Oh no. Of course. Why did I tell this story?

"Oh, Quinn, I'm so sorry."

"No, no, don't feel bad. It was fun to laugh like that. It's just . . . I just . . . I got a letter back from Oral Roberts."

Quinn takes an envelope out of her pocket and then a thin sheet of paper out of the envelope.

"Oh my God, what did he say?"

"It's not good."

Quinn stares down at the letter, reading words she now seems to know by heart: "'A child has a right to come into the world as a result of an act of love between his or her father and mother, not as part of a laboratory experiment. The process of in vitro involves implanting more fertilized eggs than are expected to come to term, a procedure called selective reduction—a euphemism for killing. Thank you for your inquiry and your willingness to seek God in all things.'"

I am furious at stupid Oral Roberts. "How does he know?"

"He doesn't know. But that's what he thinks. He thinks in vitro is never a part of God's plan."

"But who's he? He's a guy whose name sounds like a dentistry school."

Quinn does not laugh, having become, it seems, instantly sober. I press, "Who cares what he thinks. I say *you* should sin bravely."

Quinn shakes her head. "No, that's not the way for me." Instead of spiraling into her own experience, she stays with mine. "But I think *you* need to. It's right for you. I can tell." Quinn reaches across the table and squeezes my hand.

Fuck Oral Roberts, I think, *fuck him and his certainty and his denial of Quinn's right to be a mother. And not just* her right . . . *he's denying a child the privilege of having Quinn as her mother.*

"Okay, I'm going to bed." Quinn rises to her feet. "Your pullout is all set." I want to keep talking, out here on our little weird island, but Quinn's already heading to her room. She turns back and smiles weakly, with her mouth but not her eyes, before disappearing down the hallway.

I lie on the pullout, staring out the window, far from sleep. I see the crescent moon in the sky above me. *He made a moon in me*, I think, and I immediately regret my sin of gossip. But not because it was gossip, I realize, but because the gossip I chose upset my friend. I continue to stare out into the night. I think about Cooper and the unequal yoke and why romance is so connected to the moon. Then, rubbing the bottom of one foot over the top of another, I think about what Dr. Benton said. What if I didn't have to worry about the Bible? What if I weren't afraid of repercussions? What if I could just trust my instincts, my innate sense of good and bad? I flip over to my stomach and rest my head in the crook of my arm. It would be like finding out that candy makes your heart strong or taking naps makes you smarter. Or that sinning brings you closer to God.

CHAPTER NINETEEN: **LOOKERS**

I SLEEP THE NEXT NIGHT in my room at Grace Point. In the morning, a ray of light pierces the window, a ray so focused it looks like it's pointing at something. My eyes, still fuzzy, follow the direction of the point, through the window, over to the dresser, where the beam lands squarely on the strip club ad I had cut out in activity therapy, illuminating, like a golden highlighter, one single line: *Amateur Night. Every Thursday. 9 P.M.*

Could this be a sign? Am I supposed to go to Amateur Night at Lookers? Lookers with the girls one "would care to see naked"? Is this sinning bravely?

What a ridiculous thought. Of course not. But this light is so focused. It's uncanny. Like God's finger.

I go through the motions of the day, but all I'm thinking about is Lookers. What if by going to Amateur Night, by sinning bravely, doing something that doesn't hurt anyone, that doesn't violate my personal moral code, my idiosyncratic authority, what if I could . . . *knock out my fear?* Like the guy in the Psych 101 documentary who was scared of flying so he forced himself to go on an airplane, to go into his fear rather than run away from it, and then at two thousand feet, found he was not so scared after all? Like the agoraphobe who went to the World Trade Center and let the crowds swarm around him like bees and discovered he could emerge from the situation, un-stung. Could this be like that?

I decide it couldn't hurt to just call the club and get some information, so after dinner that night, I go to my room and dial the number from the ad. A voice growls back at me, "Lookers, girls you'd care to see naked. This is Dave."

My voice shoots up an octave, as if I'm applying for secretarial school in the 1950s, certain that pleasantry will secure me the position. "Hey, Dave, my name is Maggie, and I'm interested in participating in your Amateur Night competition on Thursday, and I was just hoping to get a little more information."

"No information. Show up with a tape of the song you want to dance to. Have a stage name. We don't want girls using their real names. Just creates problems."

Before Dave can hang up, I jump in and ask him for some examples of stage names. Dave tells me a lot of the girls are going by food names this season—Candy, Cookie, S'more, Tasty Pudding.

I hang up and go straight to work on a list of stage names. I begin with food references: Honey, Juicy, Licorice; also Chocolate and Brown Sugar, which I'm unaware are the exclusive domain of African-American dancers. But none of the food names really speak to me, so I consider more Biblical ones: Jezebel, Bathsheba, Delilah, Babylonia, Oholo and Oholibah, but ultimately I decide on Magdalene. If I am going to sin bravely, I want to do it fully and without compromise. Magdalene will be my name, Magdalene the unrepentant prostitute who washed Christ's feet with perfume and dried them with her hair.

The next morning before breakfast I scrap my Lookers plan; by lunch it's back on, then at dinner, it's decidedly off. I reprimand myself for even considering this clearly dangerous, ludicrous, ill-conceived plan. But after dinner, back in my room, I reevaluate, pondering my "sin bravely" campaign. Could this be the right thing to do? What did the silence say? I try to listen. "God, please tell me if going to Lookers Amateur Night is sinning bravely or is just a screwed-up—can I say fucked-up?—thing to do."

I decide it won't hurt to practice my Amateur Night competition song. But what song should I dance to? I look through my small collection of tapes. And then I know what it has to be. I know what song will have the symbolic power I'm looking for, the power of boarding a jet or standing my ground in the World Trade Center. Patti Smith's song "Gloria." Dancing to "Jesus died for somebody's sins but not mine" will be sinning bravely. Could this be Martin Luther's path? God's path?

So I put the tape in my portable tape deck, prop a small hand mirror on my dresser, and get to work creating a routine. I incorporate the shuffle ball change and time step I learned in Glenview Park District tap class, the tour jetés and pliés I practiced for ballet, the kick-out lay-back, arms-spread thing from *Dirty Dancing*, and the swivel hips I tried to perfect for my role of Maryanne in *I Stand Before You Naked*. I also decide to mouth along with the lyrics, to underline my expression and personal connection to the song.

I know part of stripping involves taking off your clothes, a significant part, I figure, since by definition that's what it is. If I go to Lookers . . . which I'm not planning on doing. But if I *were* to go to Amateur Night at nine o'clock on Thursday, I would have to take off my bra. When would I do this? *How* would I do this? I remove my T-shirt and shorts, stand in front of the propped-up hand mirror on the dresser, and try to figure out the best maneuver. Just in case it comes up. On Thursday at nine P.M.

How do I remove my bra, sexily, not like I'm undressing in a chilly doctor's office? Should I reach behind me with one hand and yank my bra off like I'm freeing myself from a harness? Or should I let one strap fall at a time naturally? Then the obvious question: how am I going to make a strap fall naturally? Maybe I should pull the right the strap down over the hump of my shoulder and wiggle until the elastic ribbon collapses onto the crook of my elbow. Same with the left side? Once the two straps are hanging there slack, maybe then I'll unclasp the back.

Three hours later I come up with a choreographed routine for the first three minutes of the song, a precisely orchestrated bra removal for the fourth, and I decide I will improvise for the final minute and a half, over the repetitive "Glorias." I notate the choreography in my notebook in case I ever need it some Thursday night at nine: *Stare straight out, lip-synch lyric "Jesus died for somebody's sins but not mine," swizzle step, ball change, hip right, hip left, scoop foot, slow-motion body wave, chest-isolation right,*

isolation left, pirouette, pirouette, freeze, hands down body, pump chest,
Dirty Dancing *kick into layout, circle hips, circle chest, circle arms, shimmy*
into time step. Bra off. Improvise with music.

Thursday night at dinner all I can think about is Amateur Night. After
dinner I retreat to my room, call United Taxi, and ask for a cab to pick
me up in a half hour. *I can always cancel. Calling a cab isn't equivalent to*
actually taking a cab, I tell myself, as I pick out what bra and underwear
ensemble to wear. It doesn't take me long. There's really only one option.
The hot pink Maidenform set from T.J. Maxx. It's the only matching bra
and underwear that I have. Plus it's hot pink, the runner-up for the international color of sex, after red. It doesn't bother me that the underwear
covers most of my torso and the bra makes it look like I have prosthetic
breasts. It's hot pink!

I put on my jeans and T-shirt over the ensemble and head outside, one
block away from Grace Point in front of Sunny and Shears, where I told
the cab to pick me up, the cab I can still cancel. I sit on the curb and wait.
When the cab arrives, I do not cancel. I give the driver, a Middle Eastern man named Farouk, the address of Lookers. Farouk yanks his neck
around to look me up and down as if I'm his most interesting passenger of
the day. "The titty bar?"

I lie, a lie I know Farouk is onto even before it's out of my mouth: "I'm
meeting a friend there. It's a good meeting place." As if I didn't already
sound ridiculous, I add, "Central location." Farouk laughs freely. "That's
great. Central location. Titty bar it is."

When we arrive, I get out of the car and pretend to look around for the
friend I'm meeting at this central location until Farouk's car merges into
traffic, becoming just one of many taillights skimming across the road.
Then I look up at the sign: *Lookers*. The neon is hot pink, which assures
me of the wisdom in my choice of undergarments. And with that small
assurance, I grab the brass handle on the door and pull. I walk through a
dark narrow hallway, feeling like I'm in a haunted house, half-expecting a
ghost or a man with a chainsaw to jump out at me.

Finally after several seconds—which feels much longer in this dank labyrinth—I turn a corner, and I am in Lookers, a small, even darker, danker room. I can see nothing until my eyes adjust to the light. All I can hear is the song "Cherry Pie" booming so loudly that I cover my ears for fear the sound will blast out my eardrums, leaving me with lifelong tinnitus. I wait, frozen, until I can make out several men plugging their mouths with beer, and then a bar manned by a stoop-shouldered bartender.

I navigate my way through the haze, up to the bartender, and using my most official, professional voice, declare, "Hello. I'm here for Amateur Night. I spoke to Dave on the phone."

"Yeah, I'm Dave."

This seems to me an amazing coincidence. Dave fills a glass from the beer tap, less impressed—well, not at all impressed—with the coincidence. "You're early."

I figure this is a good thing and pop back into to my 1950s secretarial voice. "Yes, thank you. I'm very punctual."

"Sure you are. Go on in," Dave says, pointing to a door half off its hinges. "The girls'll be shits to you, but don't mind them. They're all coozes." I've never heard the term *cooze*, but because of my strong reading/verbal comprehension skills, I understand it is definitely a pejorative.

"Get on your costume and then come back out here." Costume? Did I need a costume? Terrified by my lack of preparation, I look past Dave to the stage, where I see a dancer drenched in a rosy light, wearing a rhinestone-studded bikini with enormous white angel wings, prancing in Lucite stilettos. Then I see other dancers, in sequined halters and fluorescent thongs, in patent leather T-backs with matching thigh-high boots—*in costumes*. My enormous pink undergarments now seem foolish.

I turn back to Dave, panicked. "I don't have a costume. I just thought I'd wear my bra and underwear and use my . . . feet." Dave slaps a tap beer down in front of a man who has obviously had too many, whose head lists from one shoulder to the other, unable to find its axis, like the patients at Garden Grove.

"I don't have heels or anything," I press on despite Dave's lack of response. "I mean I own heels, but I didn't bring them. Maybe I should come back another day."

Dave tosses his hand up dismissively and grunts something that sounds like, "That's all right, nobody gives a shit," then points again to the door with the struggling hinges.

I squeeze my hands into fists and march toward the door. When I pull the handle, I am immediately assaulted by a pungent mix of hair spray, perfume, and mist deodorant. Through the haze of aerosol beauty products, I see five girls lined up in front of the mirror, and feeling I need to say something, to account for my entrance, I go with, "Hey, thanks for having me."

Thanks for having me? Why? Why did I say this? I don't know. The girls don't know either, but fortunately, they don't seem to care or to have noticed my presence at all.

These girls are not flawless like the flaxen-haired, golden-skinned, "daring the world" girl from the ad. These girls have pimples, cellulite, and razor burns around their bikini lines from impatient shaving; one has an almond-sized growth above her left eyebrow, one limps like she's been shot in the leg, and another sports a protrusion from her abdomen that reads as *first trimester*. The tallest, who I guess is the queen bee of the stubbly, paunchy, perfumed crew, is mid-story: "Yeah, so poet dude, you know, who told me he had a 'hair piece' and I thought he said 'herpes,' he wrote me a poem."

I take off my jeans and T-shirt slowly, pretending I'm challenged by the basic activity, so I can hear the tale. Dabbing lipstick on her already–bright red lips, Queen Bee continues, delighted with her reflection in the mirror. "You wanna hear?" The girls join in a chorus of exuberance, "Yes! Yes, we do!" Queen Bee, happy to appease her followers, removes a sweaty napkin from the top of her thigh-high boot and recites, "Your lips are crimson. Your smile is winsome. Your thighs are moist like pound cake—" The room erupts with this last line, the girls' echoed cackles bouncing off the walls.

Then Queenie shushes her bees. "You have to listen to the end."

The girls stop painting their faces, spraying their hair, and they turn to her, rapt. Queen Bee, once due attention has been paid, continues. "My ring—will you take?"

A ghostly blond with translucent skin and hollow eyes claps her hands. "Oh, take! Take!" She reminds me of zombie-stripper Maryanne, a character in a play who never existed but who I'm convinced I know. I half expect this woman to have stage-makeup strangulation marks and vainly placed bruises on her face and for us to, in some way, reunite.

A rough-looking redhead, with an unlit cigarette clamped in the corner of her mouth, coughs out, "Yeah, take it. Then you can live your dream of being an out-of-work plumber's wife in an apartment with shitty paneling, raising your fat schitzo children!"

Queen Bee folds up the poem and puts it in her bra. "Who still suck their thumbs and shit their pants."

The blond ghost smirks. "Just like their dad."

And the girls howl.

Amidst the exuberance, I silently lay my jeans and T-shirt in a neat little pile and look in the mirror. I'm embarrassed to see the locket from Cooper that I still wear around my neck. It's too dainty. It seems comically small and silly in front of these brazen women. I unclasp the back of the necklace, let it fall into my hands, and place it in the pocket of my jeans, under my neatly folded T-shirt. I pat the little stack of my clothes for some reason, like a mother assuring her children she'll be back.

I walk back out into the dank club in my hot pink ensemble, barefoot, my Ross Dress for Less purse slung over my shoulder. I know I look ridiculous, like a little girl padding around in her underwear with her mom's discount dress-up pocketbook, but luckily no one seems to notice. I hold my ears closed against the pounding bass of "Black Velvet" and cross my hands over my ribs, embracing myself. Why am I doing this? Is my motivation righteous or sinful? How do people know their motivations? Or do they just pretend they do?

Then I know. I know what will help. Alcohol. And a cigarette.

I march up to the bar, taking a cigarette and a wad of cash out of my extremely faux-leather purse, and say to Dave, "White Russian," (a drink I for some reason believe to be the libation of the sexy.) Dave gives me the white Russian, and it is a magical one, a sweet sugary syrup coating my nerves. I have the instinct to thank God for this white Russian, but I don't because . . . I have to prepare for my audition. The clock is ticking. Time is running out.

I close my eyes and go over the routine in my mind: *swizzle step, ball change, hip right, hip left, scoop foot, slow-motion body wave, chest-isolation right, isolation left, pirouette, pirouette, freeze, hands down body, pump chest,* Dirty Dancing *kick into layout, circle hips, circle chest, circle arms, shimmy into time step. Bra off.*

I see a pair of leather thigh-high boots walk past me, and I look up to see they're attached to a smoky-eyed girl in a plaid schoolgirl skirt. I remember the Marianne Faithfull quote from the picture I tore off my wall: *Later I went to convent school. Later I rode in leather. Later I took some sleeping pills. I needed to lose.* I tell myself I can still leave. It's not too late. I haven't done or lost anything yet.

Dave's oily voice oozes through the club. "All right, let's give it up for Candy. Good enough to eat. Take your hands out of your pants and put them together for . . . Tasty Pudding." Tasty Pudding takes the stage, the light from above bathing her skin, hiding any imperfections, bestowing a soft rosy glow. She is balanced on a spiked-heel version of ruby red slippers, wearing a piece of neon fabric slung around her neck that reaches down over her nipples, the two straps meeting between her legs to form a thong. Her hair, the color of strawberry jam in the light, is pulled back childishly in baby barrettes.

Tasty Pudding undulates lazily, patting her butt as if it were a pet, then absent-mindedly juggles her left breast, the sling still covering her nipple. But then in one quick, expert move, she hooks her thumbs on each side of the sling top and pulls the straps aside, sending her large balloon breasts tumbling out in the middle. I remember the harlots from the felt storyboards and imagine this woman as a felt figure among the others, right there with Delilah and Jezebel, Oholo and Oholibah.

Then Tasty Pudding approaches the quintessential symbol of strip clubs, the staple in every representation I've ever seen but for some reason I've forgotten about until right now: the pole. She grabs the silver pole with one hand, hooking her opposite knee, and effortlessly twirls in circles she appears to have travelled a thousand times. I hadn't thought about a pole. *What am I going to do with a pole?* Tasty Pudding scrambles to the top then flips over to dangle upside down, the large mounds of her breasts covering her mouth and nose, making me wonder how she is still breathing. And if her small ankles will hold.

Then in an instant Tasty Pudding jabs a heel, flips a wrist, and squeezes her thighs. There is a swirl of red tresses, and before I can worry any more about her, Tasty Pudding is upright, sliding back down to the ground, like a sexy fireman, as if there were never any danger.

It's ten minutes to nine and it looks like I'm the only competitor for Amateur Night, which heightens my anxiety and soothes it at the same time. But then one by one, they trickle in. First, there is a stringy girl with stringy hair, pretty enough to be attractive even without the bath she clearly needs. Next, a solid block of a woman with hard bangs, who appears dressed to deliver a "welcome to the theater" speech. Then a petite slip of an Asian girl with a ponytail on top of her head and a retainer that looks like a horse's bit. Dave motions them all toward the dressing room. I'm grateful that the crew looks as amateurish as I do, grateful that like me they pass the mark of "girls you'd care to see naked," but just barely.

But then one last girl strides in, a fresh-faced beauty with cascading white-blond hair, pouty pink lips, and aviator sunglasses that she doesn't remove despite the almost pitch black of the club. She struts with such confidence, with such movie-star aplomb, that I assume she must be the club's star performer, until Dave yells, "Fuck, Dallas. I told you, one Amateur Night a month."

Dallas removes her aviators, revealing a pair of ice blue eyes with naturally full lashes that she bats at Dave. "Oh, c'mon, sugar. Please. I drove all the way out here from Downer's Grove."

Two guys in trucker hats moan in support of Dallas's cause. Trucker Hat Guy on the right slams his beer down like a revolutionary, launching into an alcohol-fueled impassioned plea: "Aw, come on, Dave. We want to see Dallas dance. It's our money . . . so it's our *right*!" Trucker Hat Guy on the left slurs in support, "The custmerzzz alwehs rahtt."

Dallas coos back, fully aware of her charms, "Thanks, guys. You put the *b* in *best*," a phrase that, though far from clever, seems the perfect thing to say, coming from her perfect pink lips.

Dave reluctantly wags his finger at the dressing room, succumbing. "Fine. Get changed. But this is the last time."

I know there's no way I will win the Amateur Night competition with Dallas in the mix, but I am far from caring. I am happy to be here, in this strange dank world of exotic creatures. I'm thrilled to sit here on this bar stool, squeezing the white Russian glass in my hand almost to the breaking point, grateful to be part of this brazen, colorful company.

Dallas emerges from the dressing room in a glittery tube dress with matching glitter lace-up boots and feather boa, her flaxen hair now teased out to look like a halo of white light. The other four competitors follow, trailing behind in Dallas's shadow, surrendering to her commanding luminosity. Then all four women take their places next to me on the empty bar stools, two to my right, two to the left. It reminds me of swim class, when all the girls lined up in their bathing suits at the side of the pool, huddled together, exposed and goose-pimpled, waiting for the coach to wave us in.

Dave pulls out a clipboard with a stained napkin clamped on and grabs a pen that's been soaking in a pool of beer. "All right," he says, looking directly at me, "you got here first. You wanna go first?"

The coach has asked me to dive in first, and I don't want to disappoint. I am appreciative of the opportunity. So in my best accommodating Christian voice, I reply, "That would be great. Unless someone else wants to go. I'm cool with whatever."

"Name," Dave spits out, oblivious to my irrelevant etiquette from a foreign planet.

I start to say *Maggie* but then remember, "Oh, right, my stage name." Then suddenly I hear my voice ring out in an unfamiliar tone, "Magdalene. My name is Magdalene." The clipboard is close enough that I can see Dave scribble down on the damp, wrinkled napkin: *1. Magdilin*. I have the impulse to correct his spelling, but I stifle it immediately. *Magdilin* is fine.

Dave takes down the names of the other girls: *2. Bambi* (stringy, unwashed girl, now in Daisy Dukes, knock-kneed, a sprinkling of dandruff dusting her cut-off plaid shirt); *3. Sugar* (theater-speech lady, now in leather, but who still seems just as likely to hand you a program and say,

"Enjoy the show"); 4. *Georgia Peach* (an unlikely name for the Asian girl and a bite problem, now sporting a fluffy chiffon number with Scarlett O'Hara full-length gloves); 5. *Dallas*, glittering and gleaming, easily managing the boa curling around her shoulders like a snake, eyes bold like the girl in the ad.

Then I realize. The girl in the ad. The one I cut out for activity therapy. This girl in front of me . . . Dallas . . . is the girl from the ad! As I'm trying to combat my impulse to stare, I hear Dave's voice seeping out over the crackling sound system: "Amateur Night. Nothing like the first time. Five girls ready to pop their cherries. Welcome first to the stage, Magabin!"

Magabin? That's me, I realize in terror. I didn't know it would be so soon. This is happening now, I begin to understand. But I can still leave, I tell myself. It's not too late. I stand up and lay my purse on the bar stool. Time seems strange, spooled out in a long, uncanny way. I panic in slow-motion about leaving my purse unattended, and then I'm yelling over the music to Bambi, "Can you watch this?" Bambi stares back at me blankly, as if part of no time whatsoever.

Okay, here I go. Evidently, I'm doing this.

I walk up barefoot onto the lighted runway, which despite the lights is as cold as the floor in the church baptismal. Ineptly I mount the stage from the runway, making sure to bang my knee first, as I hear the lyric I was supposed to be mouthing along to, "Jesus died for somebody's sins but not mine." Shit. I missed the beginning. That's okay. I'll just jump right in to the shuffle ball changes and catch up.

I scramble to the center of the stage, pause to get my bearings, and then launch into my choreography. Tour jeté. Hip swivel. "My sins, they only belong to me. Me." The bass line kicks in, and I start my pirouettes. While my body participates, my mind looms above, thinking, *Why are you doing this? You are shamelessly naked in front of a bunch of men—dark, sweaty men, probably married with kids, sweaty men in a sweaty club, men who should be home with their wives and children, helping with homework and paying their taxes, but who are instead leering at you.*

But my body keeps going.

I get dizzy from the turns, from the lights, from the absurdity of my situation and must take a wide stance for a moment, creating a strong base, to keep from toppling over. I get back in step with my *Dirty Dancing* kick-layback and go through the next moves as planned. Then I remember the pole. I have to do something with the pole. I've never practiced with a pole, I have no upper-body strength, and I lack any hint of natural gymnastic ability. I stare at the shining silver post . . . then walk straight up to it, with friendly determination, as if I planned to introduce myself. I hook my elbow around it and circle, like I'm do-si-do-ing at a square dance. I do-si-do again.

For the first time I look out past the lights, out to the smattering of men in the audience. I can't make out their faces, but I can see one round fellow in a cloud of smoke give me a thumbs-up. I love this round smoky man and wish I could thank him properly for his simple gesture. People can be kind, I think: that little thumbs-up was a gratuitous act of generosity. Then I realize I've stopped moving and I'm just standing there, like I'm waiting to be x-rayed. I need to take off my bra. I'm behind on the choreography. As the chorus of "Glorias" begins, I struggle with the clasp in the back, a clasp I've never had difficulty with before, but which now becomes a mystifying mechanism. I try to direct my fingers, but they fumble futilely.

A voice from the audience spits out, "You want some help?" Out of programmed politeness, I instinctively mouth, *No, thank you, I'm good.* A swell of laughter rips through the club. I smile as if in on the joke, despite having my doubts. Finally, I manage to unhook the clasp in the back and, relieved, sling off my bra. When the weight from the pads makes a loud thud on the ground, several men clap. I am startled by the sound and have the instinct to bow, which I fortunately manage to suppress, continuing to move my arms and my legs in a pattern I hope is sensual, or at least not like a traffic cop. For the remainder of the song, the improvisational part, I copy the body waves I saw Tasty Pudding do earlier and try to replicate her bored facial expression, but I feel so intoxicated I have trouble not smiling.

When the song ends, I grab my five-pound bra, heave it up, and flatten it over my collarbone, until I realize it's not covering my breasts, and so I drop it down lower. "Let's hear it for Mandolin." I wave out ridicu-lously to the audience at no one in particular as I fasten the clasp in the back, one notch too tight, but it's on. I've done it. I've *sinned bravely*. As the popcorn smattering of lukewarm applause dies out, I scamper off the stage, back to my familiar bar stool, my chest heaving with excitement. "Next up, Bambi." Bambi dances to Billy Idol's "White Wedding," slinging her stringy hair with abandon. I feel the drumbeat in my chest and press my lips together, attempting to contain my exuberance, trying not to grin like a fool.

But then . . . everything changes. *In the twinkling of an eye.* My heart keeps beating at the same rate, but in an instant the tone changes, or at least, I perceive the racing differently—and that changes everything. Excitement is disfigured into panic, panic like when I watched *Dreams*, as I watched the boy who couldn't be forgiven, watched the men frozen for eternity and knew it was too late.

As the familiar taste of blood seeps into my mouth, I think, *Dear God, I've done the same thing again. I've made the same mistake. What is wrong with me?* The throbbing bass of the song "Centerfold" bangs in my ears. *My blood runs cold / My memory has just been sold.* It's loud. Too loud. I press my hands over my ears. Was sinning bravely really just an excuse to sin? I can't tell. My eyes smart from the dense smoky air, my contacts sticking to corneas, my eyelids sticking to my contacts. The air and the volume are punishing. "I'm sorry," I say to God over the throbbing base line banging into my head, "I'm sorry. I got it wrong." Everything is too dark, too thick, too loud. I have to get out of here. I grab my purse, hug it to my chest like a terrified child who needs my attention, and run to the dressing room door.

The dressing room is empty except for the ghostly blond, who man-ages to both ignore and watch me at the same time. I go to my little stack of clothes and get dressed. But when I reach in my pocket for my locket, it's not there. I check the other pocket. Empty. *One of the girls must have stolen it,* I think, as I try to remember if I saw a bathroom on my way in, in case I need to vomit. My eyes sting and start to water. Everyone is going to think I'm crying. Then I scold myself in a voice without mercy, *Why do you care what other people think? You should care what God thinks. Why haven't you been thinking about what God thinks?*

When I open the dressing room door, I see Georgia Peach whirling around the pole, her ponytail making smaller concentric circles, and I feel dizzy. I look down at my feet, steadying myself, and then go up to Dave, attempting to keep my voice even. "Excuse me, I was wondering if you could call me a cab when you get a chance."

"You're not gonna stick around to see who wins? It's audience applause, but yeah, it'll be Dallas. You're a smart kid. Get out while you can."

I sit on the curb outside, feverish, as if bathed in fiery consequence, with blurred, distorted vision and a ringing in my ears, feeling desperate to take back what I've just done, but realizing with horror that I never can. I get into a taxi and give the driver, a heavyset Russian man, the address of Grace Point.

I ride in the backseat alone, bewildered and horrified at the girl who made the inexplicable decision to do what I'd just done. I try to buckle my seatbelt, but I can't get it to work. I slam the two pieces of metal together over and over, trying to get them to fit. After I've struggled for close to a minute, the driver explains, "No seatbelt work." I wish I could at least have the security of a seatbelt. Can't I at least have that? My heart is beating fast, a hard insistent warning.

But then, unrelated to any thought that pops into my head or any comfort or assurance I offer myself consciously, beads of sweat cool my face. A gift. Undeserved. I find a delicate mist gracing my face. My fever has broken.

I look out the window. We pass a gas station and I see a boy pumping gas with a girl hugging him from behind, her head draped on his shoulder. I see a man sitting at a bus stop with his dog, both gazing out into the night, neither fidgeting nor scratching. We stop at a light and there's a flashing neon sign: *O'Brien's: Fighting Temperance since 1945.* Two men stagger out, one tall, one short, clearly fighting the good fight against temperance, holding on to each other, balancing their weight, their arms like a yoke binding two oxen, unequal. I reach in my back pocket for a lighter and find crumpled up, nestled in the bottom corner, the locket. My locket. Small mercies.

I watch the trees passing by. I look up at the sky. It's periwinkle blue, a sky graceful and forgiving, a sky without retribution and limitation, holding no vindication, no damnation, no peril; a sky open to everyone, blanketing all without discrimination, saying to no one, *Depart from me. I do not know you.* I'm not foolish enough to believe this feeling will last. I will forget it again and again, only to be flooded once more with fear. But not tonight.

Tonight life is sweet. God is kind. Whatever else happens, this was a night unlike any other.

CHAPTER TWENTY: **UNRESOLVED**

I DON'T SAY A WORD ABOUT my time at Lookers, but I hold the memory of the night in my head with care, like a precious stone, unwilling to let it go or share it with anyone else. I know my venture was ridiculous, but it was also brave, and I'm proud that no wave of guilt has knocked me down. I am not drowning in remorse. I am standing. And I feel God is standing with me. I can't explain why, but I wonder if it has something to do with grace.

My last week with the gang, things seem different. Bethanie irks me less. She still seems narrow-minded and obtuse, but now also, mainly benign. The rooms that I once thought of as murder-mystery rooms seem cheerier, as if the case had been solved and the pardoned suspects were moving on with their lives. Even the solitary boy from the painting in my room seems more at ease as he gazes up at the heavens.

A new patient arrives: a heavyset Latina girl named Luciana, whose face is covered with thick pancake makeup a shade lighter than her natural skin tone. Luciana introduces herself at morning check-in by saying, "Okay, so this is bullshit. My mom made me come here because she thinks I'm gay. Just because I made out once on a stupid field trip to the Field Museum with my fat friend Julie." Luciana wears a short skirt and sits, unapologetic on the high-backed couch, with her thighs spread proudly apart. I expect Dr. Lakhani will soon reprimand Luciana for compromising the men's spiritual recovery, but I'm sure she will survive. It seems—at least temporarily—like humans were built for survival.

I see Dr. Benton one last time. I thank him and tell him how much better I'm feeling, before adding, hoping to extract a last bit of guidance, "But the thing is that I still feel I just can't be certain."

Dr. Benton points directly between my eyes, as if wishing he could drill his finger into the spot for emphasis. "And you won't be. Never ever ever ever. You got that?"

I don't quite know what is happening. I'm unsure how to respond to his sudden ferocity.

"You're never going to be certain of anything," Dr. Benton drives ahead, "because certainty doesn't exist. Not for you, at least. Not for me."

"Yeah, but I'd really just like to be certain about this one thing, so I can relax."

"You won't be. I promise. Seriously, you won't."

This is the last thing I want to hear.

"Uncertainty is here to stay. You might as well shake hands with it and invite it to the party. You and me—we're doubters. We will never be at ease; we will never be *one of the certain*. Accept it." Dr. Benton does his familiar little head cock. "There's an old saying: 'Stop looking for certainty; you might find truth.'" Then he rights his head quickly. "Sounds like a highbrow fortune cookie, but still, there's something to it. There's a point at which further investigation leads you further from what you're looking for."

Then with no warning, seemingly without even an inhale, Dr. Benton slings out, "You should meditate. Every day." Dr. Benton delivers his final points with an urgency I find increasingly touching. "Find a class. Read a book. But basically, the deal is you just sit there and watch your thoughts go by. Like what I've been talking to you about, but make it a practice. Train your mind. You'll learn to tolerate the anxiety, to just sit with it, unsoothed, to give up hope of resolution. That's the way out. To stop seeking a way out."

"Yeah, maybe that will help calm me down."

"No!" Dr. Benton fails to keep himself from shouting. "Trying to stay calm will destroy all chance of calm! Remember the double bind. Let your mind be stormy if that's what it's doing. Ride the surf. Be a basket case if that's what you are." Dr. Benton's face goes pale. "I don't mean . . . not that you're a . . . bask—"

I laugh. "No, no, it's fine. I'm not offended. I am a bit of a basket case. Plus, now we're even for the accent speech-impediment mix-up."

Dr. Benton's eyes rest on mine, steady for a moment, then flit to the wall behind me, then back again. "Well, all right then." I think he might shake my hand or give me a hug or something to mark the ending of our time together, but, instead, he awkwardly stands up before sitting right back down again, picking up his pencil and urgently scribbling something onto a pad of paper, as if he'd all of a sudden received an important assignment. Even though Dr. Benton doesn't look up to see, I still wave goodbye to him with an appreciation it takes no effort to muster.

On my last day, I have a final session with Bethanie, who chirps, eyes bright as a bird, "I've got something for you." She reaches into her desk drawer, the one that held the stock of rubber bands, and pulls out a certificate with gold embossed lettering. She hands it to me as if she were bestowing on me the international prize for peace and success, a prize I've been gunning for all my life. Bethanie waits for me to absorb the reach of the honor I'm receiving, the significance of the document before me, which reads:

> *This hereby certifies that* **Maggie Rowe** *has completed a three-month rehabilitation program at Grace Point.*

I know this dubious honor is well-meant, but the pomp and circumstance of the lettering on the Xeroxed glossy paper makes me feel like an underachieving student in need of reassurance being given a parade for consistent attendance. Bethanie, reliably oblivious, takes my embarrassment over the ridiculousness of the award as evidence of a lack of self-confidence, and assures me, "You deserve it. You really do, Maggie."

"Thanks, Bethanie."

Bethanie puts her hand on her heart and makes a grand bow. "You are welcome. It has been a pleasure." Her eyes glitter. "And I've noticed you've gained some weight."

It's true. For the last month, I've followed a committed diet of whatever the hell I wanted to eat. I don't mind the extra pounds, grateful that my elbows are no longer so bony that they could be used as weapons, that my skeletal face has been filled.

But Bethanie knows otherwise. "I know it might be hard now. But like I told you from the very beginning," Bethanie takes in her moment, "God loves you . . . even if you're not a size six." She can't resist adding the line clearly well-received by someone in her past: "And you can save those pearly whites for the pearly gates."

Later that day I say goodbye to the gang. I hug Quinn, as images of our nights together play through my mind: our sleepovers, sitting on the balcony like it was a porch in the country, watching nothing go by, talking about silly, precious things. As I pull her close, I feel like Dorothy with her Scarecrow, thinking, *I will miss you most of all.* I am pleased when I feel my eyes water with tears, grateful that I can show Quinn how much she's meant to me. I pull away, looking right at her, making sure she sees the evidence of my affection streaming down my face.

Then I take my duffel bag out to the waiting room. I remember how, sitting here three months earlier, my mom skimming the surface of my hand with her finger, I had hoped for a therapist with wizened wrinkles on his face who would show me ancient texts and allow me to uncover their hidden meanings. Then I think of Dr. Benton explaining that *pecca fortiter* meant "brave sin."

I look up at the picture of Jesus, the one of Him with Pantene hair and the sheep. This Jesus seems somehow less likely to turn on me, or on anyone else, than He did three months ago. The menace may still be there, but it's harder to see.

Bernie, the kid from my first day, again magically materializes. "Can I help you with your stuff?"

"Sure, thanks." Bernie picks up my duffel bag, and I follow him out to wait for my parents. "Do you work here? I haven't seen you since the first day I came."

"It's kinda like a part-time summer job. They just call me when someone's coming or going. My job is to be friendly and welcoming," he adds, pulling at the sprouts of hair on his chin. "I'm working on it."

I sit on the bench, and Bernie sits down next to me.

"Do you go to school around here?"

"I start college in the fall. I'm nervous about it. But my dad says I just got to put myself out there, to not be afraid to fail big. He says fortune favors the bold. He says I should sin bravely." Bernie nervously wheezes a laugh through his nose, and I realize this is Doctor Benton's son. I can hear it in his odd, awkward, but appealing speech patterns.

"Your dad is great," I say, and for the first time I realize how much I will miss talking to him.

"Naw, he's a loser." Bernie picks up a stick and cracks it. "But I guess he's okay. I can deal."

On the car ride home, I sit up front with my dad. My mom tells me that the Cornell theater brochure arrived announcing the fall season, then reaches up from the backseat to hand it to me. "You might want to check it out, see what I'm sure you'll be auditioning for."

I take the brochure from her small hands and feel its weight in my own. The pages are thick, glossy, and satisfying. It's addressed to me, Maggie Rowe, as if everything were normal, as if Cornell University knew nothing of my spiritual crisis, as if nothing were ever amiss.

I see that the main stage fall season consists of two plays, *Cyrano de Bergerac* and David Mamet's *Speed-the-Plow*.

"Thanks, Mom. I think I'm gonna see if I can order the plays so I can prepare for the auditions."

"We thought of that."

My mom leans forward again, testing the length of her seatbelt, and hands me two scripts. I run my hand over the covers, front and back.

"Thanks, Mom."

"Well, it was your dad's idea. He called Sam French. The store in Chicago was out of stock, but they had them shipped from New York."

My dad says, "I know how you like to be prepared."

I look through *Speed-the-Plow* and discover immediately that the only female part, the role of the ambitious, sexually manipulative Karen, has a sex scene where she seduces a man who is not her husband. My family's car flies down the open road, away from the hospital, away from Bethanie and her insistent misguided diagnoses, back to normalcy, toward a new beginning, but my eyes pin with dread on Karen's line: *We want love. Why should we deny it?*

The sun slants down into the car, direct, bright, and hot on my neck. I read through the words of Karen's monologue, forgetting to breathe: *I know what it is to be depraved. I've been depraved. I know what it is to be bad. I've been bad.*

The familiar needles perched above my head sharpen and prepare to stab into my scalp. The heat in the car rises and thickens, moistening my skin. I know this feeling. This warning. I think, *Oh no, no, no, I can't audition for this play. This is not the kind of theater that glorifies the Lord. This is worse than zombie-stripper Maryanne.*

I look to the front of the script to see who played the role on Broadway. 1988. The Royale Theater. Karen was played by . . . *Madonna*. Madonna has not made her career by being on God's side. If this is the kind of role Madonna would sign on for, it certainly isn't one I should be doing. This play and my portrayal of Karen, if I got the role, if I did it well, if I "set fires in my work," could lead people away from the Lord.

This is just like me playing strangled Maryanne shimmying up the pole post-mortem for her regulars, or Cavale, with her dead crow squeezed in her armpit, reaching for her rock 'n' roll savior. Or like my night at Lookers.

I cut myself off.

I remember "sin bravely" and pause. I roll down the window, letting the breeze rush in. I reach my elbow through the opening, hooking my armpit over the hot metal, and clutch the side of the speeding car.

I am uncertain, unsoothed, without clear answers to my continuing questions, but I manage to look up at the sky. It is still there, large and unresolved.

ACKNOWLEDGMENTS

THANK YOU TO EVERYONE at Soft Skull and Counterpoint; Megan Fishmann, Shannon Price, Kelly Winton, Bethany Onsgard, Barrett Briske, Nick Gomez-Hall. And big thanks, Dan Smetanka for your insight, exceptional editing skills, and for knowing without looking it up that onion rings were at no point a McDonald's menu item.

To Stacy Testa, thanks for believing in this peculiar story and helping me shape it. It would have been a much narrower tale without your perspective.

Kelly Hughes, thank you for your support of books of spiritual questioning.

To my friends who generously read first drafts and shared their insight, Ilyse Mimoun, Jane Brucker, Jill Bailin, and John Martin. Thank you especially David Chrisman for the writing lessons.

To Sarah, my best friend and life-travelling companion. I'm so lucky to have met you in the second grade on that propitious day in the playground.

To my sister Lisa who read this book before anyone and responded with a kindness befitting her faith, who listened to my concerns about sharing this story and gave me wise, generous counsel. Kid, you are certainly no Bethanie. Thank you.

And to my husband Jim, who said to me when we met— five years after the events in this book took place, "I just love how... sane you are." Thanks for being fooled.